Laozi's Way to Wealth,

entropy and time.

Edward Brew is an independent Australian author, with no affiliations with any institutions or foreign bodies.

Laozi's Way to Wealth & the Holy Grail

Laozi's Way to Wealth,

entropy and time.

The deal with the future,
& the Holy Grail.

By Edward Brew

Laozi's Way to Wealth & the Holy Grail

ISBN 978-0-9876291-9-7

Contact; edwardbrew42@gmail.com

Entropy and Time

This book is dedicated to My Parents,
Especially to my mother for showing me the ancient economics
of plenty from nothing – credit for merit.

Contents

Laozi's Way to Wealth & the Holy Grail

Foreword to The Laozi (Daodejing)

There exists in society a delusion caused, not only by an ignorance of contemporary facts but in so far as they are known, a drawing of wrong conclusions from them.1 Bernard Shaw.

Laozi was an economist, he wrote a book called the Daodejing, it tells of his early life BCE, his Prince, and the peoples' wealth. We learn of our time, through his exile that we are leaderless and have reason to be ashamed. Because Laozi says of the old days, they had better ways.

China BCE, had the highest living standards in the world, peaceful relations and a voluntary economy. The people cooperated willingly to build the States, aqueducts and bridges, because they shared the benefits, of water, and travel. Great works need many hands, and the people pitched-in to have them, to use. So, building the nation was helping themselves. Architecture and engineering were their obsession, their wants were needs, manifestly had in their built infrastructure.

Building great things was not an obligation for the people BCE, it was their pleasure, and the more infrastructure, the greater use from the State, the happier they were. They had an agreement with the Prince to use, and a contract with the future to build, both relationships made them wealthy.

In later times, Qin Shi Huang noticed the buildings not maintained, fields in despair, families fighting, and the people sick. He made himself emperor, let the people fix, he restored the State, and the people became wealthy again.

Shi Huang, was advised on how to make the people rich by the Daoist Han Feizi; he said to kill all the intellectuals and

11

burn their books. Han Feizi was an economist. The Daoist philosophy was so practical that it was called 'legal' because commonsense was the whole of their law.

Today we would call legalists -Republicans. Qin Shi Huang successfully rid the society of its only two problems; intellectuals, and rent seekers, and the country was reborn, the Yellow place of the Yellow Emperor. Reborn, because legend told of an earlier emperor, and of the Daoist called Laozi.

After the emperor's death, the surviving intellectuals destroyed the Qin legacy. They reinvented themselves in the ensuing crisis as priestly, and actively mocked the Daoist knowledge with faint praise, for naive mysticism.

The priest-class have lied about the history of the Qin for 2000 years, denying the knowledge in the Daoist texts. They have feared the discovery of the sage instructions by another yellow emperor because Laozi warned them, his Daodejing had no peer, and he was coming back.

Laozi has modern-day acolytes in John Ralston Saul, calling bureaucrats *Voltaire's bastards*, and Nassim Taleb calling company men - *intellectual yet idiot*. After Qin Shi Huang killed the intellectual class, China hosted the world's first industrial revolution. Today we know the Qin's enemies as Professors and National Security Advisors.

The intellectuals' self-preservation has been costly for the world's people and particularly for the Chinese, who are having difficulty progressing with their foreign advisors knowing better. Their indigenous knowledge denied is being given back in the Daodejing, with this telling of the Laozi economic wisdom.

Xi Jinping, the Chinese President, lamented to UNESCO 2015;
...'the Chinese people are striving to fulfill the Chinese dream of the great revival of the Chinese nation, the Chinese

dream is about the prosperity of the country, the rejuvenation of the nation and the happiness of the people, it reflects the ideal of the Chinese people today, and our time-honored tradition to seek constant progress. The Chinese dream will be realized by the balanced development of material and cultural progress. Without the continuation and development of civilization or the promotion of prosperity of culture the Chinese dream will not come true.'

Xi wants for China, what is today unknown to the world, the known-unknown is the Laozi of BCE, here explained as, the Thermodynamic economy of the ancients. Xi senses this knowledge was once well known, for the *Chinese dream [of wealth] always had*, must have come from somewhere in the memory of the nation.

Introduction to this work

The Laozi, with comments by this writer, is a revealed work but also a created one. It was partly transliterated from petroglyphs and interpreted from other translations of the Daodejing. The society is imagined working, from Laozi's valley antidotes those suggest a thriving economy in an industrial topography.

This treatise is a transposition of the Daodejing, not a translation. It is the recreation of the model state described in the final chapters, and an interpretation of them from the preceding text. The Daodejing is here a part treatise on the industry from the dark side of the valley, and an observation of the society supporting it on the bright side.

Dao was Laozi's word for *Economics* which had a different meaning to him than it does for us. Laozi's economics was a sophisticated science with proofs, and not our dogma that equates wealth with rights, and fairness with work. Dao meant Zao (creation) in ancient China. 'De' was the virtue *of Wealth*, and the subject of his jing (book of changes - I Ching), but Laozi's concept of wealth is not ours.

BCE wealth, was the countries promises kept, by the honoring of currency issued in good faith. Honor was a trust given by the state, and that was the wealth of the present generation, won by their keeping faith with the future generation.

The preceding admittedly sounds strange, but it is a scientific introduction to wealth creation, which will be useful to the now and for the future. The appendix to this work is part titled *a deal with the future* and it is a full plan for a modern economy gifted to us from ancient China.

Entropy and Time

The Daodejing has nothing to say about the Greek virtues taught by history (quoxue) as de, or the way of the Buddha, because Laozi never wrote about those things, or knew anything about them.

Economists will acknowledge the silk road started in China, and that it was the first country to industrialize, but they will prefer to discuss the shops at the end of the road. They rather talk of distribution in Samaria, than the more interesting; production of everything in China.

Laozi will show that the origin of a productive state is from industry, and that most private wealth is held in trust by the commonwealth, not in the home. He will describe how to get rich from the beginning, and from nothing. He suggests forgetting what has been taught about economics and politics, and to approach his protocol with an open mind (Chs. 20,41,51). Let us go back to BCE, and learn how the ancients got rich.

The Qin emperor's tomb evidences industrialization, knowledge and wealth equal to that in our time. His chariot made of 4,000 parts, crafted by skilled labor, using advanced metallurgy, tells that thousands of workers and hundreds of factories worked in unison to achieve this one item. The extraordinary thing about the chariot and the other found objects is how ordinary they seem. The country did not stop working to build what looks to be a grand project, more likely; the emperor was buried, tomb supplied within three weeks of his death, because it is now, and always has been disrespectful to plan a death.

Such was the capacity of Chinese industry BCE. By the time of the emperor's death, China had an economy that was, USA productive Circa 1945. The emperor had learned how, from the Laozi. He had an intergenerational agreement with the future, and a contract with the present to act in good faith.

The emperors dealing that made China wealthy is the subject of this book, it invites thinking of treating with the future, and with our decedents, like the Emperor did with his.

China had a paper money system 200 years before England discovered tally sticks. The Laozi, tells us that China was issuing unbacked currency 3000 years earlier. This book will tell of the emperor's methodology of issuing and redeeming money so that it got work done in the present and retained its value in the future.

No review of found artifacts or text can support the assertion of the religious mysticism said to be in the Daodejing by academics. The evidence of authentic ancient texts proves only that the people of Laozi's time sought wealth, and had a system to cooperate that made them all rich.

The most ancient of found texts are the Samarian, they deal solely with legal and economic issues. Aside from poetic flourish, none deal with mysticism. The poems in praise of Urukagina and Gudea condemn rent seekers and praise the good kings that banished them. Rock carvings condemn priests and bureaucrats. Clay tablets advise silver money and fair exchange. They all speak of Laozi's subject, political economy.

The Laozi is comparable in sentiment to each of them. Praise of Ur-Nammu says that people are secure in their homes without soldiers (police) because the king builds infrastructure to make the economy thrive, and he lets the people keep what they produce, so they protect themselves, almost quoting the Laozi chapters 17 - 19, & 30 -32, dated to the same time.

China's system of wealth was called the Laozi after its creator – like Marxism is, Dao is named, like ours called capitalism. The Laozi encouraged people to take the initiative by engaging another in an enterprise, that was having productive relationships. The relationships were productive because they were vetted with hexagrams. The hexagrams were made by asking three questions of each party to a relationship.

16

Entropy and Time

With Six questions a Daoist could tell whether any relationship would be profitable. The questions come from the Daodejing, and not the i-Ching the Hexagrams are demonstrated at the conclusion of this introduction.

China had the most successful economy in history because the Daoist hexagram discipline vetted all of its commercial relationships, there were no frictions. Laozi cautioned the leaders against interfering in those relationships. He warned that diminishing returns could be got from the healthy relationships if there was pressure on them.

The appropriate relationships, known to the Qin, are explained in exquisite detail in a companion text to the Daodejing called the Gui Gu Zi (400BCE). Its Twelve psalms (two are missing), and seven scriptures, support this work.

The embarrassment of inconvenient facts surrounding the Laozi text makes a mockery of modern explanations of history, science or philosophy. Reading forward learn, the Daodejing was called the Magnum Opus, and Laozi - Solon by ancient Greece, the Daodejing was called the philosophers stone in medieval Europe, and the Kabbalah, by the family of Mosses. Laozi preceded Pythagoras, he was the one known as 'Thrice-wise,' he was paraphrased by Machiavelli, and his economic theory was called the holy grail, by the Knights Templar (who kept it secret).

The economics of Laozi was the real alchemy practiced by the controller of the Royal Mint, Sir Isaac Newton. His translation of the Green Tablet, is a direct translation of the Laozi first chapter introducing economics. There is no coincidence in Newton's $F=Ma$ being his counterpart Copernicus's theory of money (Copernicus was the controller of the Prussian treasury), because the cosmology came from the economics in the Hermtis Trismegisti, and that derived from the Daodejing. The Laozi in other translations explained gravity to Newton, and relativity to Einstein (an early and lifetime acolyte of Laozi). Money is the force in Laozi's economics, and cosmology was his metaphor for the gravity in economics.

This economic knowledge from China BCE came by way of the silk road. Later in Jerusalem, the Knights Templar discovered it and used it to establish the Kingdom of Switzerland, banking in Cyprus, treasury in London, and finance in Paris. The formula for alchemy was the Laozi that worked, not the political & economic system called Feudalism that did not.

Alchemy is a one-word definition of economics; its formula was always and is still the holy grail. Here in the Laozi, and in the appendix to this book is the Cup called by history the grail. Cup was Laozi's word for his economic model. He described it as a cornucopia (ch.4). This book will give the original version, which is both better explained, and superior to any economic model we know today.

This introduction has already made and will continue to make what appear to be heuristic claims; however, it is an introduction to a work done, these assertions will be the settled knowledge of the future, and this book is their evidence unqualified.

The importance of the Laozi to our history

The Laozi economic system introduced here is the final recovery from an actual theft. In 1440 Lorenzo Valla, exposed the catholic church for lying about the donation of the Western Empire to the Catholic Church. The church was asserting. They owned the *known world* because Emperor Constantine willed it to them. Valla caught the church with the fabricated titles.

This book will tell of the greater wealth stolen from humanity. It was the income, we call it banking today, and the church got away with it. Banking was a perversion of China's Seigniorage money system, never invented by the Templars or their predecessors'.

Assertions of right have always established ownership of land. Herbert Spencer, P.J. Proudhon, Maurice Allias, Henry George, et al., have claimed; that ownership is not a right. Valla did more than argue; he proved the ownership of everything was fraud, the church fabricated the provenance of everything, in the middle ages, by writing.

The middle age fabrication was earlier in China's history. Wang Bi and others scrubbed the Daodejing of its subject (economics) at the end of the warring states period, making it meaningless for the un-illuminated that have naively translated the deception for 1000 years.

While the Catholic Church got caught stealing the lands, it cared little, because the worth of land is infinitesimal, compared to the value of the Holy grail (the formula for wealth) contained in this right impression of the Daodejing.

In the Chronology of Ancient Kingdoms 1728, Sir Isaac Newton questioned histories dates. According to him there are a thousand added years in history, the past time of Christ was closer than we know, and he proved it by references to the timing of comets in the ancient texts.2 Could it be that the Russians are right, the middle ages lied the past to create history?3 Orwell told us in1984 that;

He who controls the past controls the future, he who controls the present controls the past.

Did the Hermtis Trismegisti code the economics from the Daodejing for the Templars? Did the Vatican introduce the Gregorian calendar and invent a dark age? Was the BCE legacy destroyed, and the past made-up, so the commons emerged owned, and indebted? Is politics played like that?

19

Orwell 1984 said it was the ministries Job to do those things, and indeed the Soviets were active believers. Book burnings, by inquisitions and the destruction of buildings (evidence), are well known of the middle ages, less known; is that the creation of books (history) was the great project of the age.

The Benedictine monks and the Jesuits were not transcribing the books written to make them more available as the history shows in pictures of them working. They were in fact as Valla proved in 1440, creating fictions, and destroying the evidence of history. Little wonder the Monks took a vow of silence to do their job, and Wang Bi died at age 24.

On Translation and the meanings of words

There is a control group that answers for the past, the whole of Eastern Europe, the Tatar lands defended from the Romans but colonized in the dark ages, renamed Russia and Byzantium. The Tatar are ignored by history because they evidence the full lie of it.

In the Russian and Hungarian language, there still exist words with meanings conveyed with great difficulty to modernity. These words date from a culture BCE and still exist with their original meanings.

Words like the 'king' that assume every head of household is a sovereign, and a 'nation' that extends no further than your homes back fence. Russian dialects use words today that shine meaning on the Laozi. Unfortunate for translators, because those meanings come from the posture of the teller, his inflection tells more of the story, than a sentence of words can.

20

The American Way and Sun Yat-Sen.

It is an unfortunate fact that in the middle ages the Knights Templar controlled the economic model of Laozi. In more enlightened hands the past may have set a wealthier stage for us.

Laozi's model was not the Knights one of controlling assets to ennoble the few. Laozi's model insists on first establishing a state, by a ruler's union with the people. The importance of a Union was that it required no concessions, the people did not forego their rights, and the leader did not agree any responsibilities. The Union with leader enabled those participating with him to Nation build at will. They could obtain an income (sweet rain), and act on land without permissions because in Union each is trusted to act in good faith.

This Laozi, the Tatar history, the work of Valla, Formenko and others including Newton acknowledges that the feudal state system was let on the world to significant effect in the middle ages, but that false claims of land ownership corrupted it, and the deliberate perversion of the currency invented in China hobbled it. Nevertheless, their feudal model still worked, and it continues to do so.

We are still using the Knights' system, except that now like then, it is not what it could be, and produces less wealth than it would in the Laozi form. The Knights Templar system of laws, land ownership, resource rationing, and money control, was called the English System by Henry Carey 1851, and today we call it capitalism, or communism.

In economic discourse, there is no pretense about the difference between capitalism and communism. Economists call the Knights Templar system a mixed economy. Communism confuses politics with ownership, but it remains ownership, and that is capitalism to an economist. Communism has its aether in a capitalist banking sector,4Moreover, it retains capitalism's, controlled; opportunity, movement, and pretended market prices, in all practical respects the systems are identical.

Economics is concerned with production and income; the ownership of assets or debts affects neither because people produce and earn regardless of ownership. Very few people get what capitalism is, Marx & Engels were not confused, they called their book (Das) Capital 1867.5

The Laozi system was not the Knights Templar or English system as Henry Carey called it in his 1851 book Harmony of Interests; 6

[The English system] has for its object an increase in the number of persons that are to intervene between the producer and the consumer. [They] living on the product of the land and the labor of others, diminishing the power of the first, and increasing the number of the last; and thus, that Ireland is compelled to waste more labor annually than would be required to produce, thrice over, all the iron, and convert into cloth all the cotton and wool manufactured in England. The poverty of producers exists nearly in the ratio in which they are compelled to make their exchanges in the market of Great Britain, foregoing the advantages that would result to them from the free exercise of the power of associating for the purpose of combining their exertions, and thus rendering their labor more effective. (p.61)

[The English doctrine of] ships, colonies, and commerce is thus reproduced on this side of the Atlantic, and its adoption by the nation will be followed by effects similar to those which have been already described as existing in England. There, for a time, it gave the power to tax the world for the maintenance of fleets and armies, as had before been done by Athens and by Rome, and there it is now producing the same results that have elsewhere resulted from the same system: poverty, depopulation, exhaustion, and weakness. (p.227)

The Laozi economic system was not a socialist mixture of capitalism; it was one where land, money, and movement were free. The people built infrastructure for the state, when it did not interfere with their production. The closest modern equivalent of the Laozi model was Henry Carey's American school wanted for China by Sun Yat Sen in the 1920's (Minsheng Zhuyi). Carey compares it to the Templars English system at the conclusion of his book;

One [the American school] looks to increasing the necessity of commerce; the other [the English system] to increasing the power to maintain it. One looks to underworking the Hindoo, and sinking the rest of the world to his level; the other to raise the standard of man throughout the world to our level. One looks to pauperism, ignorance, depopulation, and barbarism; the other to increasing wealth, comfort, intelligence, [the] combination of action, and civilization. One looks towards universal war; the other towards universal peace. One is the English system; the other we may be proud to call the American system, for it is the only one ever devised the tendency of which was that of ELEVATING while EQUALISING the condition of man throughout the world. (p.229) [capitalization Carey's]

Laozi called what Carey described as the American System, the Dao and it follows this introduction in its superior form. The American system (associated with aspects of the Lincoln, Jackson & Kennedy presidencies), has not been practiced in the USA for 200 years, it was overcome by the Templar English

23

system (assassination, central banking, war, & free trade) and forgotten by history.

The Laozi guided the Qin to unite China and begin the world's first industrial revolution, here historical evidence of the Laozi being an economic theory. The Qin industrialization answered Malthus before he was born. Here the theory of Laozi is known more thoroughly than it was by the Qin, but it is evident from the first emperor's rule, that he used what he had of the Laozi with confidence, to industrialize.

Laozi wrote in a code for the same reasons Da Vinci did. He spoke in geometry because his fellows understood it before, and better than Pythagoras. He hid his knowledge from the eunuchs (his enemies) in poems topography, and antidotes. Now it is transparent; we know quantum mechanics, chemistry, relativity, polygons and gravity, the Eunuchs BCE did not. We can decipher the poems (court language & lingo) of the Qin because we talk statistics in moles now, large numbers like the Qin poetry did and Laozi does.7

In a feudal court, knowledge was survival. The first emperor had no link to the man Laozi. The emperor is said to have died seeking the elixir of life from a Daoist priest, but we should intuit the more likely journey; he died seeking the full text of Laozi's economics (alchemy), something more complete than he had, like the appendix attached to this work.

The Yellow emperor sought more for his only interest; the Chinese dream of industrialization. The emperor was immortal, only if China was. An emperor extending his mortal life with a potion is ridiculous, but A Daoist Emperor that sought a formula to extend his countries wealth is the commonsense pursuit of President Xi Jinping today and the motivation of every competent leader.

This Laozi is a significant contribution to the re-evaluation of history from the perspective of kings; the tedious work of wealth creation, and industrialization was the emperors' day job. The leader of a wealthy people in a growing country is more concerned with city planning, and sewerage, than wars and court intrigue.

The Kings of past were competent, and their people were happy. Our past was dull, it was peaceful, and everywhere it was productive; our survival is full witness to the old kings' wisdom.8

How to know the Daodejing

Today's academics have not recognized, Laozi the Economist, because he adapted language, intended to confuse. Laozi even made an apology for his profession being esoteric and a little too obtuse in chapter 15 of his text.

Laozi never spells macroeconomics or GDP. He says Dao and the Ten Thousand things, else he calls the economy a vessel, the stream, a sea, and the actors baby, wasp, buffalo. Laozi's, peers on wall street will recognize his lingo. Tiger, Buffalo, Wasp are today, terms used in the business press of China, they describe rouge economic elements and financial players.

Sometimes to save lengthy explanations reconciling this version of Laozi to the familiar ones relying on translation those rejected for the reasons given, new words substitute for the Laozi word translated into our language - because those better convey his meaning to us.

Three examples suffice, where 'Dao,' or river (stream) then *economy* (market), and where he says infant or uncut block, 'entrepreneur' is written because that is our description of an enthusiastic unspoiled participant in the economy, and what Laozi meant us to infer from his description of a wide-eyed, creative, hard worker like Edison. Where Laozi says army, 'Police' because the army were police in BCE China. Laozi is nearly always talking about domestic affairs, and about autarky.

Priests and translators assert the Dao is their unknowable way. Those with Buddhist, Zen and Christian training are each uniquely mistaken by the pet terms, and descriptions used by Laozi to describe an economic system creating wealth. They see Laozi's awe for the political economy making everyone rich, matching their love for god, and hopes for others.

In fairness to the priests - there are correlations between religion and economics; it is no coincidence because religion learned its doctrine from economics.

Laozi described production, as creation. The Chinese word Zao is Dao in aristocratic speech affectation, Laozi describes creation beginning from nothing, and in silence in stillness, everything is made.

Laozi, the economist, made stars of men, and from materials, he created them skilled, and things useful, from nothing (Chs. 1, 16, 25, 42, 51).

The priests could not make up a story that good, so they did what Sigmund Freud told us they had always done, in his story of Moses. Freud said the priests adopted the stories of Kings as their own. God had no part in the creation story that his priests copied. Laozi agrees with Bastiat, that nature is free, value and purpose come from man - not god.

On the method of understanding the Laozi;

Shaw praised Upton Sinclair by saying.

'I have regarded you, not as a novelist, but as a historian; for it is my considered opinion, unshaken at 85, that records of facts are not history. They are only annals, which cannot become historical until the artist-poet-philosopher rescues them from the unintelligible chaos of their actual occurrence and arranges them in works of art. When people ask me, what happened in my long lifetime, I do not refer them to the newspaper files and the authorities, but to your novels. They object that the people in your books never existed; that their deeds were never done and their saying never uttered. I assure them that they were, except that Upton Sinclair individualized and expressed them better than they could have done, and arranged their experiences, which as they actually occurred were as unintelligible as pied type in significant and intelligible order9

Be thankful for the artist-poet-philosophers that rescue unintelligible pied type from history and arrange it in works of art; no other way has ever found understanding from the past.

Academics say words are precise, and they have a divined authority in their qualifications. Yet they ignore the word read. To read is known by history and before writing as *to listen*. The word read was given its proper meaning by the Webster Dictionary (1928), guess was read (since revised). See forward that we are reading, and getting by guessing and not translating.

Knowing by guessing, is rightly the pride of children, Laozi will tell in many of his chapters, to be more like children. Creative people like Hannes Alfven and Richard Feynman made-up reality, and got Nobel prizes for it, others like Nicola Tesla used guessing to create ac power, and radio. Tesla made ac electricity, he created the remote control, made pumps, and motors, he invented them all and discovered nothing. The Laozi assumes this is obvious, and we will have to adjust our thinking because his conception of work, Tesla's too, is more useful than ours.

In the physical world, we will be discussing as economics, and as useful; things are created and improved, not discovered and lost.

Academics call guessing hermeneutic, ironic here, but applied to texts such as the Daodejing; they would call the work of this author an exegesis of the Laozi and insist on its inferiority to a strict translation. However, this work is the creation of a system, not the discovery of a text, the Laozi has now a superior proof in the appendix model and the Hexagrams given below.

The propositions put in the Laozi are that; neither nature nor capital are factors of production, new things come from nothing valuable, no law can prevent attraction. Wherever fictional limits are more creative and valuable than a reality imagined, we enter the Brave New World of Huxley 2540, where titillation usurps progress, lawyers are superior to engineers, and the future is by design, limited to their poxed imagination and therefore dystopian.

Wherever discovery, there will be patents, ownership, and entrenched poverty. A promise cannot be sincere if made with an offer of discovery, Huxley knew only soma extends incredulity sufficiently to deny invention, and pretend a control by scripture.

Trust in society cannot exist with discovery because the lack of discovery limits it. Trust thrives only with the expectation of creation (an idea, or plan). Trust dies with titillation, partly because the senses cannot distinguish opportunities from distractions, and otherwise because expectations of discovery are not realistic.

Wherever the academics are known for their predecessor's scripture (Keynesian), we will be referring to their authority, and to its limiting scripture, not its usefulness. The things wanted or imagined from knowledge will be nonexistent, and the subject's unknowable.

We will look at the economic model of Laozi soon, and know more about the past, its community, and economics than reading could ever teach. These are difficult topics to study, but intuitive subjects to know by seeing them demonstrated, and by experiencing them differently than the experts taught.

Non - Action - is do no harm.

We will be discussing the origins of Chinese medicine, and learn that the temples of Luxor and Beijing were the economic models of the female state. Acupuncture was Eunuch banishment, and problematic officials were a form of cancer, toxins that needed extraction from the palace model, for their poisoning of others' relationships. Laozi's nonaction in the economy is what we know from medicine as the Hippocratic oath. Be sure, then do no harm to the patient, remove the disease (always an academic), don't attack the patient (entrepreneur).

Laozi and Macro Economics.

The challenge in resolving the received Laozi was in creating the economic model it hinted at in the Daodejing, and in imagining the political machinations necessary to accommodate massive new wealth in our society.

The model had to work for it to of operated, and it needed to be useful in our world for this work to demand attention. IT DOES. The appendix is a full explanation, and its origin in the Daodejing, therefore commands attention.

The Laozi BCE is feudal ownership, free markets, free money, free resources, and no capital. The economy changes some energies into useful forms and creates entropy in making products. It changes some combinations of energy (qi) into other forms of energy (qi) and makes them useful. It takes labor, solar energy, and fossil fuel, and changes things made with them into food, clothes, and warmth.

This description is the by-line of the i-Ching - the book of changes. Entropy is a word derived from the Greek, meaning changes. The by-line of the i-Ching belongs to the Daodejing; it explains the changes in energy that Soddy and Laozi call economics.

The Daoist system is not explained at all by Marshall and Freidman (classical & monetary theory) but has consistencies with Riccardo, the Physiocrats, and Walrus. It foretold of P.J. Proudhon's observation that capitalism [a competing system] ends in deflation, with the fatal destruction of assets by capital. Therefore, the Laozi could not have been a capitalist system, with a debt based money, because it would have failed, and the Qin proved, it did not.

Many of the institutionalist ideas espoused by Thorstein Veblen, and Stuart Chase, are evident in the Laozi. Henry George, The Science of the political economy 1850, partly described chapter 25, and 42 of the Daodejing. Allias agreed with all of Laozi's ideas (without knowing any of them), he shared with George the idea of expunging the rentiers and thought the only viable interest rate could be zero.

Laozi will mimic the contempt Veblen had for marginal analysis (supply and demand) in the text.

Entropy and Time

Frederic Bastiat Economic Harmonies 1850 explains economics, politics and the law like Laozi does. His insights introduce the problematic early Laozi chapters 2 & 3. The Law 1850 by Bastiat, is referenced, and it is an excellent companion piece to the Laozi.

The early Laozi chapters (Chs. 2, 3, 11, 12), were the obsession of a renegade group of radical economists in ancient China called the Mohists, their work evidence how difficult economics can be at its limits. What little of Mohists texts exist, directly support this economic interpretation of Laozi. The Mohists were interested in how asymmetric relationships were to be navigated by trade. How is exchanging a rare peach for a common plum with an infirm neighbor a good deal? Was then and is today an exciting question, requiring an answer.

The Mohists explored the value of the commonwealth as the private and productive wealth, they believed like Laozi, that intellectual property belonged to the Commonwealth, and that it could be used effectively there as private wealth. Their ground is being re-explored today by those looking at patent laws, the costs of polluting the environment, and the essentials of improving, not denuding the commonwealth while making money. Their work is similar to Georg Simmel's Philosophy of Money 1900 and his sociology, it shines over today's confusion of State education with the domain of parents, and illustrates the problems of confusing the public welfare with peoples' private wellbeing.

The American System of Henry Carey, was similar to the Laozi, in many respects an example of the Laozi working, (Lincoln's greenback was Laozi money).

Bastiat lives with us through Henry Hazlitt's 'Economics in One Lesson' 1946, a book that has never been out of print, that does deliver on its titles promise by simply repeating Bastiat's Broken window allegory, *What is Seen and Unseen.*

Laozi's Way to Wealth & the Holy Grail

Asserting, that this Laozi will reward any effort made to understand Hexagrams, and Thermodynamics, with the formula for wealth, is no more heuristic than Hazlitt's and he. quoting Bastiat, and only Bastiat has not been accused once, of hubris in seventy years.

Learn how to increase the Nations GDP 10% p.a. Every year by working less, retiring early and debt free, participate in the polity and work in Nation building. It's all in this Daodejing, and proved in the appendix.

Review of the Daodejing literature

Hongkyung Kim concluded his introducing Old Master, 201210 by saying

'I primarily view Laozi as a political text.'

Hongkyung Kim is a rare commentator to disagree with the mystical interpretation. His book is a companion to this work. Hongkyung Kim will give the reader a complimentary history to the one given here, and a worthy comparative text, he offers the reader many word choices, and a full review of the literature that has been ignored here, because it is an area well covered by Alan Chan Laozi, Stanford Encyclopedia of Philosophy, (2013) and others.

Hongkyung Kim spends much energy defining his Chinese words, and choosing their English counterpart; he emphasizes how important a correct interpretation of the words is to understanding Laozi. His translation methodology is similar to the one made by Jonathan Star, Daodejing Definitive Edition 2001.

Entropy and Time

Comparing their translations, *using the most meticulous care* by Hongkyung Kim, and *definitive* by Star, the differences exist greater in deviation and quantity than their agreements, proving the previous discussion on translation, and what we should intuit from reading texts from BCE; it is near impossible. To wit, had the Chinese dictionary had been revised once every two generations. While the language, or the morals, science, conversation, or industry, or any combination of them changed just five percent per revision, then that calculation would be done compounding (rule of 70 over 30 iterations) and the meanings of the pictographs, and ideographs would be near random as they were found to be comparing Hongkyung Kim & Star.

Direct translation produces *Chinese whispers* after 4000 years, it plays a part in understanding the Daodejing, but a minor one. Hongkyung Kim, Star, and others that rest their authorities on translation are mistaken to do so.

The Dao is oral knowledge, in any event, proved by the six summarizing, and six explaining chapters, planted throughout as memory cues. Chinese speakers write in the air with their lips and with fly sticks, their explanations are illustrated with their bodies, and not given in writing.

For those not familiar with the Chinese language it is exclusive. Meaning is intended for receptive and permitted listeners. Ordinary exclusion is by dialect, tone, and pronunciation. Extraordinary exclusion is by way of coded geometry, numbers, and science. Ordinarily written words and spoken words have radically different meanings in each of the 13 regions of China, and many scholars have been additionally confused by where Laozi was when he wrote his text.

The language spoken and written by Laozi was very private, his words, had his meanings, and only guild members knew those. In any setting, the Chinese language is not understood by reading outside of the place, time, situation, or at all without the express invitation of the writer.

An experienced listener, reading the talk, imagines the speaker, conjures the power point and must know the speakers subject in part, to hear the words knowing. The listener reads, understanding words from knowing their context in surroundings. Laozi himself says in the text that the great speakers are awkward, the meaning is got by the knowledgeable listener in quantities more than the speaker gives. The text is never the full authority or the only source of knowledge available from reading. The Laozi references a plethora of knowledge that is assumed, and if it is not known, he excludes.

The way to know the Daodejing, and the economy of the future, is by imagining Laozi as he is commonly described, an advisor to a king, as the treasurer of a kingdom. He hated wasting money because he said so. Laozi wanted people to be productive, to not burden the state, because he said those things too. He wrote a book, like Jack Welch did, *Jack Straight from the Gut* 2001. Laozi's book describes what he did in his day job as an economist advising a king. The jacket of Jack's book says *here he reveals his philosophy and management style.* Jacks book was about sacking, Laozi's banishment, both to get rich.

Laozi is a character similar to Jack Welch, neither have empathy with Jesus Christ or the Dalai Lama. If Laozi had a caring thought, it was for the king's survival, by the king keeping a modest palace to escape the peoples noticing him, the thief collecting taxes.

Knowing the speaker, and his subject is the obvious path to gaining knowledge from a new text. Words are meaningless in any language if they have no context in the subject. Here explaining how academics have missed Laozi's cues to the economic model.

Entropy and Time

We will approach the words of Laozi with an intuition; our advantage is having the model & the hexagrams, it allows us to appreciate Laozi's emphasizing, and his elaborations from the start. In the comments to chapter 25, there is a new definition to the subject of economics which will significantly assist appreciating the worth of knowing the Thermodynamic economy of BCE China.

Let us call our process of understanding Laozi an exchange between a professor of economics and his graduate student; Laozi assumes the student's pre-knowledge that he is an economist. Then call it gestalt, teaching is the production of learning. Production is our subject described by the example of gestalt, the scholar produced. We are using the Laozi method now to learn by creation, the exchange between teacher and student produces results, the product of the student knowing is the proof, how the student learned is irrelevant, because she did.

If we choose the Laozi way, we choose creation for progress, then as Nicola Tesla and Dr. Suez showed, we will make better substitutes, and do it by leaps (exponential), not rungs (linear). The only thing Buckminster Fuller discovered was to create everything better with half the material, everything else he invented. Moore's law tells us that power doubles and price halves by the invention of better. Anything discovered, like land and resources gets used, depleted and scarce. Everything created, like aluminum, and graphene gets lighter, cheaper, and more plentiful.

Addressing the rump of the Daodejing literature, kindly a scholar skilled in translation cannot be expected to recognize the strange economics encoded with descriptions of shape in the words of an ancient text.

The philosophy industry has worthy foot-soldiers who write essays on the various commentaries. Typical of the genre is Two interpretations of De in the Daodejing by Erin M. Cline

2004 Journal of Chinese Philosophy. Her essay arbitrates disagreements in the opinions of Laozi authorities; if we could salt her article with more candor, Cline would give a good account of the deplorable discourse existing in Chinese philosophy, typical also in economics today.11

Hongkyung Kim is less circumspect on the commentaries; he chooses Robert Henricks (1993) as a representative and typical interpreter of the Daodejing. He says Henricks edits chapters or ignores them altogether; he has Laozi saying what he does not say while ignoring the symbolism inconvenient to his narrative. Hongkyung Kim concludes that the combination of these compounding errors is fatal to those commentaries.

In fairness to Henricks, most Daodejing scholars stop at the translations of words (after a mysterious transliteration never explained) and offer no interpretation of the 81 chapters.

There exists a very much smaller collection of scholars that have attempted to know Laozi with a direct comment on all of the chapters. Kwan-Yuk Claire Sit 2010 typifies the very best of those few, but they also share the Henricks flaws, and by degrees, they too extrapolate his errors.

Here each chapter of the Laozi and the whole is treated as a single subject, and as a monologue. Each chapter resolved as Laozi would have done. This Laozi is a comprehensive and complete economics text, no part mysticism.

The i-Ching, Hexagrams, & Confucius.

The oldest known classic is said to be the i-Ching (yijing) The book of Changes. It is known for its eight trigrams, arranged in two sets on an x,y, axis. Their sums make hexagrams. There are 64 possible solutions these were arranged as a matrix and numbered by King Wen while he spent seven years in prison. What could be their meaning and why would a king be interested in the yijing?

The i-Ching scholars say now that the hexagrams are picked-up by throwing sticks, the dropped sticks generate random trigrams, these are combined to make hexagrams, and those divine the destiny of a simple people and their superstitious emperors in China.

Each of the 64 possible pairs has an explanation in the scripture of the i-Ching. Confucius is said to have spent twenty years writing its text and wanted to spend fifty more guiding the seemingly foolish people and gullible rulers of China, that believed in the wisdom of dropped sticks. Wang Bi too was an authority on explaining random sticks.

Wang Bi is the go-to authority for nearly all Laozi, and i-Ching scholarship, not heeding the warning of his youth, academics refer to him more than any other as the fount of Chinese philosophy. All of the little known about Wang Bi is that he was to conflate the Buddhist, Daoist and Confucian thought to concoct an acceptable uniting philosophy for China at the end of the warring states period.

Wang Bi was retained to write a reader's digest of the Chinese classics which he did as a 19-year-old. He was a one-person, *Council of Nicaea* that invented a uniting philosophical creed to be accepted by a [then] too diverse intelligentsia;

37

Wang Bi was to simplify ruling a nation in the process of post war reconciliation.

Wang Bi and later the Jesuits (with their Catholic Confucius) did in China what Akhenaten did in Egypt impressing Aten (the sun god) as the only god. Akhenaten purported that the sun god had the powers of the other gods. This Aten fraud was accomplished at the Council of Nicaea by Constantine like it was by Akhenaten and by the Emperor using Wang Bi at similar stages in their respective nations evolving.

By the leaders destroying, rewriting, and altering the physical evidence of the past, and discovering it the next day as the history of Jesus, Aten, and Confucius, or Buddha, the leaders got divine authority.

None of this is controversial; these are facts well known, all of the Confucian material was burned 223 BCE by the Qin. What is interesting for our purpose is that buried in the i-Ching concoction made up. The tricksters left the footprint of Laozi. The Yijing is the proof negative of the Chinese dream to enrich the country.12

It is irrelevant to people's lives, what the church agreed Jesus told Peter, or whether Aten ever did control the river because those things are of no physical consequence. An academic using the authority of the Nicene Creed, or the king's ode to Aten can be tolerated as a harmless twit, writing about a subject of no importance. However, an academic using the authority of Wang Bi, or Confucius to discuss the i-Ching as random numbers, or the Laozi as mysticism will have extended humankind's impoverishment and denied generations of their material wellbeing.

The purpose of Wang Bi and others changing the past in China was to discredit the Laozi; then the only of understood economic philosophy. By their making hexagrams appear random numbers, they mocked the relationships at the foundation of Chinese prosperity.

The Laozi was respected after the tricksters pretended the i-Ching, but with the hexagram key in the Daodejing text (chapter 22 -26) removed from the Hexagrams in the Yijing, all the usefulness was lost, the Laozi got faint praise, and was called unknowable, the Yijing a mystery. Wang Bi's purpose was after-all to unite China with a dominant philosophy. He chose to elevate a Confucius cartoon character for that purpose. The made-up Confucius, promoted subservience, obedience, devotion, and duties, in short, the slavery we think of as associated with feudalism.

The Jesuits shared a new emperors purpose at a later date and built on Wang Bi's work. The Jesuits had multiple agendas; none included the Chinese people learning their indigenous economic model. The Jesuits wanted the knowledge (science) useful from China to support their European banking business, and also to control China with Catholicism, but at a later date, and by their ownership of China. The ownership of China was a long term project, a generational plan to make the Chinese ignorant of their indigenous knowledge.

To those ends, the Jesuits for the pope & emperor re-invented Confucius again, as Mill did with Smith13, and over a 500-year span the cartoon Confucius was promoted to become the familiar presence we know. Confucius, version one fictionalized by Wang Bi, and version two, catholic Confucius invented by the Jesuits.14 Catholic Confucius said everything and thought of everything as the apostle Paul, and sometimes he does sound exactly like Jesus himself; the golden rule of Confucius is; to *do unto others*. Coincidence before Christ was born?

Wang Bi and Catholic Confucius refer to the Laozi in nearly every hexagram interpretation; they lacked the imagination to think of 64 new ideas, and only obfuscated the Laozi as the i-

Ching. The invented word ren is an excellent example of their dimness, wherever it appears in a Confucius text, it has an origin in a Daoist text and meant money. The philosophy of Money by Georg Simmel 1900, is an 800-page explanation of the word ren.

The tricksters effectively made a slot machine out of the Hexagrams; every stick throw was a propaganda message to obey, respect the betters, work for the new owners.

The legalist emperors remembered as fools divining sticks, and even then, Confucius was to be better at it, and everything else, to dominate the future.

Neither Wang Bi or the Jesuits could interpret random numbers, no-one can pretend that conceit. The ham-fisted editing in the Yijing and the simple-minded commentary on the Laozi in it shows a Keynesian contempt for the average man [sic.].

Typically, introductions to the classic books have faint praise for the Chinese people; they embed their pretended respect for the i-Ching and the Laozi with the loaded mockery associated with tarot cards, random numbers, dropped sticks and mysticism. It is always fake Confucius that is to be the clear thinking and ultimate authority.

The academics control fake Confucius, and he provides the philosophical foundations for the laws and policies that have damned the Chinese people to poverty in a declining empire for five thousand years. Their control of him has been the academics meal ticket, now taken from them, by this works proofs in the hexagrams, and the economic model built from their relationships in the appendix.

It will not be necessary to read the i-Ching (or much of the classics) ever again because the i-Ching was never a book, and the classics were the Confucius backstory made-up. However, the hexagrams were real and were a valuable tool used by Laozi to ensure that commercial relationships were profitable.

Entropy and Time

In ancient times people saw the Daoist's make the hexagrams from a distance, while the Daoist was in a private conversation or alone. People outside of Laozi's guild never knew how they were derived.

How to read the hexagrams from the key in the Laozi? To be clear there is no authentic text in the i-Ching. The Hexagrams were made by the Daoist entrepreneur to analyze relationships, some people like King Wen matched them to the Laozi, by studying the Laozi.

The hexagrams of the ancients were not random but made by a scientific and very modern asking of six questions. Their answers form one of 64 hexagrams that can correspond to a chapter in the Laozi here.

Laozi explains the political economy as a solar system inside a space; he says profitable relationships are made like gravity (chs. 1, 22 - 27).

Gravity is the attractive force determined by distance and mass. Laozi says all things and people have a mass, and we are familiar with the idea because a person has gravitas. Laozi says the person is the subject of economics, and the person is Laozi's star, a star suspended in the community by the attractive force of another's gravitas. Laozi tells that an economy is a network of exclusive relationships based on trust, and those enclose the community, to make the system.

The surplus created by good relationships is the product had from their synergy's, say the more from the division of labor is the profit made from good relationships. The economy seeks profit (product), Laozi says that is a synergy expressed $1 + 2 = 4$ (alchemy).

The Hexagrams of Laozi have their modern counterpart in the decision matrix tools generated by management consultants like McKinsey and company. Their purpose is to predict the synergetic profit from a relationship, every combination of relationships has a value, some are positive, others not ($1 + 2 = 2$).

The three questions that determine gravity between Two objects in space also determine the trust between Two people in society (Laozi chapters 22 - 27).

Now starting with six matchsticks (or a pen & paper) to record data, enquire about the prospects of a productive relationship with another party. Ask first; Is the stranger in the neighborhood, or on my trade route? If the answer is; yes, place the match, then ask; Is there potential (sufficient gravitas) in that opportunity? If answer; no break the match, and place the broken match above the first match, then ask of yourself; Have I the gravitas to pull that other party into my orbit, and make use of them if it suits me? If the answer is yes, place the unbroken match, above the other two.

So you have asked one distance question, and two mass questions, because there is one distance but two perspectives of mass, (In the appendix the Lorentz transformations are used to reconcile the mass) therefore, three questions.

Now imagine you are the other party, using what you know of him, answer the same questions referring to yourself. Is he (you) or could he be in my galaxy (neighborhood, trade route)? Answer; Yes, and place an unbroken stick above the other three, ask again as if you are in the shoes of the other party. Do I have the gravitas to offer the other an attractive opportunity? Answer; Yes, place an unbroken match above the other four. Ask from your knowledge of the other party; Does he have the gravitas to suck me into his orbit? Answer; no break a stick and place it broken above the five, to make a hexagram. Now analyze the relationship without looking yet at the Laozi.

Reading from the bottom up, your trigram (three) first, the other is in your orbit, but he has nothing to offer you, although you could take advantage of him with your superior gravitas. Then reading his trigram; Yes, he is in your neighborhood, or could be, he would love to have a relationship with you, but he has not the experience, smarts, or gravitas to make it possible or worthwhile.

First, note the wisdom and insight extracted from asking six intelligent questions of yourself about a potential relationship. It appears evident from reading the hexagram that you would need to make a great effort to have a relationship with a person you are not interested in, and that has little to offer you.

Now, let us use the King Wen order of arranging the hexagrams in a matrix, and we find our hexagram described is number 49. Using the Mawangdui arrangement of the first 66 chapters (found with the King Wen matrix), we find an excess of two chapters in the discovered (agreed) Daodejing, when I merge Chs. 15 & 16, and or Chs. 17, 18, 19, 20 or combinations of these whole chapter subjects to create a 64-Hexagram arrangement to match the King Wen matrix. There is an oracle-like instruction from Laozi for the hexagram story told above. Using the King Wen, 49 is chapter 47 from the Laozi reduced.

The Laozi at chapter 47 advises on the relationship described in the hexagram derived above by saying; you should know without asking, you should trust intuition, and not have the relationship described by the hexagram (take no action - avoid). George Harrison put this advice to Music, and the Beatles titled their song; The Inner Light. Be honest and have good relationships without making an effort to move, look, or think (logically).

By founding a countries economy on relationships that make sense, the king (commonwealth) will enjoy their synergetic benefits (the natural profit). Profitable relationships are the wealth of the nations. The essential Hexagram is the one made by the citizen, asking about his leader, and this one explains the Union that Laozi says is the fundamental to be sound, for the States productivity (Ch. 42).

To be clear nearly all hexagram descriptions derived from asking the six gravity questions, match a relevant instructive chapter in the Laozi (reduced to 64). Where the hexagram does not match, I have found the hexagram instructive and insightful without the Laozi. Frequently where no fit to the Laozi, I reconsider my answers using more honesty about the distance, or my gravitas, or the other's attraction, I then get a different hexagram story to tell about my relationship with tools, or material, or people that do match the relevant Laozi chapter.

Let no cynic think that all chapters will say the same thing as they do in the i-Ching fiction; each Laozi chapter is a discrete topic, there is specific not universal instruction in the Laozi. Remember that King Wen had seven years in Jail to derive his matrix with the Daodejing. It is more likely that the Hexagrams stood alone, they were a tool useful to filter fellows well met.

The Laozi is merely a reference guide, knowing the Laozi is to draw on it like a master. The hexagrams are tools that say the obvious; good relationships are founded in honesty from the beginning and made by a productive exchange.

The Laozi is all about beginnings. The experienced will intuitively make hexagrams of every situation; their Laozi intelligence acquired, is a ladder thrown, that a happy life with productive relationships and lots of money. Maybe it explains why the world's richest man Jack Ma, carries a copy of the Daodejing with him at all times, and he recommends it to everyone that asks him for advice, on how to make money.

In the interim access to the Laozi is with hexagrams, and by being honest. Honesty forces a reappraisal wherever the hexagrams fail to reference the Laozi. The clearest Hexagram demands a lack of denial in asking the questions. Honesty has this different meaning (lack of denial) when you intend to form a relationship than it does when you are in one (sincerity).

Entropy and Time

The Hexagram measures the involuntary and superior relationship caused by attraction, you are as a body in space motivated by passion (not compelled by logic or need) you have a certain gravitas; a quantity known to you by not denying where you belong, or how attractive you are, or how much you have to offer.

With realistic appraisals of the other party's potential, a hexagram analysis will show that the laws of attraction will decide *the whether* of all relationships without any resorting to logic.

Where the hexagram analysis denies the relationship should be, like our example did (even before looking at the Laozi with the king Wen), then it was honesty that told the story in the hexagram. If the relationship has with the hexagram approval it will be a productive one; if lost; retrospection or its forcing will tell the hexagram assessed early and right.

Relationships are joined or avoided by trust like gravity; no effort should be made to either form a relationship or to avoid one. Either will happen, for the practical reasons told by Newton's laws of attraction, used in the hexagram analysis without using logic, or desire.15

Laozi will teach society is our universe, we are suspended as objects in society by the trust (honesty) existing in it. Trust in society is measured by the money supply introduced by extending trade credit.

The two simultaneous events that happen with a relationship in a Laozi economy are that its potential is recognized, by the room made for it in extending trade credit (the money supply).

Trade credit stretches the fabric of society to accommodate the synergy to be had from a new relationship - new gravitas. The basis of sound money is a certainty, and that a backing, which guarantees a currency deserves the full faith of a trusting people.

The six gravity questions asked of a relationship, not only strip denial to force an honesty (like a lie detector), but they create a (financed) reality. Where is the money found? How does an emerging country get rich? How can a man with nothing feed his family? Will be answered for tomorrows economist in the appendix, and for us by the Laozi witness BCE.

An honest assessment, one free of denial, gets a hexagram that gives a realistic indication of the potential in a relationship to be had, together with its financing. In the hexagram is the potential, and the opportunity, and the work, and the money, and the reward.

Has there ever been a more beautiful explanation for how to start productive relationships or make money than by; honesty finding trust? Does a self-fulfilling proposition, end-all poverty and make everyone wealthy? Laozi will prove that it does; intuit how quickly by using the hexagrams and reading this Laozi.

Just some of the suggestion in the hexagram or a relationship based economy is that people get their wages, business, or wish, in advance, because they are honest about their relationships, they will return with the fish, dig the hole, deliver the goods, if the are in a relationship and more effectively as principals of one - trusted, than wage earners checked in arrears.

A country using this system will know only full voluntary and useful employment. Henry Carey's only lament for his American system was a lack of people to do all the work, and to take advantage of all the opportunities, to enjoy the abundance for the taking. Unemployment and scarcity could only exist in the English system.

A word on induction.

The Laozi tells the extra not told; Where's the money? How does society accommodate the stranger? A young person never asks; Where do 'I' come from, is a question requiring its suggestion. What the child asks of their life is; Where is my place? How can 'I' be accommodated?

Where do I come from? Is a telling, you are a foreigner, you have arrived in the empire, there is no room for you, we own it all, it will not expand to accommodate you, so obey its rules, and beg for favors, and you might get a crumb from an owner.

Can a stranger, or a new child be accommodated? Where is the room - has always been the question? If you want to live well in a wealthy economy, it will be in the one that accommodates you and appreciates especially you. These are the questions answered in the Laozi, and in the appendix.

Intuit how the knowledge offered by Laozi, is superior to any taught. Laozi's economics is not about the distribution of a scarce resource discovered ad-hoc, and owned by the church; it is about the creation of new wealth and yours for the making of a relationship.

Can you imagine the efficiency of a nation founded on a system of vetted relationships, all starting from the beginning valuable? You know there is gold in the hole, you want a relationship with the gold, you are standing over it with a shovel, no one is stopping you from digging. Why the wonder in wealth? Where the limit to how much except exhaustion?

The Hexagrams tell, what the Knights Templar, Aten Confucius, and his Catholic descendants did not want to be found out. Getting rich is the natural product of having honest relationships. If a third party mediates in the relationships they will not be profitable; more likely not be had.

Honesty suggests trusting relationships. Those that exist are the societies gravity. The society is made from relationships, commercial ones extend trade credit, and you will learn variants of trade credit determine the quantity of money circulating, their strength tell of the trust in societies relationships. Einstein described gravity as the fabric of space; The appendix will use his theory and thermodynamics to explain what Laozi does, money is the fabric of society. Money (backed by a trust in its redemption) supports people in society like gravity supports the planets in space.

Money backed by a trust (Lincoln's greenback) relies on honesty in exchange, this money is potential energy in the hands of people it has the same characteristics as a nuclear fuel rod. People and things are as nothing while inert (unemployed), sitting, but when activated, realized with the energy given by trust with money, and in a relationship their potential flows, and becomes powerful (in a workplace).

We and things are full in varying quantities of this type of potential energy, in various combinations of relationships, by organizing (community), these potentials have the further attribute of resonating with others and amplifying their individual and collective potentials (Feynman).

Power is, energy, and that is money. Money backed by the full faith and credit of the people using it, because trust backs money as it does in Singapore today (the full faith is the credit-money of the people). To Laozi; trust is the creator; it is the maker of paths (form) and also the tension that binds a money system based on relationships.

Laozi is the Wealth.

There is only one Chinese classic, and there was only ever one classic of money that deserves the title THE WEALTH OF NATIONS, and it and only it will deliver the dream always had, it is the Laozi economic model based on the hexagram relationships.

48

Entropy and Time

I have spent Six years studying this text, and when I reviewed my work, I had a similar proof to that found by Leo Tolstoy Gospel in Brief 1896. The Laozi written as two books their final Chapters are 37 and 81, in each, I found my work summarized by Laozi.16 On finishing the Gospel Tolstoy found his work summarized by the Lord's Prayer, and he delighted in the confirmation as I do. Moreover, I had a triple blind test in the extracted model from the text, now the appendix to this work, and the gravity derived hexagram. The formula of the ancients, for nation building, and wealth - the Templars Grail, was a thermodynamic economy, trading with the future - bridging time.

The Daodejing listened to by Edward Brew.

1. The Mystery of Production.

Things are never fully described.
There is more to know - subtleties to intuit.
Say the stars appeared spontaneously,
like the things on earth do - by trusting them stars to be.
See how we learn the universe,
gravity and trusting do the making.
If full of desire believe,
that enterprise and work make things,
however, know by living,
that attraction inspires movement,
and movement creates wealth.
Although things do result from an enterprise,
they begin with ease,
that begins an attraction - a power.

The subtlety.
The mystery of mysteries is that gravity,
and trust are the same energy,
both move objects.
This attraction is free, and it takes no effort.
This movement given from attraction,
is the gift of living well,
it is the thing wanted - got.
Attraction is grounded in exchange,
moreover, trading tends to wealth.
Wealth is the subject of this book called the Daodejing.

The subtlety and mystery of production.

Laozi will teach - that wealth is a trust in beginnings. Trust the Matter in useless things and idle people to get wealth. The matter has energy, its valuable. Learn from the house of Yin (Yellow Emperor), that trusting releases energy (qi), and it does the work (yang) that makes a virtue called wealth (de).

A man is attracted to a pile of rocks. With some effort, a valuable wall makes a useful Stonemason. The rock had the potential of stone, the man of skill. Those potentials were not described in their names but realized in their attraction. The gravitating man, and the accommodating rock - made an arrangement, a wall, and Two things valuable.

The rock and man existed as potential. When the rock was imagined useful, it was trusted and became stone, and when the rock captured the man's attention, he became a mason. See that work, merely describes what is manifested by the allure of a potential energy - movement. Gravity tells how the wall *became from the energy trusted to be* in the Mass's attracting. Laozi is introducing the (Kinetic) gravity theory of value, to his economics class BCE 4000.

Laozi's mystery is that trust has the same value as gravity in the beginnings. Trust is an alternate name for gravity. Trust and gravity are both synergies - Ones that describe the origin of kinetic energy in potential, and of becoming from nothing.

Free of desire, a flower can attract a profitable exchange from a bee. Full of ambition, people compete to purchase, with the diminishing returns from working.

Laozi thinks of the economy as a flower. The Commonwealth's potential is the beauty of the state; the people attracted to it, are rewarded by its satisfying arrangements, and never exhausted by work.

Laozi will explain wealth; as the product of attraction. Production describes the movement caused by beauty or the kinetic energy harvested from relationships with potential. Wherever a society encourages relationships between things and people they find attraction, and things are their by-product.

Laozi will advocate freedom. He asks for the removal of all societal barriers standing between potentials and, says that freedom will let trust create on earth as gravity does in space - without effort.

Laozi will talk of making wealth in a political economy as children's play; as imagination rewarded. Trust is the child's currency, and it is backed by seeing the potential of sand imagined as a castle in the beginning. Laozi will praise the child's intuition, mock capital as a chimera, and hard work as stupidity.

Laozi rejects the economics taught, for the satisfaction of demands - full of desire. He sees the things to be, and their being - before their manufacture, as the science to be discovered.

2 Value, work, wealth.

Wealthy is great;
it is better than being poor.
Recognizing a better is knowing the difference;
seeing the good - learns the bad.

If wealth comes from work, then coercion is accepted,
the good is a vice.
Where neither wealth nor work has a standard,
ask; What is enough wealth?
Is that too much-demanding work?

The Sage unpick this knot;
By diminishing the work,
the Sage reconciles its worth.
Society is confused by exchanges of work for wealth,
it needs the Sage.
The Sage teach economics without logic;
they show it by example,
the society adopts - the Sage way as standard trade.

The Sage demand no obligations of people,
nor do they claim ownership of others' things;
They ignore laws and enable people.
The Sage do nothing, yet everything,
because all mimic the Sage.

Introducing the Sage.

The Sage does not welcome more, because more creates less. Today, if a new house is made available it is demanded and expensive. Innovation stops production. What curious explanation says; make fewer homes because the better ones are unaffordable?

Both the beauty of work and the guile of deceit have values in things exchanged. It's impossible to know what is priced worth, in the chains of confusing asymmetric exchanges of things for effort. This parsing of price with value confuses everything with quality and even labor with quantity.

Academics call these confusions, Economics. They assert assumptions-are foundations; and those limit explanations; good to avoid the paradoxes. Keynes called this economics an amusing game one invented to distract the average man [sic.]. Keynes made no defense of the classical theories he merely asserted them.17

Laozi will explain; what none other have - how nations make their people rich, he introduces economic quandaries early in his book, because he will unravel them in the following Eighty chapters.

Laozi's Sage is an actor, a participant, and not a teacher. The sage acts by not explaining which of effort or axiom determines price, nor how the syllogistic arguments reconcile, because the nonsense questions are not posited by the wiser people.

By altering how we perceive the better things, the Sage affects our demand for them and thereby the efforts people exchange for them. The Sage will acknowledge the better thing's uniqueness, but champion the old thing's utility. A person need only work, for what they can afford, and eventually, everything will be affordable.

Perceiving a different value is a nonaction, Laozi will explain the nonactions as enough action for society to thrive, producing much from plenty. Not demanding is the *all done* to avoid scarcity, and that enough to save efforts working.

Thus, the Sage destroys value, while preserving energy and wit. Less demand is spread across more choice, reducing all prices. Lower prices cut the amount of work or trickery exchanged for goods. All of the economic puzzles disappear. How odd to ask about the value of nothing, in-particular, requiring no effort to acquire?

Laozi argues that progress makes a better wealth. Work makes leisure. While the superior bridge impoverishes the ferry operator, his society wins the freedom from work, by not fare-paying.

Work is only required to overcome the obstacles between wants and satisfaction. While private wealth is appropriately made removing obstacles in the path of satisfaction, wealth is more customarily had *maintaining them*.18

Laws focus on living with problems like regulating river crossings. Progress is bridge building; progress creates private wealth for a bridge construction once and negates the laws to protect the ferry boat forever.

Great private fortunes are a temporary beauty. The superior convenience in the bridge disappears the perpetual rent-seeking of the ferryman. The permanent wealth is in the community and forever by using the new bridge.

The public wealth is useful private wealth only it is shared as technology, in wheels, and screws, or in the convenience of bridges. Public wealth is the gift of previous generations and grows when new generations remove obstacles or solve the commonwealth's problems.

Entropy and Time

Laozi introduces us to clear thinking by suggesting the quandary of Bastiat's petition to the French government. Bastiat complained about the unfair competition of the sun on behalf of the Candle makers. He asked for the law to block windows so the Candle makers could solve the problem of creating light during the day, and without the unfair competition of the sun. According to the Candle makers, the sun unfairly, and at a high cost to the Candle makers, provided light for free during daylight hours, the sun was limiting their opportunities for work and for accumulating private wealth.19

3. unique and absolute.

The Sage grant no favors,
thus, preventing rivalry and petitions.
Whenever people produce what they can,
they will trade fairly for their needs.

By not tempting with exotic production,
the people are free of dangerous ambition.
The Sage encourage enterprise,
by ignoring the peoples' fantastical wants,
a surplus of necessities compels their exchange,
that lets all dreams live.

See that by weakening illusions,
the trade is more.
When people do not contend in exchange,
say - by bidding foreign luxuries with local goods,
then common sense dictates all production,
moreover, the clever agitators cannot pervert efforts.

The Sage seemingly does nothing,
so, the state is perfection

.

Value

Laozi's needs are to be fed and clothed; everything else is a want. Choices can be made between desires because luxuries are comparable. Luxuries are subjective and therefore relative to other luxuries. Whereas, needs are absolute, and objectively not a choice.

People that confuse needs with wants, seek and get wants but only by assuming obligations. Their fantastical contrivance is called a right, and enabled by debt. They spend on wants, and petition for rights with debt, they get their needs, but end fretting over their obligations.

This confusion of things and with the convenience of debts starts *a cycle of covetousness for luxury* and causes a scarcity of necessities; economists call it *demand and supply*. The status-quo encourage a demand for luxuries and cause a limited supply of necessities, it is the formula for a compliant and indebted society, one easy for them exploit by suggesting, rights are the necessities supplied by benevolence but with obligations (debt).

Laozi tells us that the appropriate mix of guile and effort to be exchanged for goods will be, discovered in the absence of a demand for them. Where needs are satisfied absolutely, wants will be got, but free of desire; by having idle whims without the pressure of demands or the convenience of debts.

Rational decisions are made about the value of luxuries when using the appropriate trades for them; the pleasure of a smile is a fair exchange for the luxury of flowers. The what's naturally exchanged for gifts are not the same work or guile exchanged for necessities. Utilities such as food and shelter cannot be compared in value to luxuries because they are experienced through their effects and known in use, by their results.

The measure of a Utilities value is energy because energy can be, measured with calories (work) and it is, used for its effects satisfying. Power is, used; with utility the energy is lost, the power and the utility are had and forgotten. When you have eaten (consumed energy), you are no longer hungry; the machine your body, and the energy is available again, or not, that is the all and only measure of work - energy.

The Sage need do nothing once the distinction between needs and wants is, understood by a people free of desire (satisfied). She grants no favors because favors are luxuries. If favors are, demanded they become problematic because of the scarcity that defines them.

The Sage denies favors to discourage rivalry. She makes people aware of alternatives to treats; a glance from her is a nod from an opinion maker, and enough non-action from an influencer to be effective. See that a Sage doing nothing does everything.

4. The Space and Time.

Barter for necessities with the neighbors,
because swapping utilities is good manners.
Exchange for wealth with the commonwealth,
because improving the public domain,
makes its utility to you more,
where the barter is less done,
Utilities are free,
and only the exchanging makes wealth,
In a magnificent commonwealth.
The infrastructure and health of the public space
Encode the wealth,
the commons signal the potential for wealth,
they invite improvement, and work on them,
back the currency later exchanged,
for their development,
See private effort makes the commonwealth,
from the public domain.
Without permission, people will;
blunt its sharpness,
unravel its tangles,
soften its brightness.
Moreover, the privateer will return its potential,
re-arranged as things or products,
all made from the commonwealth.

Enterprise is a boldness not taught,
only done,
production for exchange with the Commonwealth
is a spontaneous and rogue activity uncontrolled,

This goodness from production is the gift of life,
it precedes any from god.

A job in the public Domain.

The workplace is the where of exchange with the commonwealth. It is a space Laozi thinks of as a cornucopia.20 Want something from it, and it will appear for you, there is no limit to its bounty.

After people are, satiated from the workplace, they as a community will contract with the commonwealth for wealth, they offer to build the commons great, making it the additional wealth they get.

The public spaces, canals, bridges, and roads are the town hobby and made with love. Thoth weighs the contributions of time given to infrastructure in the book of the dead - like Laozi values the contribution of energy given for the same purpose.

Here is an answer for history - the full explanation for the division of days, and time; was to get paid for building the future; it had nothing to do with its metaphor-analogs, religion & cosmology. The stars told time, they measured the distance moved into infrastructure, and that weighed the present community's currency, Thoth was the bill discounter, he estimated the current value of the future wealth, and gave it to the builders.

For Laozi, a wealth-creating exchange in the workplace is ultimately and always made with the common of the future. Most of the work done from the past and in the present, is useful, and necessary but worthless to the future because it is used and consumed, while the jobs done on the common comprise our wealth, only that work is paid from the future.

An agreement exists with the next generation that authorizes our progress beyond survival - wealth now, in return for building the infrastructure of tomorrow. *Rewarded by the future explains the How of wealth.*

Wealth is made purposefully, meaning that additional work is done - and gifted to endow the commons beyond our needs in the present. Work for survival, or variants of barter explain our living, while the public domain gets improved utilities. Survival takes less effort in the improved commons, and the barter trades become less too, as the wealth-creating exchanges with the Commonwealth and the future are more.

Work that creates infrastructure and wealth might seem to be the same work bartered for survival, but they have different accounts, the former credits living, the latter are exchanged for - living well.

The three types of work are; a) blunting sharpness - Ignoring laws, responsibility, or obligations, b) unravelling tangles - fulfilling contracts (knots in a string), and c) softening the brightness – offering desirable alternative things that are cheaper and better.21

The economy exists as a system controlled by nobody. Not even the king; nobody can control the currency to facilitate exchange, or the natural resources required by production because those have no value, only utility. People will exchange natural resources amongst themselves and use as much currency, chemistry, and resources as necessary, or they will not exchange, won't use, don't need or want.

An idle populace ignores roads and has no use for money. Assets and cash have no value to a community excluded, from land and trade, by ownership.

Laozi ignores ownership claims on the free domain because when resources are made-assets by laws, they have no utility to the people excluded from them. Nature and infrastructure are free or ignored. Free, they are employed, do most of the work (sun, water, land, chemistry, wind) and account for most of the production (resources). Owned, they are wasted or idle.

Economics and value are concerned exclusively with an exchange, and that only happens outside the home for it to have value - with, and in the Common.

5. Free energy

Nature is practical;
it treats things as disposable items.
The leader is realistic;
he treats people as expendable.
The Sage is sanguine.

The space between potentials is empty,22
the Sage erects a bellows between them;
as the potentials attract, the bellows close,
converting the energy from attraction,
to a useful potential energy from the space that was.
This energy substitutes for work,
moreover, it saves time spent in production.

Physical energy harvested by attraction.

The Sage encourage others to seek potential and free its energy. They want a movement, to re-arrange the surrounding common. Nothing is sacred in the endeavor of making and building, called; taking and replacing in the commonwealth.

Trade demands no effort and gives pleasure. When a potential attracts, it is towards. Movement is captured by the bellows, the emptiness between two bodies, is a space, that compressed (air) is made useful by the bellows turning it to stored energy (potential) that can surpass labor effort.23

How much of the free energy replaces labor, is the political decision that determines a societies well-being. Rulers prefer the employment they control over the attractive power they don't. Laozi will show the rulers are mistaken, and control is unnecessary, because more energy is got from the bellows closing with the force of attraction, than by coercing labor to make.24

Trust assists effort, inspiration resonates with effort, attraction increases momentum and the latter harmony of attraction with effort amplifies both energies to finish products in less time.

Here is the How of the pyramids; they started with energy, they inspired enthusiasm, and they gave energy. The power of attraction is sufficient enough to supply and encourage the energy to produce. The inertial energy had from a potential, causes the combustion (effort), that makes a sufficient rearrangement, to know that something seen from the beginning can be finished by momentum in the end.

If a ruler allows people freedom in the Common, the people will move on its potentials. Their closing distance charges the bellows to fuel production - using less labor and resources.

Size is irrelevant to mechanics because velocity is the equal of mass. Attraction powers the free economy so every relationship and all of their potential can be encouraged with freedom. Laozi wants to remove the laws that prevent potentials (things & people) closing on each-other in the beginning so their contribution - moving can be added to our production (GDP) in the end.

6. Due diligence.

Trust never dies.
It is a mysterious female spirit;
the laws of nature are her secrets.
She is delicate and ephemeral,
however, use her,
moreover, take advantage of her;
she is inexhaustible.

Trust is made valuable by doubt.

The freedom to move on a potential is an opportunity to a free agent. Laozi will always advise caution, here he suggests doing a risk analysis on the chance before wasting effort on it. He says to consult the mysterious female, she is a propositions filter.

Potential is only an opportunity if it could be made profitable. If the plan complies with the laws of production, it will likely be worth the effort. Least resistance and diminishing returns were Laozi's two laws. His mysterious female weighs the impractical ideas. Her wisdom is called *due diligence* today and adequately done it protects entrepreneurs from wasting their energy on a poor potential.

If the potential passes the due diligence, it will be seen by others as a worthwhile endeavor. Later when the proposal floats and co-operation is sought, it will be by persons respected for its conception.

Laozi's Way to Wealth & the Holy Grail

Due diligence and planning involve the delicate processes of gaining support for new ideas. Due diligence loves the eyes of wisdom, the insight of Laozi's mysterious female analyst, infuses the solicitous mannerisms and sense helpful in approaching a potential opportunity.

7. To live, evolve.

The cosmos is reliable, and the earth is resilient.
What is the secret of their effervescence?
They have no concern about their existence;
they always survive.
The Sage mimics patterns
always participating;
the wise element, within but never in the lead.
The Sage are enablers,
not leaders,
so they are always safe in their achievements.

Stasis is death - change is life.

The entrepreneur is the Sage one.

The patterns of the cosmos are evident in all movement. Movement is life, the patterns Laozi admires are life observed. The Constructal Law of Adrian Bejan explains that living things are systems of elements moving and transforming. Birds flying, and people working are systems - they are flocks, and gangs affecting a topology by their energies moving.

The energies in living things transition from potential to kinetic, this is noticed by their emerging as a thing. Maneuvering is the creation of the enterprise. Topological patterns make, they are the by-products of movement, Laozi calls those parts of everything (GDP).25

The Sage joins in creating these patterns, Laozi knows what the enterprise is, and how its products become, he is here explaining it from where an observer sees production.26

Adding energy to light creates a laser, the additional energy excites the chaotic energy displaying potential - into a pattern; the combined power makes a form, that becomes a laser, the thing laser is a product of the arrangement of energy. Cymatics also, describes this spectacular process; sound energy spontaneously arranges matter into shape.

The Sage entrepreneur is one-only part of an energetic melee called society. They are detached but amongst present at the transitions of potential energy becoming arrangements as things.

A form is something from nothing; it is energy by Laozi's description, but others call it a coherency, or a shape recognized by appreciating movements; the others describe Laozi's power, and both stories are accurate - however Laozi explains it better by its beginning.

The trinity of heaven, earth, and sage (form, materials, and trust) are the framework of all economic activity. Heaven (trust-gravity) is the topological pattern, the land is the supplier of matter, and the Sage is an enabler, a free agent.

The achievements are the people's arrangements, in their movements are the patterns, these are in temporal surplus. The Sage is the holy ghost that ensures no rules interfere with a people's freedom to trust potentials and move on them in patterns.

8. Be respectful at work.

Producers are like water.
They nourish everyone establishing an enterprise,
moreover, when they do, they settle with it,
at the lowly workplace,
they make sure that it flourishes.
When a Producer acts,
she finds the prepared are below.

By her joining the workplace,
the producer nurtures the essentials.
In her friendships there,
she is promiscuous and faithful.
By her speech there,
she is listening.
In relations there,
she appreciates and gives respect.
By being experienced,
she is competent,
moreover, she co-operates in her enterprise,
She does not contend in the workplace,
so, avoiding all conflicts.

Get Smart.

The producer (entrepreneur) reaches down to the workforce with her opportunities because she is attracted to their potential. Doing that she follows nature: Water is drawn to the low like heat is attracted to the cold. The producer has a hot idea: she warms those (below/cold) who are ready, energizing them to exchange efforts with her.

By presenting a non-judgmental demeanor in the workplace, the producer joins the workers, treating them with respect. To begin production, trust like heat or water flows one way. An active producer acts like water; she is a nutrient to the plant that feeds from her.

Trust is welcome at the lower socio-economic levels where it is least given and most needed. Trust is a free good, like the air, and sunlight: people only take what they need, which is more than nothing and all they want.

Not contending is Laozi's way of reminding that the producer is one only element of the many needed to create. The producer is not more special than others in the workplace. She is as able to influence its patterns from within as any other element engaged.

9. The law of diminishing returns.

Tension a bow with great force,
and you will wish you had not.
Sharpen a weapon to its sharpest,
and it will soon blunt.
Collect great wealth,
and you will not be able to keep it secure.
Too much is the child of arrogance,
that is the disaster of incompetence.
Temper ambitions with modesty.
Whenever enough retire;
it is common sense.

When to stop working.

Trying too hard causes disaster (stretching a bow to breaking point). If you perfect a technique too well, it becomes ordinary (sharpen a weapon to bluntness). If you amass great wealth, the burden of its existence will invite its loss. Laozi advises that you should retire when there is enough done.

Laozi proclaims the economic law that is foundational to all economic thought: it is the law of diminishing returns.

Over-stretching a bow, over-sharpening a knife and over-filling the larder are all examples of wasteful effort. Knowing when to stop doing useless things, is the start of living a long life - well.

10. If Kippling said.

Could you be the accommodating female,
and host as the leader
let all indulge the wealth?
Could you breathe like an infant and ignore crisis?
Could you unlearn reason to act instinctively,
and judge yourself competent?
Are you responsible if you trust others?
Could you shape things without coercing them?

If you were the ruler;
Could you play this female role of accommodation?
Will you nurture what appears, and without favor?
When your curiosity extends beyond the state,
could you remain focused on the commonwealth?
Could you contribute an effort,
without leading an endeavor?
Will people be productive without your demands?
Would you use violence to effect?
These are the profound questions,
that test your readiness for leadership.

Teased to journey - curious to doubt.

These questions caution the protégée to reject responsibilities early so they may prepare more thoroughly for them later when they are abler.27

A ruler need only mimic the female tendencies to nurture, to know the enterprise of making a nation. Countries are productions. The feminine ruler will have the intuition to be an effective leader.

If you appreciate the gift of those that contribute to the state, then you will be wise to let them enjoy the Commonwealth's potential according to their will.28

Tenantry describes matriarchal ruler-ship, the Tennant ruler entertains in a free commonwealth and always prepares for the Tennant ruler, of the next generation.

A society will expand if the leader is attractive to the present and accommodative of the future.

The female is Laozi's; model of the state.29

11. Intellectual property.

Thirty spokes arranged around a hub make a wheel.
It is those that bear no weight they make the wheel,
a useful thing.
Mold clay into a cup;
it is the space within the cup that makes it useful.
Cut holes into walls;
its the lintel that makes the room useful.
The thing seen has value, it is wanted, and made.
However, the thing useful is the commonwealths,
the effort of working is useless,
without the Commonwealth's knowledge.

Public knowledge.

The thing unseen is the technology; the tension making the wheel, the displacement making the cup, the arch making the window. The intellectual property is the all of anything's utility, and it is public property.

Intellectual wealth is a significant part of the useful wealth. It is your birth-right held in trust for everyone by the Commonwealth. Which wealth is valuable? That wealth owned, by you, or the one protected for you?

Heidegger uses the three examples of the bridge, jug, and hammer, to say something similar. Heidegger's hammer is only noticed when broken, because of its lost utility.30

The technology of the wheel, the ceramics of the cup and the lintel framing a window are all things in the public domain. These were once thoughts purported owned as patents; those said rare and expensive. To Laozi, they are general knowledge, one dividend of progress. Their usefulness has an explanation: they are appreciated from the past. Thanks to a free commonwealth.

Without the public knowledge of how to build things, measure and make them, all efforts beyond survival would be useless, and there would be no opportunities to create wealth, other than to opportunistically take necessities by violence for extortion.

12. Passion the decider.

Too many colors confuse the eyes.
Too many sounds prevent hearing.
Too many spices destroy the taste.
Appreciate the simple,
moreover, the absolute in necessary things.
The body cannot distinguish between luxuries;
choice confuses the mind,
indulging curiosity damages the wellbeing.
Enjoy the surprise of luxuries when offered,
However, know the simplicity of necessities,
And their joy from production.31

Passion is demands superior.

Demand is the result of confusing needs with wants; it is not a desire for either. Laozi mocks things preferred for their attributes rather than their utility. Choosing between luxuries is impossible because the senses cannot distinguish indulgences. Choosing between utilities is unnecessary because they are not preferences and they are free.

Wherever luxuries demanded as wants are needed, it forces unnecessary work to get them. Wherever utilities required like luxuries are wanted, it too forces unnecessary work.

The impossible values made by competing for work and in demanding for things invites contrivance into the supply, and exchange of goods. Those deceits in trade, diminish all relationships and herald future vulnerabilities in society.

Let *passion* do the work of choosing, let passion move you to get without having demands make work necessary for luxury.32 This passion is a force, that acts as if it were a source of supply (a self-fulfilling demand). Passion has a pressure release; a safety, passion is fleeting, its force is measured by commonsense. Passion has only a causal relationship to the luxury demanded, and one easily broken when it is not appropriate. Laozi will call passion frugality at chapter 67, a jewel, the foundation stone of a strong economy.

When passion is the force desire can be fully satisfied, say by a smile, or forgotten by a change of mind, proving sensible people do not always want luxuries, so an economy should not work to satisfy their demand.

Always new production can create substitutes for things, or circumstances can create new preferences; demand for items is a measure of wisdom and time, both exist in unlimited quantities, as utilities in the commonwealth and had there for free.

13. Profit and loss.

Success and failure are both problems.
Success is the greater disaster,
because protecting success causes death.

Failure is good;
it is the opportunity to succeed,
where you are competent.
What do I mean when I say,
'treasure problems as your own life'?
We have problems because we are living.
If we have no life, what problems can we have?
Therefore, welcome the problems as your life,
so, you will engage with the world appropriately;

When the problems are your life,
you will be trusted to solve them.
Whoever loves their life more than high rank,
will be trusted with the dominion of the empire.

The limit to logic and hubris is the exhaustion of trust.

The avatar is an inferior son. Which would a mother prefer?
The avatar's subjugation to reality is the one condition for decision making.

Entropy and Time

The virtue of artlessness is clarity. The archetype blonde is the exemplary entrepreneur; unspoiled with cleverness, she survives tribulations by limiting her ambitions to the necessary and matching her efforts only to them. She treats each problem as a test of competence by tackling them at the modest levels she can.33

An avatar is the archetype male, he expects success but neutered by ambition and education he is misguided by agendas and embarks on grand schemes. He relies on work; he is even prepared to risk his life for his crash through plans.

The feminine actors rather cooperation, and by taking a path of least resistance, their modest ambitions do not waste other people's efforts on diminishing returns.

Those that recklessly indulge their avatars endanger lives. The CEO that risks his company for his ambition, based on a risk calculation or a temporal fact is like the soldier that risks his body. In short, do not trust someone who is so reckless to bet his life on a calculation or a fact. The successful entrepreneur participates in the economy like the artless blonde; their living decides all actions.

When the female takes on her most important role as an expectant mother, she becomes economical. Without any training or preparation; females;

Don't risk their production contending in unequal competitions.

Forego luxuries for necessities.

Take no unnecessary risks.

Make no work or unnecessary effort.

Get cooperation in their production - to be sure.

Here, Laozi is giving us the measure and standard of the trustworthy leader. The person focused on their creation will always disgrace their avatar to produce. That person will have a (rightly) selfish, therefore feminine intuition of life, and that person will be thinking of the next generation, and that will be a person qualified; trustworthy to rule the world.

14. The measures and area.

Look for the efforts exchanged,
and you will not see them; call those;
the invisible black-market.
Listen for the efforts exchanged,
and you will not be told of them; call them;
the unheard or barter economy.
Reach for the efforts exchanged,
and you may not touch them; believe they;
the illusive opportunities.
These; black, barter, and illusive activities,
cannot be understood,
so, we merge them as one on a flat plane,
and call their meshing the economy.
Above that plane is not revered,
and the activity below is avoided.
The plane is the space where all things belong,
for their potential,
and where they later return,
used or consumed, as nothing valuable.
The economy is dynamic, formless, indefinable,
and elusive,
traverse it, and you will not find its head,
chase it, and you will not see its tail.
Only by being attracted to the economy on the plane,
will you know how it works,
and then only by exchanging with its potentials

The economy is a Cartesian space.

The illicit, unreported black market cannot be measured or controlled any more than the unheard, unnoticed satisfactions bartered amongst friends and family. The opportunities given by exchange may never be appreciated or understood because they are unfathomable. It is the combination of these unseen, unheard and illusive transactions that account for the whole of the economy. Righteous ambitions - say, charity work (the above), and nefarious activities - like crime (below) are not economic activity, everything else is.

In describing the economy as an area in space (workplace), Laozi is alluding to the same plane that Frederick Soddy called *Cartesian economics* (referencing the plane's map coordinates; x, y, z):

'In each direction possibilities of further knowledge extend ad infinitum, but in each direction diametrically away from and not towards the problems of life. It is in this middle field that economics lies, unaffected whether by the ultimate philosophy of the electron or the soul, and concerned rather with the interaction, with the middle world of life of these two end worlds of physics and mind in their commonest everyday aspects, matter and energy on the one hand, obeying the laws of mathematical probability or chance as exhibited in the inanimate universe, and, on the other, with the guidance, direction and willing of these blind forces and processes to predetermined ends' (*Cartesian Economics: The Bearing of Physical Science upon State Stewardship*, Hendersons, London, 1922, p. 6). 34

The economy is societies forum, how much use, and how well it is accepted is all that determines whether people will be wealthy. Only by being a party to the economy, and by transacting in its forum can you access the power to exchange the energy created by it.

The experienced participant finds the economies satisfactions happen by surprise and not by planning, or demands over time. Life's prizes are got chasing the illusive opportunities with the energy to do so.

The most rewarding experiences are the enterprises that encroach on the free domain: those things done in the public spaces to make the commonwealth free. Achievements' are the forgotten jobs that negated the need for them, that solved problems forever, that gifted the commonwealth with either infrastructure or knowledge.

15. The chain of ponds that makes.

Of old, the best economists
were subtle, obtuse, and mysterious,
their quixotic ramblings humored,
so, it happened that their eccentricities,
also, follies became our joy in the commonwealth.
I will describe them from observation.
Reluctant, advising economic interventions
(Hesitant, fording a stream).
Alert, like a person in danger.
Their demeanor was that of a guest.
They would be like ice waiting to melt.
They were sincere, like uncut wood.
Moreover, seemingly vacuous too,
like a cave.
They watched streams connect muddy pools,
(roads connecting cities)
wanted that flow did not fill them,
that flow never disturbed the pools,
that activity brought some things and cleared others,
saw pools unaffected, just improved enough.
By the economist's nonaction,
they maintained the streams flowing,
to keep the pools attraction. 35

The economist described as an irrigator.

'I have just spoken of the flowing of streams to the sea as a partial image of the action of wealth. In one respect, it is not a partial, but a perfect image.' - John Ruskin. Unto This Last, 1860

'The economy is a group of buildings, mines, farms with machines and connected by lines of energy, and transportation; founded upon a series of scientific processes and inventions, and a set of human habits.' - Stuart Chase, The Economy of Abundance, 1934

Populations exist as workplaces, Laozi's calls them pools that struggle if isolated. His connecting stream is Guy Debord's passing spectacle, it that interprets the societies enterprise, a moving fair that leaves behind impressions and sends signals to elsewhere of the people's potential.

The stream's flowing was the Ancients connecting with commerce, Laozi is talking Monetarist, Milton Freidman style; velocity, and money supply (M1), just enough movement to create activity, but not so much work that the community is disturbed by industry.

'Economics deals *not* with quantities of energy [as things and communication], but entirely with the flow of available energy, and its transformations into useless forms ... [and also] physical wealth as a product of the control and direction of this flow. Wealth is 'derived from and produced by the flow of available energy in nature; it represents a draft upon or a deduction from that flow ... for the production of all forms of wealth.

> Available energy is required from the natural flow, and either enter into the wealth produced or is used up in producing it and converted to waste heat.'36
>   - Frederick Soddy, Wealth, Virtual Wealth and Debt, 1926

The irrigator of old is a feminine economist, and later, Laozi will describe her market as a river (ch. 34). She can influence the market against its natural inclinations, encouraging its connectivity. She is therefore hesitant to act against its tendency; alert to danger; polite; uncomfortable with exposure (ice melting); has no philosophy, allegiance or agenda (uncut wood); is open to ideas (hollow & Vacuous); patient and calm. She trusts in the currency, it is flowing, she is careful that it does.37

16. How things are made.

The Sage sees that the pools have capacity at the top,
so, a population has room to expand,
she maintains the energies in stillness at the bottom.
The pool primed is still,
the signal shows from the stream above,
the energies below resonate to its image,
they re-arrange spontaneously,
watch the ten thousand elements transform,
becoming by moving, a show,
the product of movement is everything good but later,
then the energies transition back to being energies,
returning to the stillness,
they can, if inspired become again another potential,
being available is the norm.
Everything moved to make was lost,
however, nothing was lost, all will be made again,
with the signals from the cloud.
Returning is the norm, and illuminated, that rooted;
by consulting the mysterious female.
Returning to the norm is to be rooted,
that a part of something, to be more?
Returning is affirming, and encouraged.
Knowing this norm is to see the potential of the economy,
it's the opportunity to improve the commonwealth
for the future,
the present is past, and the norm is impartial about the
present,
being available - a nothing in the present
is looking to the future,

is to be kingly,
being kingly is to be part of the stillness in the norm.
Stillness begs the joke, and that starts spontaneously.
From the stillness comes all things.
When the efforts made in production stop,
the effects had - continue by momentum, not effort.

Production is creation.

Where natures contribution to the creation of things, is the equal & better of labor.38 39 40

Nobel laureate; Frederick Soddy, discussed economics, as a living system, likening the economy to a living plant. He introduced the topic like Laozi does - from the beginning, not with the roots in the soil, but with the plant getting the energy to live.
The following is Soddy's explanation of the Laozi witness.

> The [plants] chlorophyll in fact effects the marriage of energy and matter. It is a photo chemically active catalyst secreted by the living plant but is itself merely a substance, neither organized nor alive. From an energetic standpoint, the human contribution is always of the nature of a transformation rather than a creation of energy, becoming as civilization advances more and more direct with the replacement of the intuitive metabolic process by [that of] others arrived at by reason.41

Laozi discussed the economy in the previous chapter - as a network of relationships, like Stuart Chase, did, now he elaborates agreeing with Soddy; those relationships are made productive by their constituents using not a catalyst secreted, but something similar - a resonance or frequency that tunes at rest ('all of life is a frequency of 3' N. Tesla).

We intuit from a business that relationships do produce things without the assistance of nature, or labor. Above, Soddy referred to the public knowledge, that of technology (Ch. 11), and said; as civilization advances, the importance of relationships, and public knowledge will become more apparent, and therefore more valuable, than labor or nature, agreeing with the observation of Bastiat; that in time, with public knowledge all things will be cheaper or free, and of Buckminster Fuller - lighter, and stronger.

Laozi uses the metaphor of the pool connected to a stream, to explain what Ruskin and Chase did; a community related to its economy.

The economy has an area to grow, and the un-agitated elements primed below. They receive signals from the clear above, these are received and made images by the elements, those resonate, causing movement, the elements arrange seeking space; make Cymatic patterns, and do coherent things; those things once recognized are the whats appreciated as products, to the clear above. (ch. 14)

Imagine the pool Laozi described with a shape forming school of fish at the bottom, and the fish broadcast a ballet to the cloud above that inspired it. Production in the pool is inspired, and spontaneous. Now think of the pool as a Vessel (cup) call it a popcorn maker, the bottom is still, the top is empty. Hot rocks are amongst the seed, all is still, the potential of the seed spontaneously appears to the top as popcorn, the product flows to the stream. Production is made life, or movement from potential energy, describes making and Living spontaniously.

Say two men trust each other with an idea to make some mortar: they mix lime with sand and water and know that chemistry is the dominant maker. There is energy in the idea; there is energy in the materials, power in labor, and also a synergy in their cooperation, the factors that make concrete are all of the energies, that constitute it. Cooperation, is described here by elements equal and sometimes superior to people and that as production.

The mixing is not Laozi's element-making. The work was a small addition to the making, work is forgotten in the cement because the effort of work is not visible in the concrete. The work of making the concrete was a thermodynamic process. The chemical process of bonding in the cement created the heat with water. The product concrete is made from energy and was only assisted by the addition of work energy in mixing.

Under the right conditions of pressure and temperature, materials transform in a closed area (volume). Concrete production is appropriately called a reaction by scientists. Economists have deceived themselves, and society by calling it work.

When a task is finished, the energies return to the beginning. The pool is re-energized, at the depth. New potentials approached, and new images are tested with the mysterious female, making new plans.

These - chatting fun things are done in stillness, they are the beginnings of better things, and the norm. Einstein defined stupidity as doing the same experiment over again – expecting a different outcome. Better, do-once, then try something new to be greater, this is the norm at the root of Laozi's production, that multiplies all efforts to good effect.42

The products and energies all return to the improved commonwealth, where they are either useful or consumed. Not all the power given to production ends embodied in the products; some of it is wasted, creating further opportunities for its capture and use in other cycles. Not all efforts made in progress are accretive. Some initiatives or expenditures get lost to the commons. These are called Entropy (S), in the appendix, not waste, rather they are the economic measure of opportunity.

The commonwealth is refreshed by production, while its satisfactions are enjoyed, the opportunities continue. The possibilities get grander with progress, because new potentials are more accessible in the common improved.

Knowing that nothing produced is permanent, or valuable authorizes being generous and kingly. The experiences of people on holidays, conflating their private wealth with the Commonwealth's, prove their useful wealth, and show being kingly.

Knowing life is finite, Laozi thinks we should always be impartial, and generous.43 Everything we have will eventually pass to the public domain; we are advised to spend our private wealth in the present; protect it never for the future because the Commonwealth was paid forward when it became one.44

Production alone creates the means to trade, and the ability to awaken desire. By being productive first, we create the product and the methods to get others. Demand does not create supply - supply creates demand.

It is worthwhile to remark that a product is no sooner created than it, from that instant, affords a market for other products to the full extent of its own value. When the producer has put the finishing hand to his product, he is most anxious to sell it immediately, lest its value should diminish in his hands. Nor is he less anxious to dispose of the money he may get for it; for the value of money is also perishable. But the only way of getting rid of money is in the purchase of some product or other. Thus the mere circumstance of creation of one product immediately opens a vent for other products. - Jean-Baptiste Say, 1834 – now known as Says Law.

The precursors for stillness are; comfort and security. Enjoying an idea shared with friends has no cost, and a proposition is not a burden to consider. Laozi will instruct that during idleness - a potential, becomes uniquely apparent. The products eventually made from the potentials attraction, are merely the energy of idleness and leisure packaged. The thing valuable in all products is the knowledge shared by the community. Laozi says a grace for the goods while explaining leisure as the enjoyable work of planning for production.

The things that come from being congenial at rest, are later called products, their value in a fair exchange, is therefore the value of other thoughts shared in stillness. The one who knows this norm, is tolerant has room for everything impartial and Kingly.

Whoever understands the source of production being from the stillness will know it by productive relationships, the most significant relationship is that of the person with the Commonwealth.

Laugh at yourself in a joke and know kingly-creation; by losing face, you give wealth to the commonwealth from nowhere. Then you are seen to be productive, and that is kingly: by laughing, you lose your avatars value, winning a useful wealth for the commonwealth. Your former worthless pride had a potential seen, it was amplified by the surrounding goodwill and realized as a good by the community.

Useful wealth is the sum of goodwill; parts are immediately available to you by your contributing a something to the commonwealth. Meaning you get credit for mocking yourself and become eligible to participate in the kingly game of exchanging. You depreciated yourself first to do so; that is how you get credit and opportunities, those create permissions to draw on the commonwealth. The kingly game is the How of creation, it is economics played well, and the what enjoyed for eternity. 45

Entropy and Time

17. On effective leadership.

The best leaders are all famous,
by the quality of the things and,
people in their realm.
Ordinary leaders are all remembered,
by being attractive persons.
Weak leaders are infamous for their repulsiveness.
The worst leaders recognized by the venal people,
and unattractive products in their realm.
Wherever the leader is a gatekeeper,
there is no approaching a potential,
attraction is unknown in his realm,
if a leader is the intermediary of exchange,
then there will be no trust in his presence,
he will rely on laws,
and, on experts to coerce production with demands.
The best leaders get their production by,
showcasing the potential in the realm,
moreover,
by introducing it to an exchange,
and giving away the opportunities to exploit potential,
the best leader is attracting trust,
he lets the energy that is everywhere - make,

and when it does, the excellent leader gives credit.

Leadership is facilitation.

Good leaders are not known directly; instead, the people and the things in their realm are known to be attractive, famous, or reliable. To Laozi, things get trusted like people, because items exude the same attractiveness as people. A chair is trusted, and a bus is safe like a guide is reliable, and a currency valuable.

A realm that can be trusted offers a natural warranty with its products. *Made in Italy* needs no explanation, and an Icelander no introduction because the origin kingdom indicates a ruler that is trusted.

The best a leader can do is be the countries host. If he can create an atmosphere, a stillness for his constituents, they will react to each other in the commonwealth as guests do at a party.

His graciousness is forgotten, and appropriately because good hospitality gets usurped by the guest's time together. He will have allowed them space to each other. Although the host leader is acknowledged and appreciated later for the arrangements, it was never his party, the guests partied, he was the host

If the host leader, doesn't create stillness at the start of his party, he will end controlling a crowd. That party is then a performance, and it will be a contrived one. A leader has no dignity, as an entertainer, he is a clown, and later as a crowd controller, he becomes a cop. The spontaneity denied by performance, is an opportunity lost. Wherever the host is a star, he is judged as a performer, and if he is a leader, he loses his usefulness as an enabler. If the host is the cop too, he ends a jailer.

Replacing spontaneity with contrived activity, or control is not a productive way to run a State. A leader that invokes conventions and scenarios ultimately crushes the people coercing their activity. He will be working against their inclination to produce on their own; he will be a counter-productive agent to the economy as a clown, and to the society as *a cop come jailer* he is the enemy.

The leader that denies the guests spontaneity to do what they will is the bore that wastes energy commanding patronage. That leader is disliked by a frustrated, and disenfranchised people made to do, and make, which is less and worse than what they could.

18. The problem with do-gooders.

Where demands usurp spontaneous production,
laws appear as justice;
benevolence heralds' rectitude
moreover, idiots get tolerated; Then,
humanitarian obligations are accepted,
sophistry will explain morality.
When meanness excuses the venal,
there will emerge hypocrisy,
worse, artificial society.
When relations are not in harmony,
there will appear,
Filial piety and paternal kindness in the home,46
The Political economy is damned.
Wherever loyal servants, sycophants are apparent,
the intermediaries are in control,
Where the people are poor, there is no good leader.

The cycle of misery.47

Where movement is restricted by the ownership of resources or the enforcement of conventions (filial piety), those that could produce, won't be permitted. A leader will be compelled by his own needs to force their contribution.

If a leader respects ownership claims from history, he will need to empower intermediaries and enforce them. He will then assume obligations to the intermediaries, for their living (stipends), and later enforce them on the people for their labor.

Forced labor creates an inferior product to what would have been from a free common, because innovation is denied by legal obligations (taxes, rent, fines), and productive talent is turned from making things, to enforcing laws.

By the king's acceptance of ownership, he excludes enterprise and makes scarcity. He effectively doubles down on stupidity by joining the sycophant tools to the owners. He turns his administration to clientelism. Here is the raison d'être for exploitation and the full explanation of most aberrant behaviors.

The hypocrite elixirs to enhance the king's tolerance of sycophants are; justice, benevolence, and duties. Justice is an insincere apology for the wrong of ownership. Charity is an inadequate restitution for the access denied by ownership (trespass), and responsibilities are the deceit that perpetuates clientelism.

Ownership creates privilege and causes conflict. It obligates people to make luxuries, while their diversion denies the necessities they are more suited to making.

Wherever there is justice or benevolence, a community damaged by cleverness is controlled by violence. That community will be relatively unproductive because obligations exist with toxic relationships.

By contrast, wherever efforts get exchanged without favor, production is spontaneous, duties are unknown, and charity is not needed.

Satisfactions are subjective; they do not have a measure. If obligations exist, then that is enough to know that efforts are being demanded and not exchanged. Wherever there is demand; additional production is evident in the stockpiles of luxuries teasing people to sycophancy and obligations.

A society is damned by its respect for, filial piety (elders'), and paternal love (slavery and obligation to dependents'). Where a free common, there is no elder ownership and therefore no demand, therefore no commitments, or needs for justice and charity.

19. Needle the experts.

Banish the sophists
moreover, discard their cleverness,
watch the people benefit a hundred-fold.
Reject all rights,
So that state justice is unnecessary,
then people will return to their natural relations.
Repeal all debts,
abandon property ownership,
robbers and thieves will cease to be.
These State remedies are not sufficient on their own.
Encourage people to embrace commonsense,
diminish their avatar roles,
so, to watch them exchange freely as neighbors,
without selfishness, or demands.

To restore the benighted Kingdom - Banish the sycophants.

Commonsense guides always to disengage from a fanciful company, it immunizes against the hypocrisy of state justice and benevolence.

Where the state excludes people from the commonwealth by enforcing trespass, simplicity will find satisfaction where it can. People will retreat to the home, they will survive, and barter in the hidden, elusive and black economy.

Entropy and Time

In a society damaged by intermediaries, where scarcity and violence prevail, a people controlling their desires in the public domain can be secure and thrive in their private realm.

The free domain will soon be available to them. The producers are better to wait for the emperor to act than to participate in; abuse by a sycophant.

Justice, benevolence, and duties are the wrongs that thrive in a weakened society. Laozi recommends; the regular surgical removal of the experts cancerous to society.48

After restoring the commons, the need for justice, and the artifice of benevolence vanishes. Banishing frees the state from clientelism. The removal of betters, lets the people enjoy trust based relations without obligations.

Ignoring rights, using common sense and avoiding obligations, implies the banishment of the do-gooders that insist on entitlements, and enforce bonds. The expulsion of academics is Laozi's gift of peace to the Commonwealth.

The companion internal remedy is the lesson learned to the future; reduce selfishness now, and never claim a right, so the society of the future, (our trading partner), won't make a demand that common sense could not anticipate. If we set an example of being unhinged, or extravagant, they might follow it, misjudge our legacy, and not redeem our currency. (see appendix).

20. The system designer.

Stop formal education confusing people,
the teaching is nonsense.
Between consent and force,
how much difference is there?
Is there any distance between good and evil?
How is it measured?
As to what others say. Should you mention as well?
Must you do what others think?
Just how ridiculous is learning?
Look at how deluded academics are,
always feasting their utterances at picnics,
moreover, confirming them *right* with each-other,
and on summer strolls (Peer review).
I wish for awareness, I want for everything,
and need a reason smile like an infant does.
I see the people struggling with the nonsense taught.
I am beyond the apologetic explanations.
I am a witness to prosperity,
and I have the experience of it,
yet I am ignored, and passed-by,
because the world is full of experts.
I am dull and stupid to them, like an idiot.
I see the problems they created,
moreover, all of them are unnecessary.
Experts are tools with roles to play,
 - they were made by education to act.
I have no role in solving riddles,
only a purpose,
to be redundant when the problems disappear.
I am the outlier now, but join with me,
let us be rich together in a productive country

(the great mother).

Laozi asks for disbelief.

The preceding chapters described a Faustian bargain between a weak leader, and a clutch of rentiers. Where the leader paid the sophists dearly, for a convincing illusion. There is no power above leadership; the dominant leader and the temporal owner both exist on delusions.49

Laozi has said to banish the experts that apologize for the kleptocracy, he wants the common-wealth restored to the king, and for the king to protect the commonwealth from predators. Now Laozi says; to make the better society in the future - stop educating more of the experts.50

While the people are educated; they will accept justice - as the king's apology, benevolence as restitution from the owners, and coercion as an obligation. While the people treasure teaching from their servitude, the Cabal will evade banishment.51

State education teaches to accept justice, it learns benevolence and knows coercion, its only purpose is to justify the status quo owning the commonwealth. It mirrors the script of monotheism - accept servitude on earth, you are less than the master, your reward for service is in death.

The cabals teaching is to entrench the cabal now as a deity. Education is used by them to maintain the plain-sight injustice of their ownership and the nonsense of power without leadership. Time and space are later and elsewhere for you, but now and here for them, it's the primary axiom and equilibrium taught.

The cabal educates confusion (gas-lighting), it teaches people to ignore their common sense. When people get taught, temporal facts as truths, theories as laws, syllogisms as proofs and myths as realities, they will accept obligations to the owners, and beg for charity as justice.52

Rudolf Steiner and many others have said as much, Steiner has given a stunning proof of what a real education could be in the Waldorf model. The Laozi disdain for academics and experts is unrelenting and will continue to the last chapter There is no mistaking his description of Copenhagen agreements, or scientific consensus; he accurately said of his own time that peer review was the pillow talk of gay strolls, and he meant it to be insulting.

Ludwig Wittgenstein's Tractatus Logico-Philosphicus 1–7, answered logic by saying 'Whereof one cannot speak one must be silent' and at 2.0121 of Tractatus, he addressed Laozi's subject of this book, and answers why teaching the discipline of economics with logic is nonsense.

> 'It would seem to be a sort of accident if it turned out that a situation would fit a thing that could already exist entirely on its own. If things occur in states of affairs, this possibility must be in them from the beginning. (Nothing in the province of logic can be merely possible. Logic deals with every possibility and all possibilities are its facts). Just as we are quite unable to imagine spatial objects outside space or temporal objects outside time, so there is no object that we can imagine excluded from combining with others. If I can imagine objects combined in states of affairs, I cannot imagine them excluded from the possibility of such combinations'53

> Wittgenstein tells us how not to know economics; it is to study it as a subject using Logic and mathematics. Above he mirrors what Laozi said in the opening chapter; parts do not adequately describe a thing, and some things

possibilities are not known, here at Chapter 20, he says - therefore it cannot be taught as we imagine it can.

Logic and learning are the enemies of a nation's development because they deny its possibilities.

An intuition of potentials hints at progress, it invites our imagination and that inspires trust and trust - enterprise. Development, therefore, has no logic, nor does it contain any facts suited to measurement or equations (ch.14).

Laozi dismisses the fanciful axioms and syllogistic trivia, of academics; as useless to progress. His final repair to a society damaged by clientelism is to stop academics, teaching a new generation to be ignorant of possibility. Otherwise said, let people, do, try, experiment, and, they will dream, discover, make and build a better Commonwealth than any imagined by academia.

Laozi is not against education per se, just the indoctrination of logic, reason, morals, truths, history, and opinions. Corporeal knowledge can be attained, as required, by anyone who needs it by acting on the advice of shift happens from YouTube. In the interim, the common sense of a motherly intuition to; *let the child be* is educations superior.

The second stanza of this chapter 20, is Laozi's curriculum vitae for the System designer. Compare it to Jean-Jacques Rousseau's description of the lawgiver;

> To discover the rules of society that are best suited to nations, there would need to exist a superior intelligence, who could understand the passions of men without feeling any of them, who had no affinity with our nature but knew it to the full, whose happiness was independent of ours, but who would nevertheless make our happiness his concern, who would be content to wait in the fullness

of time for a distant glory, and to labor in one age to enjoy the fruits in another.54

Laozi is an educated product of the system, a Sophist himself, but he asks not to make that judgment of him. He has learned what's taught, and he has surpassed it. To paraphrase he says: please forget the useless instruction and listen to what I am going to tell you in the next chapter.

The great mother that sustains Laozi is the land, made country by a trust (Wu), the beginning of production is the way - to wealth. Trust is the energy that sustains all life; it is the nemesis of knowledge. Wittgenstein proved the nonsense of logic in Tractatus and removed the ladder, Laozi is doing the same - there is no going back to formal education. Learn only to trust an exchange with the commonwealth by experiencing one.

21. The three factors of production.

The economy enables means,
wherever the potentials attractively presented,
moving on them,
is the all to do.
The economy is the Country.
The State is a nebulous vessel,
containing the energies of;
images (people),
substances (resources),
and their essence (pure energy).
The essence is trust - that contained in a potential
it is proved by the synergy of people cooperating
(by their movement).
Trust is the origin of all things valuable,
from the past, trust is known as a warranty,
and to the future, trust is guaranteed,
by things made for the commonwealth.
Things done well, contain the essence of sincerity.
How do I know the creation of all things?
It is by the essence,
that which causes movement on substances,
and,
by the production, and availability everything.

The three forms of energy.

These three are interchangeable in the production process (Ch. 16), and the workplace - economy Chs. 14 & 15.

The State is a workplace. The economy describes the country, and Laozi tells us that it works by being free, by allowing access and enabling opportunities. Laozi's full explanation of the rich country is, *a barrier-free economy*. Where the people are encouraged to act, and allowed resources; they will approach others and together with their fellows develop the countries potential. In a free country, people are invited to form an image of their merging with the countries potentials, and they do make arrangements, they will join to others and those relationships will later become enterprises that will result in the Commonwealth's betterment.

Laozi sees the workplace from a galactic distance. From his vantage, the product is on the shelf, and its being made on the factory floor, and is being designed on the draft board, and all simultaneously. From our vantage in the present time, we see only the product at the shop. When Laozi considers the product, he acknowledges its teleology.

He wants us to learn economics by intuiting the origin of products as he does. See the pencil as the image once had by an entrepreneur, attracted to a substance, and by trusting the dream of a writing implement to be, as an image of the pencil had. The image is impressed before the product or work to make is aired; Laozi wants us to channel the 1958 essay I, Pencil: My family tree, as told to Leonard E. Read, when looking at what fills the shelves of shops. Products from the past and into the future seen this way will empower the faith necessary to allow making what society needs in the future by making the arrangements now, to give permissions for work.

The workplace produces forms, and it arranges what we see in other dimensions, those are called products (services anticipated). Mostly they are made with intention, other times they appear, by the serendipity, of an unexpected arrangement.

A found value, is the wealth had from engagement - like three people meeting, becomes Apple Computers, or three strings tangled; are a tassel, a profit, not waste. Laozi wants us to acknowledge this fantastical gift of the workplace that some activity in the workplace defies Newton's first law, creating wealth is making [potential] energy from synergies. See the workplace sometimes conserves energy being idle, wasting may be a signal of wealth and a potential store of energy (scale model building). At other times the workplace accumulates energy being unproductive, these maybe synergetic interactions, and may end being the most profitable of wastes (the long lunch).

Society gets more from the workplace than the peoples' contribution to it, and since the population's needs are more than their abilities. Laozi explains here; how the impossible is observed as the reality that sustains us.

The economy works like a perpetual motion machine; it makes *the more* that is known to be necessary. What Marx wished could be had by the promise of sharing work, Laozi explains as a gift given from freedom. It's obvious says Laozi, the evidence is the synergy of a society that trusts its fellows. The cornucopia is the country that encourages each to approach, it's like a party enjoyed more than the surrounds suggest, and approaching fills the bellows with power.

The economy is a vessel (ch. 4) containing - three elements that are indistinguishable; images, substances, and essence. These are what combine seamlessly in the workplace to make alloys from themselves.55

Each person can give more than they had at the party, and get more than they did in the economy because the total product of the workplace is a synergetic product, an alloy, which is something more than the sum of its parts.56

The images are by people, creations of themselves. They may be ephemeral, and ridiculous, or lack practicality, and be without logic.57 However, they will be more than ideas because images have form, and that is a thing of itself.

The enterprise, for example, is in the form of the image, if the entrepreneur were to stop thinking about the enterprise, it would disappear. Images are exclusive to the person holding them. The Image a person has of the thing is their reality, but by necessity, their Image is the form shared in trade, because we ignore the person in a profitable exchange, and deal only with their image. The image is a well-known intuition of phycologists and proved by sales-persons.

The substances are matter, the resources. These things have no value, only utility.58 Resources are part of the public domain and are gratuitous. People are carbon, so they too are a subset of matter, all matter is energy. Laozi did not need Einstein to know that wood creates heat, Matter has the essence of power, he only had to see it burn, to understand its nature as energy.

Essence is pure energy. It is the energy that Laozi says has the evidence that proves it to be the origin of all things.59 The existence of energy needs to be understood because the senses (smell, sight, touch, hearing, and taste) don't recognize potential energy. Until energy has evidence (moving), it will be unknown and therefore unnamed.60

Synergetic energy is potential energy, like hydro or nuclear. Potential energy is stored and un-obvious until seen moving (kinetic) and proved by its effects. The potential of Hydro is called gravity by us. The possibility of nuclear is called the weak force by quantum physics. The potential of trust is called the attractive force by Laozi, and he knows it like Maxwell did, as an electrical effect. Laozi will call the kinetic (active) form of Trust energy *the way* [power] in chapter 25, but now he thinks it as a potential like un-enriched Uranium, and that trusting in a relationship will (with enriching) attract labor energy and he calls this the potential energy - *essence*.61

Laozi makes the same distinction we do in discussing energy that between the Hydro dam being potential energy, and the Hydroelectricity, being its *potential in use*; kinetic energy.

The three energies combine seamlessly in the workplace: two men use wind to sail a boat; a scientist uses chemical reactions to make glue; a farmer uses sunlight to grow food; a composer makes music with an orchestra. All were images of what could be; each inspired by the potential of the other energies in whatever form to be trusted to make the image of something moving, sticking, feeding, playing a thing made in its arranging.

The products that emerge were images that became things - Ones that had their potential seen, or known from the past, and thought into the future as an image, realized as a product trusted to be in the present.

Work is a misnomer to production. Products are the transformation of potential energies, sometimes but not always assisted by work. Production with this understanding is described correctly by the thermodynamic process; energy transforming, and elements reacting to power by their changing.

Laozi appreciates that the essence is a factor needing further explanation; because this discussion needs elaboration. He reminds that it is the same mystery he introduced in chapter one, as the synergy that makes like gravity (with energy).62

When Laozi says that; the essence has the evidence, which proves it to be the origin of all things, he is offering a big bang explanation of production; observing the workplace, he guessed that the inertial energy at the beginning, in stillness originated from antigravity. He called antigravity - the mysterious female - her doubt (due diligence), is what precedes trust.

The matter is energy; Laozi says for example the potential energy of a substance (a rock) and the other energy (a man) are tricked into moving by the mysterious essence called trust, and that is the currency of the space we call the State. The currency is the fabric of the economy, it is the economies gravity, and acts like gravity. Gravity is the fabric of the Universe, and Trust is the fabric of the nation measured by its currency.63

In summary, the three factors of production, take two forms, both energies. Matter, contained in substances inclusive of carbon-based people is the first form, and the second is the essence, known as trust. Matter as energy has the evidence of thermodynamics. The laws of gravity prove essence (attraction). The images, when acting as entrepreneurs, are essence; the pure energy of trust, but as people laboring, they are a subset of matter. Images are the full set of the essence when creating, and part set matter working. Images wholly contained within the set; energy (substance & essence).

22. Newton's Laws.

To yield is to move, and to move is to be alive.
Becoming straight, and wanting life,
be bent;
becoming competent, and wishing wealth,
become entrepreneurial.
Grow rich, by not being rich.
When you lose wealth, you attain more;
With too much wealth,
you are only poor.
Enjoy the commonwealth as your playground
work pro bono for the public,
and the nation returns the favor,
moreover, getting back wealth is the pattern to wealth.
The entrepreneur does not brag,
so, she has merit.
She does not boast of her ability,
hence, she gets credit;
nor does she brandish her deeds,
accordingly, she gets sought after in the quiet.
The entrepreneur does not compete,
so, none compete with her.
Therefore, the ancients say yield and overcome.
For gravitas energy is renewable;
by its returning,
after allowing and enabling others.

.

Trust the essence by analog to gravity.

All people have a measure of merit, for their endowments and credit for their achievements. Laozi sums those and calls it gravitas. He discusses individuals or institutions as a Mass with a physical presence. The Mass effects and affects all of the movements made in society. 64

Gravitas is societies prime-mover; it allowed, acts. Wherever not prevented by barriers; say in a vacuum of laws, the only power that moves is a person's gravitas, it *acts* in society as mass does in the universe – to move, Laozi says *people gravi*tate.

To yield with a measure of gravitas according to Newton's law; is to react to another's gravitas. Using those laws people act by joining, and avoiding other people-masses, otherwise, orbit or avoid some of them at appropriate distances. To yield is to survive by orbiting or avoiding.

To become wealthy, be poor, be accommodated orbiting and made wealthy later when others are attracted to join your moves.

By being productive, respectful and polite, in the economy, acquire merit and get the credit called gravitas. It's a type of capital in the economy, and won from nothing. Gravitas is a mass of potential energy; we can intuit it as a synonym for wealth. That derived from attaining merit; Gravitas is the merit invested in production - credited.

Gravitas begets respect; it attracts opportunities when people join to share in its power. The gravitas of each image is a complex mix of attractive and repulsive qualities, and their quantum causes the patterning in society, similar to that of the cosmos. In a galaxy some stars are light, others are small. The light mass could be substantial, and the tiny heavy. Each mass has a unique makeup, a presence whose being, influences the arrangements of the whole.

Proper behavior in society gets demonstrated by the actor that reads gravitas well; reacts appropriately. There are no conflicts when actors abide Newton's rules of attraction. These laws are not taught, because they are lessons experienced.

The critical insight is that apathy and disinterest beget merit for avoiding, and credit for the decision. Attain gravitas in society, by joining a relationship, but get more by avoiding one. A toxic relationship avoided - gets respect in navigation, and that is credit in a productive society.

Gravitas is free from logic, it moves all parties into place and positions them like planets - according to their mass and distance. Thereby it is gravitas that constructs a society into the nodes, or workplaces, using the way of galaxies.65

When the ancients say yield to overcome, they mean to get more gravitas and come back. To yield is to gain experience in the workplace, and get respect from society for navigating there. Yielding is to follow the laws moving, being preserved whole until you are sought, then you are joined, or orbited for your gravitas; that is your time.66

23. Meet the rentier.

To be always commentating
moreover, always demanding is against nature.
High winds and rainstorms exhaust themselves;
nature knows when is enough.
How can rent-seekers not tire?
Can endless force protect their wealth?
Can wealth keep growing without it moving,67
Wherever wealth is not circulating,
people are not thriving,
wealth is the treasure of the State,
all people share it like air when it flows,
if the sky be denied, people would fight for breath,
see wealth is like air, it cannot be denied,
only exhausted into the commonwealth,
and used by it circulating in the State,
it will get returned by trade.
Those not exchanging, threaten life,
a rent-seeker - protecting their wealth,
only beg its total loss.
Wealth is safe circulating as currency,
it exchanged,
makes work a pleasure and not a necessity,
movement is life, its an absolute,
and absolutes are fought for.
Be warned friends of the Commentar,
if the dead are preferred to the living.

Wealth is to circulate by exchange.

Commentators (the rentiers insisting) haven't the gravitas to create. They are the blowhards that waste others energy, with their demanding certainty from the state, or with the gods (above) about their concerns for the public domain (risks below). Their demands and insistence are the cause of conflict, their insecurities, the making of stagnation. Wherever the rentiers threaten to withhold investments, they impair the commonwealths progress.

The productive act on faith, risking their worth in the public domain to improve it. Participants will clear the States obstacles, and find its opportunities if they are enabled to and allowed their reward for doing so.

Hoarding wealth creates the unbuilt bridge, those not made things, force the fare-paying community to work. Wherever wealth is let-stored in property rights and quarantined from circulating it stops the entrepreneurs from acting on the commonwealth.

The commonwealth grows at the expense of private property, and that is a good, not a problem. The State is an area measured by circumference (r^2), it increases to a power when the state grows. Private assets are a quantity, and they too grow with progress, but by addition. In chapter 25, we will discuss the measure of private wealth as ($2r$).

The owners are enriched by spending their assets to improve the commonwealth, they will have more in the improved nation, and better access to it, than they had, or could hope for by protecting their private property.

Progress is the transfer of private wealth to the free domain; spending is part allowing, and allowing describes the useful wealth that will be had by future generations. The protected asset is the excluding one because it has a No-Trespass sign or a patent mark on it. The given, invested, or spent asset, is a welcome, productive, and useful one. It will be the greater good invested, a share in a commonwealth improved, is the dividend of progress, the source of income, and income is the only good of wealth.

Progress is investing the private wealth to work in the public domain. The risking choice inspires people to build a bridge. The bridge will destroy the ferryman, but he will benefit more from the Bridge as a member of its community, than he ever did as the owner of its boat.

The rentier's habit of preserving wealth, and withdrawing efforts harms their share of the more useful, more significant benefit to be had in the commonwealth growing.

Wherever the State makes progress, private fortunes decline, because wealth is not an absolute and it is always relative to the commonwealths. The rentiers battle with growth is a fight for less or none because a small fortune can only grow-relatively by losing less, and when the commonwealth shrinks, while their share of a failing commonwealth is a loss no fortune can cover.

There are no losers in a progressing Commonwealth.68 According to Laozi, what goes on in the production of wealth stays in the production of more. Only the rentier-owner resists progress, he alone petitions against growth in a law court or a title office, and by doing that he disqualifies his wealth from the societies protection.

24. Rock, paper, scissors.

On tiptoes standing is difficult,
always preening and posing is dull,
moreover, affectionate displays are tedious.
These meddlers that promote themselves are pathetic,
Ignore them.
Those that know,
don't solicit attention,
yet, all get drawn to their gravitas.
In the workplace,
see-through people are known as
confidence tricksters,
rent-seekers
also, do-gooders.
Even they detest themselves;
thus, all images that are productive avoid them.

Avoidance is the first and best response.

Merit and credit are acquired with achievement, and lost by failure. The gravitas trade is exclusive to productive people. Those not participating in the economy, Laozi says the tiptoeing; boasting people have no gravitas to trade. Those poseurs have been previously called rentiers. Laozi is advising, the obvious; acquire credit by avoiding them.

The energy trust is acquired by real attraction, not pretension. If one projects height, the experienced see instability and keep their distance. The action of avoiding encourages the tiptoeing bragger to adopt more stable and productive habits. Therefore, avoidance is the purest display of sincerity - it signals the pretender to adopt better habits. Productive people do not practice the do-gooder's cruelty.

The entrepreneur engages only with merit, and she will not credit effort. Laozi explains moss and rolling stones; the do-gooder, gathering useless clowns, forming institutions from nobodies does not make gravitas.69

A mass without gravitas is unattractive, those joined in them are unable to make connections, their existence will depend on deception or cupidity. The tax-exempt churches example a virus interceding on the active vectors; they construct barriers to movement, mimicking the modus-operandi of the license holders, that suck energy from the more productive relationships.

A proper understanding of the braggart is unnecessary for the sage because they avoid them. Society becomes wealthy by avoiding (even banishing) the irrelevant. Full by empty; more by less, rich by poor, the affluent know to avoid confidence tricksters.

All choices people make within the economic system are one of the three actions allowed by gravity: join, orbit or avoid.70 Any choice made by reference to logic, morals, or rights will be less productive than the one made by the laws of gravity. Therefore, the Laozi system is exclusive to bodies with actual gravitas, and gravitas can only be had by participating.

25. The Dragon in the electric sky.

Something exists to form the cosmos.
In stillness, by ignorance,
and without substance or form.
I do not know its name,

qi (energy) maybe.
I think of it as the way.
If I were to name it,
I would call it a force that shapes things;
it functions everywhere that is beginning,
and returns to what is made.
As the heavens have this powerful force,
so, does the workplace,

and the king.
Within society there are domains;
the king has one of them.
Man abides by way of the king.
The king abides by way of the workplace.
The workplace follows the way of the heavens.
The heavens abide by the laws of nature.71

The way introduced as qi (energy).

Where a law has evidence, and what follows proves it.

Here Laozi talks of the essence acting, *the way* is energies potential used. Its use is what that shapes society. The way is the movement made by attractive energy, it is what affects arrangements, those make the patterns that become things.

Everything is something by its arrangement from the way (energy in use). The way arranges the solar system, it arranges the court of kings, and makes the patterns in the workplace.72

People are attracted to energy in use because their needs exist beyond their abilities. Each individual's production is inadequate, so they engage others and seek a potential in action to make the difference they want, for a trade needed. Exchanging places and tokens is the movement that starts momentum, it is the spark neither party had in equilibrium. These arrangements that start in the workplace are the conventions trusted to release a potentials kinetic energy, it is to start by trading it. **The fur induces the rod with rubbing.**

The domain of man explains the wonder of the universe. Exchange compels man's movement, and that is the movement observed in the arrangements of heaven. A man will gravitate toward another by necessity. His necessity is the other's want. They both need the other for the more neither has; the patterns made by a man getting, is the order of yielding to Newton's law. The rule is determined by the gravitas of the parties and their distance from a potential. Therefore, Laozi observed it must be in the heavens by this gravitas too.73

To talk of economics following laws is not new. Laozi's has a prescription, it is a science mistaken as alchemy; although, he mixes factors that make a product more fabulous than the ingredients, and he refers to that process with reverence, he follows a method, makes observations and has evidence. Therefore, his economics is science.

Henry George gave a full account of this Laozi science in 1890 when he imagined - how of production, by using energy alone. Without knowing it, Henry George got close to saying $E=Mc^2$ by postulating that the factors of production and the products of it, were forms of energy twenty-five years before Einstein.

Henry George, in The Science of Political Economy (1890) wrote;

> 'The three factors of the world – showing the constituents of all we perceive.' In summary, 'We distinguish three factors; That which feels, perceives, thinks, wills; which to distinguish we call mind or soul or Spirit. That which has mass or weight, and extension or form; which to distinguish, we call Matter. That which acting on Matter produces movement; which to distinguish; we call Motion or Force or Energy. We cannot, in truth, directly recognize Energy apart from Matter; nor Matter without some manifestation of Energy; nor mind or Spirit un-joined with Matter and Motion. It may be that what we call Matter is but a form of Energy; and it may be perhaps that what we call Energy is but a manifestation of what we call mind or soul or Spirit; and some have even held that from Matter and its inherent powers all else originates. Yet they may not be in fact separable by us, and though it may be that at bottom they are one, we are compelled in thought to distinguish these three as independent, separable elements, which in their actions and reactions make up the world as it is presented to our perception.'

Henry George said that energy took three forms; spirit, matter, and energy. Laozi called those, essence, substance, matter. By either set of labels, they are the only factors of production, and their mixing is the full explanation of creation or the subject of the Daodejing, explained as economics.

George explained production as a pure science like Laozi did by observing it; neither studied the universe or quantum mechanics, yet they both understood those subjects and described their laws by finding society producing things in workplaces, and talking of it as a subject to know called the Political economy.

The scientific proposition of economics is:

The process of production is one of the conversions of some types of energy into others. That of labor, trust and matter into work, those manifest as matter in products, and entropy enjoyed as satisfaction, potential income, and community health.

The scientific proposition of political economy is;

The arranging of the social environment to allow
the, most possible productive outcomes over time by ensuring the greatest freedom to do so.

These new scientific propositions are proved with science of Thermodynamics, and the mathematics of time in the appendix.

26. The cold start of an economy.

The heavy is the anchor of the light;
it is gravitas alone that invites orbiters,
moreover, it that makes genuine relationships,
gravitas is the start of production.
Therefore, if an entrepreneur travels,
It is with their enterprise.
Distractions do not tempt them from trade;
They orbit on arrival,
to let their gravitas attract others joining's,
and those will be relationships',
also, the beginning of their contributions,
at their new place.
How far then can the ruler roam?
Can he leave a palace with ten thousand chariots;
can he be the societies anchor and be absent?
No, he denies his gravitas,
He is lost to them,
moreover, they lose their place;
wherever an absence of gravitas,
all relationships vaporize, there is chaos,
Wherever the presence of gravitas,
it is useful, and all relationships flourish.

Gravitas explained working.

A people, joining, orbiting or avoiding in Detroit will be making cars. Their movements are called work, and it necessitates cooperation by Michigan. We call that society working a State. Participation in work starts with many agreements, and they are relationships not needing enforcement, just trust.

The measure of work is, therefore that of trust, not effort or law. Trust makes the nation a society, just like gravity makes dust a planet. If we know the gravitas of each party to a relationship as a quantity, then we learn the effort to make things, as the distance or time to trust an attraction.

The traveling entrepreneur carries her gravitas, as her reputation. Her gravitas is more than a curiosity to a new society, it's an attraction. Her gravitas will attract orbiting images by her being still, and those orbiters will want a relationship with her if they see an opportunity to turn her potential to use with their cooperation.

Success for the settler in a new place, is forming relationships. Those are made afresh, like they were acquired in the old place; by letting Newton's laws do the work, and by making no effort.

The ruler is the entrepreneur of old; he has an observable pattern of orbiting images surrounding him, the traveling entrepreneur is a witness. The new society mimics the old, and the Solar system too.

The sun cannot disappear without losing all of its planets. The entrepreneur cannot arrive without attracting; the king cannot leave his court and expect society to remain in his influence, the entrepreneur, can't force a relationship. All movements are for connections; they are made by trust, not effort. Trust is the power that creates links, and always has been.

Trust is the power that captures images at all scales. It is a universal constant, and scalar invariant. Laozi describes its effects as gravity (G) while discussing its power, as trust.

Laozi tells us to ignore what has been taught as business, or trade. His prime mover is Gravitas, and it requires exchanges to exist. It is an unknown quantity admitted, but not a denied one. A transaction is a form of maintenance that makes, an induction, and it takes time for the energy to come, and time is measured by distance.

It is possible to rely on knowledge for a time with pretending gravitas and with rules, but it is essential to know the limits of education. Stray from an enterprise, and find there is a distance, or pretense too much. That limit is found not learned, and in the heavens it is by feeling the Gravitas pull of the other body in the relationship.

The limit in our society is gravities equivalent - trust. The tolerance of others determines the limit of confidence. In a relationship, the patience of the other is either exhausted by a relationship's diminishing returns or exhausted by its excessive ambitions. These are the bookends of trust. They cannot be taught, only learned.

Laozi suggests, to stop working and use the observations to make relationships, into wealth. Move only by attraction, and the gravitas will determine how far, with who and when. Why is a question easy - because trust is the measure of wealth. To stray from his instruction is to ignore the value of effort, and lose (credibility) Gravitas.

Laozi illustrates this most crucial instruction with a vignette of a traveling tradesperson, she arrives at a new community, with her mobile workshop, and awaits approach for her merit

and credit. In telling the story of the interloper, Laozi describes the birth of an industry, and by that a city, its society, and State.
*****

Visualize the economy working, see the plane described in Chapter 14. Say an entrepreneur joins another, they orbit the resource on the plane and unite with it; they develop a strong relationship with each other and the supply on the plane. Their enterprise with the supply is represented as a stick, so the (x,y) plane now has z-axis making a skyscape of sticks. Now wrap the plane so that it closes on the skyscape.

We now have a sphere, and its surface is made from the sticks turned in, they are now the spheres struts - its polar tensors. The plane has become a ball of sticks.

Nothing is added to the plane, but now it is a sphere, it has an additional area, a new surface, new possibilities for relationships. The new area on the surface enables non-exclusive relationships that were not possible on the plane, because on the plane it was the resources that had the potential to attract. Now the parties to the resources can connect to others that are not a party to them. They join anew as the interloper on the surface, and increasingly ignore the tensors attached to the resources.

The new surface enables promiscuity, and the constituents prefer it, they skip across the new surface, and find new ways to relationships, and additional uses for them not imagined. They travel paths across the ends of the polar tensors and find profitable ways to move on the surface of the sphere; others mimic them. These movements on the surface pressure the tensors inwards - and force them less, while they also reach above the surface into the spheres atmosphere - extending from the surface.

The economy we know is now near-fully described by the balls stratosphere. The old relationships that underpin it become increasingly irrelevant, as they are more reliable pressured. Most of the wealth circulates like the interloper joining and orbiting on the surface, she moves for exchange to maintain her gravitas by trade, making a difference is a distance closed a movement made - is the work done. The economy is born and the computer industry has been explained.

The original relationship tensors, are still exclusive to the contracting parties, the new surface alone is attractive to others, the interlopers gravitating on the spheroid appreciate the ball of sticks, and respect the first relationships, but ignore them.

The interloper's surplus energy circulates the spheres perimeter. The tensors explain the increasingly rare exclusive relationships, while the greater surface topology accommodates the much more numerous transitory relationships of the many.

The more numerous create their vectors - tending to the great circle paths of the spheres surface, and counterintuitively avoiding the seeming more efficient routes through the center using exclusive relations.

Wealth loves movement, and speed conquers distance. Trust loves difference, and passion finds a way to prefer its attraction.

Interlopers avoid inertial accidents on the sphere because they restrict themselves to the known paths. They intuit the spheres travel conventions as; Newton's laws.

Trading forms the commonwealth a sphere. Trust in the original relationships, or the real wealth, has attracted the new and greater wealth, that wealth is the currency, it an energy extra that can ever expand into the stratosphere, if not restricted.

Exponential growth in a finite world is still impossible. However, the society and its economy exist on the sphere's surface, both expand into its atmosphere, which has unlimited potential for growth. Wealth can grow circulating in the atmosphere as energy, but not on the finite plane claimed as assets. An expanding wealth - made by a progressing society is maintained in motion by increasing movement on the sphere.

Some useful wealth moves through the tensor paths connecting the first participants trading, but the greater wealth runs on the spheres great circles. The surplus wealth pushes the balls stratosphere out, the model shows room for growth, in the possibility on the horizon, and that teases society to move with greater efficacy on the great circles, such that some images will sling-shot on the momentum and reach for the sky.

Since there are no limits to trust, there can be no limit to wealth, so long as wealth is circulated as energy and not protected in assets, the economy has room to grow. Power as trust is a currency; it can only be used or lost. There are no assets in a growing economy, just potentials, new space for expansion and the currency to trade.74

27. The mother's intuition.

An entrepreneur's movement leaves no tracks.
Her speech needs no explanation.
Her reckoning requires no abacus.
Just as
a well-shut door needs no locks or bars,
yet none can open it;
a well-tied knot uses no rope,
yet none can untie it,
the sage can,
like a mother does,

it's called being sensible.
Therefore, the sage is the torment of law-makers,
and the authority of authority.
She drives the nobodies toward opportunities,
that is where confusion and failure ensure movement.
Here is the essential subtlety of economics;
there is no generosity,
yet it is not cruel.

The play of mass and distance is the subtlety of the political economy.

The Sage tease the nobodies into the economy. Those that may have got knocked out in the rough of the workplace, losing their mass, or the inexperienced yet to acquire gravitas. The sage creates opportunities for them to enter the workplace again.

These light images may have lost their gravitas in a melee; they may have been done over by an entrepreneur's action (movement), warning (speech) or calculation (logic). They may lack qualifications (the well-shut door with no locks that cannot be opened), or they may have been bound to a contract (a knot without a rope that, cannot be untied). These are what the sage can sort out, and they are her raison d'être. She offers the idled images opportunities to acquire gravitas, by their joining, or avoiding and orbiting others.

Therefore, it is the sage that takes care to recruit them back to trade. Trust cannot be forced, but it can be shown. The sage subtly places experiences in the paths of the lost. She hosts a potential so that trust can be discovered in it afresh.

Leaving no tracks does not mean the entrepreneur's movement did not affect. A clear direction from a boss need not be the final word. By the best calculation, some things are forgotten, and a decent sum takes account of factors that can't reconcile. Shut doors can be opened because unqualified people can be given opportunities. Contracts can be changed.

These things are done by the sensible sage that cuts through conventions, rules, and history. A mother knows the time to swing her *Alexander's sword* and cut the Gordian knots.

Entropy and Time

Nurturing and including, are necessities to production. The sage does the obvious for expansion, mixing and reaction. For work to happen, the Sage prepares new potentials as the holy ghost. Her newbies becoming available makes progress possible.

The Sage's effort gives a society's its efficacy. Connecting people with opportunities is the ambition of the sage. The essential subtlety is the play between mass and distance to make attraction happen without force. Newton explained the skill of the ancients, Laozi says to use it to make the nation great.

Time is distance, both are trust. This is another subtlety: belief exists in time or by distance, paying one forward in time, is down the track in the distance, and both are done with a mother's faith.

28. A mother's advice.

Know the male role in society,
however, be feminine in its business,
then to participate in the commonwealth,
join, orbit and avoid society,
do that with a gentleman's politeness,
however, in trade; do it with a female's aversion,
then you will thrive in the Commonwealth.
Trust the State as the infant does his mother,
and you will know the bright side of society,
as a favored son,
as a matriarch; the dark places, of its economy.
Being the master is attractive,
however, the producer is the one approached,
so be both,
return to the other always.
Wealth is made by;
being the bright, but useful dark too.
Know and live honor,
however, play the role of the nurturer,
then you are a model for the country,
be uncomplicated in your thoughts (uncut wood).
If you shape your thoughts with education,
you will be a tool,
like the official or magistrate.
The greatest carpenter does no cutting.

Where being an entrepreneur is nonaction.

A society necessarily organizes around its production, and because females are the natural producers, the more productive society will be the matriarchal one.

Power and work are necessary for production, but not to initiate it. The female has a unique energy that attracts others; hers is a superior power to force, it compels a voluntary society, without demanding effort.

Females demure to get co-operation, usurping the efforts of men, they get movement without force. Their way of doing is what we call entrepreneurial (Ch. 13). Their idea of getting things done works well in the unheard, hidden, and illusive economy, that describes the ideal commonwealth (Ch. 14).

By politeness the state is attractive, and by its reserve, the state inspires trust in exchange. By the State yielding, efforts are made taking advantage of its potential. Experiences are had accommodating the female state, and where its economy is voluntary those arrangements are made with her.

The entrepreneur is Laozi's actor, she joins the state like children join games: with care at the edges, quietly at first and with respect for the game; willing it to be good, wanting that the players invite her, knowing she will be better for them and understanding that they wish her included.

The successful entrepreneur wants to play, she trusts the economy and acts in a trade like an infant. Babies initiate the movement by taking liberties from their mothers; entrepreneurs do the same, they respond to exogenous opportunities and ignore caution testing their competence.

Yes, know the bright side of the society (its affairs, and demands) but return to making and doing things: accept accolades but stay immersed in the game. It is the How of gravitas.

With gravitas, return to the plane of non-being and expect opportunities. Wealth is attracted to those that are competent. People are best rewarded doing what they can. Overreaching courts failure and invites diminishing returns.

Laozi urges us to be feminine so to fully experience the economy as a producer, otherwise 'If you shape your understanding, you will be a tool, an official, or a magistrate. The greatest carpenter does no cutting' (chooses not to).

The daughter is born perfect as an entrepreneur, a child cut (educated), is ruined.

29. Taxidermy.

If you plan to take over society
to create a nirvana of its economy, you will fail.
The society and its economy are marvels,
to control either is ridiculous,
they both depend on the others freedom.
They are as living rhizomes;
so, complicated that to disturb one,
is to destroy the other.
Some of their flowers are bright,
however, most are dull;
some are enthusiastic,
others are lethargic,
some have attractions,
others have none;
some are healthy, many are not.
Therefore, the Sage sees no unity in the people,
or their activities.
Only the benevolent agitators demand;
homogenous arrangements,
want;
humanitarian fantasies and extravagant luxuries,
those are the inadequate excuses for coercion.
The sage wills the plant to live,
When the economy is free,
the people bloom on their own.
When society is free,
the economy blooms without assistance.

Demographics prove no homogeny.

The workplace sustains society, and society supports the workplace.75 If a ruler interferes with the people trusting each other in their workplace, its enterprises get picked to extinction. The Sage ruler knows that no amount of interference in society is wise; any meddling in the relationships that are blooming or not damages what was developing or unraveling for the better.

The ruler can only encourage the plant. An effective ruler is an enabling host and an observer. They nurture the plant, and never pick at the flowers. Veblen described the florist leader as a taxidermist, the state that chooses the brightest, and preserves the dead, destroys the plant.

The Sage's role in the work of society is to be present only at its phase transitions. A flower emerges and grows without an obvious trigger. A leader cannot influence the state's blooming, but he can allow it. Altering the enterprise of the people either impairs their production or invites the communities, unwelcome reaction.

Acting on the inequities of society denies the good of its unheard barter and hidden goods. Removing the illusive opportunities destroys the relations exchanging to benefit from an enterprise.

Laozi sees each demographic of a population as sociologically and physically unique. The individual stems, elements, and branches of society continuously evolve with time: by description, age, vitality, and preferences. Meaning there can be no homogeny in either the home or the workplace. Any attempt at unifying a population as a society, or imposing a commonality on a place, is incompatible with living and doing because they are evolving.

Entropy and Time

There is a clear distinction between the flowers and a plant, the former is irrelevant to the individuals, and the latter is necessary to all.

The governing authority for non-action given in chapter five; be realistic, people die, so the sage does nothing to interfere with their living. Pandering to special interests in trade, or demographic groups with needs is a waste of effort, their evolution is older and wiser, both goods, that compel non-action. There can't be one agenda, purpose or ideal when the lot is always changing. The Sage need no plan because they accept change is the order (ch. 3), they are disinterested in how people are, or what they do.

30. Using the police.

When advising a ruler,
advise him against using police to coerce production.
Violence births reprisal.
Wherever coercion and taxation,
discord and poverty,
is followed by scarcity and revolt.
Advise the ruler to trust the production,
and not force it.
If coercion is necessary, then use the police,
however, do it without arrogance.
Produce with police without boasting;
use violence on the people without bragging.
The police force is a wilting one,
the active state becomes the weak one.
Success with force obeys diminishing returns.
What is against the people will perish.

A closing window for violence.

Leadership is not power. Leadership is benign. Power coerces a society to act against its nature, to flee where it would fight. Violence has no role in the attractive process of relationship making. The violent force prevents freedom of association and diminishes faith in trusting to make.

However, if a leader needs coercion, if he needs to tax people and to force labor from them, to take from them, police are a useful tool, for a time.

Power is a mix of violence, persuasion, and bribery;76 Each is thought a political weapon, but they are exclusively economic tools.

Violence is the forcing of production by demanding, and violence is a thing made by services, to enforce threats with jail and death.

Bribery involves the giving and denying of privilege; it relies on violence to confiscate, and more to give exclusion value.

Persuasion is part violence, and part bribery, only wrapped as oratory to get surrender with appeasement.77

Power is the product of economics because violence is a production. To partake in force is to produce it in a workplace. In a palace, experts work industriously to draft laws, and train police, they will be very productive in making weapons and designing jails.

The gates of heaven do open, Chapter ten explained how. Laws are made to advantage, and people can be forced to cooperate. Excepting that; the sage will have a mother's intuition of violence. A society used to attraction will co-operate with, or tolerate violence until they will not.

Power requires a feminine intuition to know the subtlety of gravitas and distance. Laozi cautions the leader using violence not to brag or boast about the police being his tool because their success will diminish his gravitas and their effectiveness.

31. Trust funds.

As for the police, they are tools of ill omen.
All productive people detest them,
the entrepreneur's place of pride is their partner,
and on the left side.
The rentier favors the weapon side;
therefore, police are not the choice of producers,
partnership and cooperation are their way,
Police are the weapons of the rentier.
However, where there are no alternatives,
then without relish,
use the police.
There is no glory in them,
or in their violations, never victories.
Hence to celebrate the police,
is to rejoice in the sycophancy of patronage,
and to undermine the voluntary exchange in trade,
whoever calls police violence - Justice,
will lose the respect of the unborn.
The rent-seeker that has resorted to the police,
and the ruler's law to protect his wealth,
is celebrated with grief like at a funeral.

Rentiers are warned.

Without police violence, the rentiers, could not purport their ownership of the commons, or enforce tithes on people.

Rent, royalties, and interest make the provision of necessities unprofitable. The police enforcement of those dues directs the people to risk trading in exotic places, and in luxuries to pay the police. The rentiers have not the gravitas to impose on trade without the threat of police. The celebration of the police is known as the tragedy of commons.78

Society tolerates rentiers by grieving their existence, wishing for their demise, and wanting alternative histories.

Laozi warns the leader about using the police to return the dead. The rentiers are the economies zombies that won't die. They portend relevance by their ownership of land, the filial piety inherent in licenses and patent rights, are merely screams from the grave until the police enforce them.

Zombie wealth is celebrated by society, like an inherited debt. The police make it visible. Laozi says here what is known, unsaid everywhere. The zombie rentier has inherited wealth, or quarantined wealth. He is the trust fund and the iron lung sucking the vitality from society. They are celebrated by all - with grief for their existence.

32. There is more than enough.

The economy has no limits;
it is a lawless space of possibility,
an uncut stone,
so, simple that none can master it.

If the king could let it be;
subjugate himself to its quandary,
and live with its perplexity,
society will thrive.

Exchange always because,
trading makes the sweet rain,
it falls evenly on those in the common domain.
Without coercion, in trade,
there is harmony in society,
however, start controlling trade,
and the stone is shaped,
the exchange slows,
and the police will demand more,
then chaos ensues,
moreover, relationships vanish.
It is prudent to not interfere in the peoples' affairs.
As the great river is attracted to the sea,
all under heaven are drawn to exchange.

The path of least resistance, ignores obligations & assistance.

Laozi thinks the economy is the people's business, let them exchange with potentials in the commonwealth, and the more they take from it for trade, the better. If a voluntary exchange is restricted, production slows, and the scarcity causes dissent.

Rulers should, therefore, not interfere with what the people do, or take credit for the peoples' achievements in trade, because it is the peoples' pride, and the rulers benefit.

The credit is given once already by each to another in the relationships trading, if a leader denies their credit paid, then he undermines the faith in the relationships that make, and the nation will fail, for lack of trust power (currency).

When people exchange in the Commonwealth, the ruler can take credit for not stopping them. The ruler is trusted to protect the commonwealth from land and patent claims that restrict exchange.79

Wherever a ruler reclaims the commonwealth from the rentiers, the workplace will occupy it. Laws have no relevance in the workplace because the society ignores them.80 The Sage ruler welcomes this form of workplace anarchy because it is the white noise that brings his rule into harmony with the people's enterprise.

The commonwealth bestows income on society: and the sweet rain (income) falls heavily in a conspiracy of silence. Laozi rebuts the do-gooder's equity, their rights, and income redistribution. The who gets what of wages, welfare, profits, crime franchises, royalties, rent, and security are irrelevant to a self-sufficient population.

The lawless economy creates a cooperative and connected society, one that relies on the ruler's distance. Efforts in a free community, are traded in the workplace for shares in single endeavors rather than stipends from ongoing enterprises protected by the ruler's police.81

Competing claims are settled amicably in a free society, because of the incentives to resolve interests quickly in the quiet. A people weighing good against better, are more interested in what can be made, than - what can be had.

33. How to live a long life.

To understand others is clever.
To understand yourself is wise.
To overcome others requires effort.
To overcome yourself requires willpower.
When you are content, you are wealthy.
To stay still is to endure.
To die and not perish is the mark of a well-lived life.

Agreements are a waste of energy.

The alternative to avoiding those that cannot be trusted is to join with them. Then an effort is spent on understanding, and more on overcoming, both demand energy and energy has more productive uses.

Differences are overcome, and new relationships can be forced, on your terms with effort. However, understanding and overcoming make problematic relationships. The laws of Newton are superior to logic; avoiding is the way.

One is more likely to perish overcoming, than avoiding. You are sure to suffer in a bad relationship by understanding. Therefore, Laozi says avoid.

Avoidance redirects energies to more suitable opportunities, saving them at the beginning for more productive endeavors later. An effort is too precious to be wasted on agreements with unfit parties. Avoidance is the superior choice in a society based on profitable relationships, because it denies bad ones.

Therefore, the ancients say yield and overcome, meaning, avoid and survive rather than perish in competitions. The necessary of a well-lived life is having the energy to live a long one.

34. The Market.

Are there enough products in the market?
The buyer expects them full of produce,
buyers want low prices,
the seller wants the markets empty,
sellers want high prices.
The prices go up and down,
the buyers and sellers are grateful,
they both get enough,
yet the markets claim no credit.
When the producer completes making,
her products are put to market,
they have no price demands,
she gives her produce to the market,
the market has no cost; it's a utility and free,
yet the market is under-appreciated.
The market is efficient, its role is forgotten,
even as it feeds and clothes everyone,
moreover, it supplies them with all things.
The market is great.
The Sage, too, is great,
She is the facilitator of production;
not noticed for doing her job well,
she only shows her greatness in the products.
Without the market,
there would be no efficient distribution.
Without the Sage,
there would be no effective production.82

The market is the river.

Producing is the source of all things; after the accomplishment, the producer claims no possession, she offers her product to the market. She has not a reserve price. Her products are sold by the Dutch auction method of the village fete, where the price starts high and is lowered until the product is sold or given gratis at the end of the day.

The market is irrelevant to the Sage because the public fully understand the market. It needs no explanation requires no regulation.

The market is a public good - efficient and free, like all great things in the commonwealth.83 People will say they made the market, let them ignore the buyer and seller, let them enjoy being in the commons. Like the producer will say *she grew the crop* without acknowledging the contribution of nature or the Sage. The consumer will say *I bought the food* without acknowledging the producer or market. No participant gives deference in public or recognizes obligations to another in the market, because properly there are none in a commonplace.

The market satisfies the society with produce and entices it with opportunities. Price is irrelevant because things are bought and sold in the same market. The market makes nothing, it spreads sweet rain (income) and speeds the peoples return to the norm - where satisfied, they stop working, and enjoy the stillness that begins new things.

Income and goods are exchanged equally at the market space and in a time singularity; Price is irrelevant in a clearance of income and products.84, 85

35. Let the gravitas work.

Embrace the commonwealth,
merge your gravitas with it,
and your potential will be apparent,
take from its bounty,
and make it useful,
see yourself the attractive focus.
Penetrate the commonwealth,
moreover, take possession of the public spaces,
entertain there, traverse and enjoy them,
engage with its potential,
furthermore, please take advantage of it.
Some will be curious about your ease,
And being in the commonwealth,
others will envy your casual manner with the public,
Answer;
that success takes no effort,
engage with the nation,
be surrounded by its opportunities,
some approach you and use your gravitas,
take advantage of them,
their initiative is your gain, their needing,
is your ease getting,
Your nothing is their advantage,
their success explains your wealth.

Wealth is for the taking in the public domain.

Since chapter two, Laozi has been instructing on the interplay between the universal and private wealth; he creates an algorithm to explain useful wealth. He says to recognize and embrace what is your useful wealth in the commons, claim it, then trade it back to the public and become wealthy.

After a period of success in exchange, you will have acquired a reputation and be trusted. You will return to the norm, and be in public. People will orbit, tempted by your fame, seeing its potential power they are compelled to your gravitas, as they were towards Solon's.

Prosperity and ease are not explained by effort in the workplace, but by being trusted in the commonwealth. Your gravitas will attract others, and they will use it to advantage themselves, their industry will usurp any effort you could make. They will habitat in your orbit and reward your ease.

Your being is enough because your gravitas begets their movement. Ease has the attractive power; it makes the sweet rain we call income - wealth.86

The economics of Laozi is so simple that it is offensive. To be offered Laozi's explanation for happiness and security seems unbelievable and inadequate. People prefer private wealth to have a more obvious origin in luck, hard work or divine intervention.

Laozi says - be spontaneous, politely avoid people, don't work, ignore logic, and engage in the public spaces to get rich. His instruction is insulting to those who are full of desire; observing prosperity and demanding to know how it can be achieved according to what they know. They want to win the owners game, but Laozi instructs on a better one, with a bigger prize.

Entropy and Time

The greatest wealth is free. Music and recipes are public knowledge, and therefore everyone's wealth, but only competent people can play music and make food.

The competent are wealthy because they access the public knowledge, and use it to problem solve in the commonwealth. Their wealth is envied by those full of desire that don't understand it as the gravitas to attract.

Anyone competent and free of desire can be wealthy in the commonwealth. Without rentiers, preventing experiences, competence is a matter of time. There is no need to envy anyone for having the front to access their wealth obvious.

36. Opportunity cost.

What will shrink was once expanded.
What will weaken was that reinforced.
Whatever imposed will be eliminated.

In time artifice is superseded by necessity,
practical people by-pass institutions,
they learn and produce what they want,
it is the virtue of progress,
wherever the producers overcome the rentiers;
so, ignore privilege, titles, and barriers.

Whenever the state teaches and makes laws,
the leader divides people,
moreover, he prevents exchange,
all fish thrive,
when they are together in the deep water,

The rentier dies. Why reinvent him?

Entrepreneurs if elevated are made weak. The state's laws advantage no person over time. The exalted fail above their cohort, because having a role in a contrived institution denies the gravitas advantage they had in society.

The elevated are not more assisted with illusory legal powers; instead, they are neutered by them. Can you keep the spirit, and embrace the [power], without parting from it (Ch. 10)? Artificial elevation disturbs society: on the way up its an extraction, and on the way down its an imposition.

Wherever the state's laws are on offer, they are demanded then later made the titles to property. Whatever is given by a King, can be taken, or usurped by others. In reality, nothing useful is given with titles and privileges.

Society operates best in the vacuum of laws and institutions. There is more potential in the whole of a community than in any part of it. There is no potential in an elevated group; they can only prey on the other in the same place. There is more wealth had by the State in letting the talented do the mundane better with the many than by having them do the spectacular with the few.

37. Summary of the Dao jing.

The economy is a living system;
self-sustaining, and resilient.
A people free of desire join it without demands.

If kings and their mandarins could let it be,
it will sustain the Commonwealth,
producing all it needs without fuss.

The Sage king stamps his presence in society,
and on the public domain,
he tempers his desire for luxuries.
He is always still in the Commonwealth,
moreover, his silence there is the all of his acting's.
His stillness invites others to movement;
and his restraint allows their reward,
both his silence and his restraint,
let opportunities,
those are the people's enterprise.

His presence preserves potential,
It's for the Commonwealth.
Furthermore, his self-constraint,
guarantees the production from it for the future.

The leader encourages a productive commonwealth,
its joy usurps his desire for luxuries.
Prosperity is a production free of the king's effort.

Being still with gravitas invites movement.

The final chapter of the Daojing summaries the pure science of economics; it has been told as a bodies Anatomy. This first book has described the economy. What it is, why it works, how to experience it and where it is found. This chapter gives cues to access the book, which is the beauty of oral knowledge instruction.

38. How to get rich.

Foreword to the de jing – Part 1

The competent man does not seek wealth;
therefore, he has wealth.
A man of merit who fears his credit
has no wealth,
because wealth is merit in trade,
not credit got by elevation.

Wealth is a currency voting for beauty.

Wealthy is having the gravitas to be attractive. Gravitas rearranges your surroundings. Entrepreneurs intuitively know gravitas as a dynamic quantity, and continuously attract exchanges to keep it.

The entrepreneur's wealth is like a boxed gift; the gift has a value in being exchanged, it draws movement without effort. The gift of the entrepreneur is not a wrapped asset to be treasured. It is an invitation to treat another (still wrapped).

Assets are not real wealth, other than possessions; they belong to the next generation. Money is not a right to assets; it is a utility to exchange with. Wealth is potential energy, only manifest useful by movement, and that needs coaxing by trade. Life is movement, and wealth lives as potential, money is the health part of wealth.

Entropy and Time

The value of an exchange is inconceivable to those full of desire for the thing of the gift. An ignorance of wealth has some confusing wealth with assets, and this explains to entrepreneurs why the poor have no wealth, even when they have money and assets, they are hard-done and idle.

Wealth is a form of energy, it is discussed by Laozi as gravity, but is equally understood as heat, by converting gravity energy (hydro) to a British Thermal Unit BTU.87 Energy as wealth is like food consumed to live, so valuable it disappears as it is used.

Energy is intuited as a movement, and by force, or heat. Neither power nor currency has value in storage, its only value is in use, and that value is unknown until it is discovered by the experiment called exchange.

Now by discussing wealth as heat and as a unit of currency, we introduce discipline to economics. Heat either flows to cold or dissipates being idle, either way - the laws of thermodynamics say it is spent. However, heat as energy can be exchanged, it is like an expense; paid out and re-captured as income. Wealthy people understand heat circulates to exist, so they refuse to be idle, they seek the less affluent, or cold to exchange with, they form relationships with them to flow their wealth, spending it so that it comes back (ch. 8).

A steward of wealth will initiate a trade knowing that he will lose to the other party directly and to the Commonwealth by doing so. Entropy sends energy one way; the wealthy will enrich the less affluent and enhance the commonwealth to get more money back.

The steward of wealth will most likely disgrace his avatar losing money but does it to maintain the gravitas of his person in the nation. Success is playing and suffering because losing creates the movement, it makes life, and that is the energy returned as wealth. In the game of exchange, the wealth lost circulates, and returns with a synergetic profit made.

Laozi's Way to Wealth & the Holy Grail

Inexperienced people with "Assets" don't participate in exchanges beneath them, because they fear losing their avatar's credit. These people are the commentators that seek elevation, then later as idle rentiers; expect the police to collect their tithes.

Instead of reaching down for opportunities beneath them, the rentiers reach sideways to their cohort. Warm does not flow to warm. With Newton's laws movement attracts momentum, and the wealth lost returns - Laozi says with more.

The architect has a reputation for innovation and reliability. He can be trusted to deliver a building on time and fit for purpose. He earns ten percent of his project's value. The more he is trusted, the bigger his plans; the higher his income, the wealthier he is. His wealth is measured by mass, using the laws of gravity. Ten percent (his fee) is his distance from the project and his gravitas (wealth).

Trust is the architect's source of income and the measure of his wealth, not assets. Trust is the currency he uses; his gravitas is what he risks daily in exchanges with the Commonwealth - building. He works to maintain his reputation in public, to enhance his Net Present Value (gravitas). His Gravitas is his wealth, and when he has enough possessions, he retires, in the commonwealth, he made great.

38. Do-gooder demands.

Foreword to the de jing – Part 2

The competent achieve by leaving nothing undone;
with merit, they act purposefully to their credit.
The benevolent leave much to do,
their escalating objectives are beyond their gravitas,
they demand support,
so, the humanitarian is invoked;
do-gooders have no merit,
they cannot exchange with authority for credit,
or get promotion for merit,
so, the do-gooders are avoided,
they resort to righteousness,
moreover, to the police force.
Then arises meritless propriety,
the demanding of efforts for nebulous fancies,
and those with police violence,
they are the sirens of ceremony,
wherever justice sings for benevolence,
the problems have started.

The cycle of misery retold.

Going clockwise, at One - the competent entrepreneurs are progressively disturbed by do-gooders, who increasingly impose obligations on them. When their demands prevent trust-based exchanges, they cause a crisis. The authorities then coerce the entrepreneurs' production, necessitating violence, ownership, and justice.

This cycle of misery, was described in chapters 17 through 20. Laozi's solution is at Eleven on the clock; banish the do-gooders and stop educating more of them. In Chapter 28, he advises against magistrates and educating them, and in chapter 36, he suggests the king never to grant status, because it denies the better opportunities won by gravitas and prevents the unproductive work made necessary by logic.

38. The gift of demand to economists.

Foreword to the de jing – Part 3

The waste to track,
and to predict this demise is the shame of mandarins;
it is their thin folly,
also, the origin of all ignorance.
The wise man deals with the roots,
not the flower that portends the fruit.
He ignores predictions,
moreover, he knows better.

Economists are called idiots.

The economy is all the invisible, inaudible, and the elusive activities; merged, those are the economy, each of its components are impossible to know, measure or predict. Meet it, and you will not see its head, follow it, and you will not see its tail (ch.14).

Then the origin of all ignorance is the macroeconomics that either describes or predicts. Economic nonsense is the pretense used by dilettantes to alarm society with unhinged talk of supply and scarcity; the corollary is - demand and terror.

The Economics taught is adequately explained by the transitive relation A=B and B=C so A=C. Then say Owners control supply, so Supply = Demand, then Scarcity = Terror, so Supply = Terror. The owners of drug patents cause terror for the sick with limited supply. The owners of development land terrorize homemakers with scarcity. That can be the only conclusion from learning the economics taught.

The wise man deals with the roots, in the stillness, Asimov told that the roots are the inverse of multiplication (production). The workplace multiplies its product; the wise man does not waste energy, so he seeks stillness to divide, he checks on the roots; to the 3; *Images, Substance, and Essence*, the three factors of production. So, he does not multiply them tomorrow in error, at work.

The flower neither portends the fruit nor indicates the plant. The flower will indicate all things, and therefore explain nothing useful. Laozi told us the fruit is disposable in chapter five, so our concerns for people are misplaced, and predictions of their future are irrelevant. For Laozi, the forecasting done in the name of economics is a fantastical, and mendacious deceit.

39. Two is One.

Always things have embraced another to become,
a something at all.
The sky obtained stars, and became clear;
the earth acquired disturbance, and became calm;
the gods got the dark force, and became divine;
the valleys captured the streams, and became fertile;
the creatures obtained their mate,
and became productive;
the kings acquired their people, and became sovereign;
all became as one by another's being.
If the sky were not full, it would not be noticed.
If the earth were not disturbed, it would be featureless.
If God were not beset, he could not be divine.
If the valleys were not drained, they would be swamps.
If the king were not of the people, he would be nobody.
Therefore, the noble only exists by the humble,
moreover, the low is the measure of the high.
The kings name themselves orphaned and widowed,
to invite their completion,
to make them - king.
Dismantle a chariot into its parts,
what is the carriage how?
Jade bells and stone chimes, can be a duet discovered,
but unimagined - they are but rocks on a beach.

Things become by joining with another.

Certainty and caution are primary to relationships.

In chapter one, Laozi introduced the pure science of the Dao Jing (book of changes/economics), by saying like Wittgenstein, that the definitions of the things are not their description.88

He now introduces the applied science of wealth the de jing, by explaining that things only exist by their constitution of other things. Both introductions caution non-action. Chapter one warns that incomplete information compels non-action, and this chapter cautions that the unseen constituents warrant consideration before acting.

The sky is known by its emptiness as the clear one. We acknowledge its emptiness in the description, clear, but the Sage is wise to see the sky as full before flying. The earth is known as calm, but the Sage is wise to consider earthquakes before building.

The first advice of Laozi is; don't act. The examples of heaven and earth are the reasons why. The clear sky and the calm earth, are also the full sky and the violent earth. That things are more than their description - is prerequisite knowledge before acting, and often the whole of the wisdom for nonaction.

Religions are full of evil, without devils, religions could not exist as divine. Police and schools would not live without their equal in the criminal and ignorant, because they make each other. The police and the schools select the upright and the intelligent, creating the degenerate and ignorant populations from those not selected. An understanding of those institutions being responsible for their other is the reason not to appoint police or build elite schools.

Creatures are known as productive, while their offspring are yet to exist. They are living because of their unborn; without them, they are dying. A society of humans able to make space for their evolving in the commonwealth is living, else it is disappearing; a species being eradicated from the land of the rentier.

Laozi's description of a chariot broken into its parts being no chariot is an additional caution towards non-action. A machine is more than the sum of its parts. A system is valuable; its parts are worthless without instruction; the whole is something; our nation is a system working with all its bits, or it is a useless box of parts. That is the all.

40. Three heuristic statements

The action of the Dao is to give back.
Natural spontaneity is the method of the economy.
All things come from being,
and being from non-being.

The action of the Dao is to give back.

The Dao (the economy) has a mechanical action. The more it works, the more energy it makes. The curiosity of attractive power is that the machine using it completes its cycle with more. Man's boundless ambition for better is teased by the gift of having improving means in an advancing society.

The energy given on trust (work) comes back as wealth, in currency. The Pharaoh builds the pyramid with seigniorage, he issues the currency against its magnificence, giving back its value to the future. What was spent forward by the builders, is redeemed in the present.

In effect, the Pharaoh gives trade credit by printing money to build the state. The produced infrastructure inspires faith in the commonwealth. Whatever is done in good faith by the present, guarantees its currency will be honored in the future.

Money now is given for later and valued from the future. The Pharaoh's book of the dead, examples Laozi's ledger being balanced - the assets provided to the future are paid to the present (in full) with currency. The money supply (circulating) values the Commonwealth of the future, and that is the settlement of generations. The Big Deal is between the dead

170

and the unborn; the bill-discounter Thoth brokered the deal - with the now to give back.

There are Three times. The past, the present, and the future. The currency crosses time; it is issued in the past, used in the gift of the present and redeemed in the future. There is no such thing as a bank. The honest society issues the currency in good faith and makes the commonwealth magnificent for the future that redeems it. (this is the subject of the appendix)

The parameters that determine that the size of a galaxy by the laws of Newton are what describe the concentrations of people in the cities because they are built on trust - with faith by work. The masses are the people building, the distance measured is the tolerance of society for the future, and the currency is the constant that determines the consideration or worth of the efforts made for the next generation.

The sums of Mass and distance triangulate, both the wealth of the kingdom and the activity of its constituents. Copernicus discovered these ancient concepts as the Treasurer of Prussia; he found the quantity theory of money, as an economist, and not the solar system as a cleric. Likewise, Newton was in charge of the Royal Mint; he was an economist, obsessed with the value of the king's money, and counterfeiting, not his telescope.

Newton turned to the Green tablet, which is a paraphrase of Hermes Trismegistus, and learned Copernicus afresh. The quantity theory of money was $F= Ma$. Hermes Trismegistus was most likely the source for Copernicus; he had access to the Vatican Library, Newton had his copy. Hermes Trismegistus is an inverse interpretation of the original Daodejing, got via Egypt Benjamin Franklin wrote *the way of wealth* 1733 referring to the green tablet, and directly quoting Laozi chapters 2&3.89

Copernicus, Newton, and Laozi were interested, employed, and obsessed with one subject, it was the value of money, they all described it with relativity, and a force called energy - trust. Cosmology was their metaphor to illustrate economics with the stars. The ages have mistaken the metaphor as the subject.

The currency is a constant, that measured by Thoth as time, was distance too; the function of Thoth results in Laozi's constant. This ancient system explains the Singapore dollar today. The country with no resources is a wealthy one. Singapore made its common great, and that wealth is given back in the currency, manifest as wealth.

The economy is no more complicated than a series of barter transactions starting with the state, each completed with an invitation to treat. There is never equilibrium: the system is dynamic, the barter transactions act across the machine's crankshaft with treats that skew it. Every offer accepted is made with a fortune cookie. Currency is the smile of an infant; a knowing wink from the father assures the child to have faith in the future - with trust between generations, the machine gives back paying forward.

Natural spontaneity is the method of the economy.

All creation starts by stillness, wherever people are satisfied and peaceful, their potentials resonate, and they self-organize. Following Adrian Bejan's Constructal Law principals, their movement seeks space; it gathers momentum, and manifests as flowing. An image resonates, the action is spontaneous.

Chapter 39 introduced the idea of a something, being two things; that things become one by embracing another. However, Alan Watts told us, that when those things embrace, neither can move without the other anticipating and preventing that move. Therefore, to live with another in an embrace, is to be spontaneous sometimes. Making space to take the other by surprise, explains the method of making movement, creating wealth and also life.

All things come from being, and being from non-being.

Laozi introduced pure economics in chapter one, by saying; a potential is not exhausted by describing it, and in the previous Chapter introducing applied economics, he said; that things described don't exist in reality, without another thing.

Being beautiful is less than not being ugly it is being beautiful, by not being nothing. Being wealthy is less than not being poor, it is being at all (is that more?). Having, making, getting better-more is merely conjuring from what-is. This craziness is the real alchemy that vexed Newton. The societies incommensurable values perplexed the money man.

All things come into existence as images from nothing, those are the ideas described, or facts made real (Hume, Dewey, North-Whitehead). Measures and shapes made descriptions of ideas become real. The idea of the farm is not in the land. The farm is produced by not being one. Ideas are their descriptions, and arrangements from the concept, make the metaphysical a reality.

It takes a physical power to shape an image into a thing with a description. The image is projected, the idea comes from a potential seen and draws movement, then a stillness, a resonance, conduction, a relationship, and a thing is made.

Trusting an image is what causes movement, then making the thing is the result of that trusting. The power of the image manifests in movement by attraction. The power of images and the force of attraction is what re-arranges the environment such that the physical thing described, ends with the potential it was trusted to have.

Being by non-being explains Laozi four times;

a) An image becomes a reality by being described.

b) Creation by gravitas; a meeting becomes a relationship.

c) The relationship has a synergy; that a product.

d) The potential of mass has a power too; in a relationship, but not on its own.

From the previous chapter; Jade bells and stone chimes are not when they were described rocks on the beach. They become Jade bells and stone chimes when an is image formed of their merit in the theatre; when the rocks became the instruments imagined, they were transformed from rocks.

The image of the rocks being something else attracts their retrieval from the beach, and the idea of trusting their potential, becomes experimentation, that an industry, once a description, later a celebration in the orchestra of a thing made fact from fiction. The utility comes from imagination, and wealth from potential, neither come from nature or hard work.

41. The reality is, has been, will be.

When the highest type of man has this Dao explained,
he practices it.
When mediocre men hear of it,
they are curious and need it demonstrated.
When ordinary men hear of my Dao de, they laugh,
moreover, they dismiss it.

If they do not laugh,
they are yet to be told;
there are many curiosities:
the easy path is not,
the brightest is dark,
the most fabulous wealth looks like no wealth,
the hardest is soft.
By these quandaries,
incomprehensible to many,
the economy starts,
it provides,
moreover, it completes all things.

Laozi asks forbearance while he explains further.

The three heuristic propositions from the previous chapter are heard as assertions, and those challenge people with degrees of incredulity, Laozi understands and sympathizes.

Neils Bohr said; Everything we call real is made up of things that cannot be called real,90 and John Wheeler said; If you are not completely shocked by quantum mechanics, you do not understand it.

They had the same difficulties explaining physics that Laozi has with economics: it is unbelievable, seems to be the timeless reportage from scientific pioneers.

Laozi is introducing chapter 42, which the reader will find incredible. It is an explanation of creation. It is the most challenging thing Laozi will ever explain, so he asks here as he did introducing chapter 21, (with its preceding chapter); for your tolerance, he asks for care with quick judgments. He pleads for patience because he will explain fully - what starts, provides and completes all things, in the following chapters.

42. The answer to the universe.

The way gives birth to one,
the one gives birth to two,
the two gives birth to the three.
The three is a One, it's a something more,
and it gives birth to all things.
Each thing Three is more,
In each, the elements,
there are the Ones embracing their other.
The harmony that binds
them is the tension that created them.
Men hate to be orphaned, widowed or worthless,
kings call themselves by those names.
because, people are elevated by falling,
also, destroyed by being successful.
I teach from experience and as a witness,
a violent man will die a violent death.
I regard this as the father of all learning. 91

The process of creation explained.

Buckminster Fuller explained how a thing becomes something productive, by saying:

As one will always be to one other, but no other, no one. Other, is four, but whereas one has no relations; Two have only one interrelationship, three have three interrelationships, but four have a minimum of six relationships in Synergetics. There is no insideness without four, without four, no womb, no birth, no life.92

Fuller was explaining creation from first principles, he elaborated further on its mechanics than Laozi did explaining the same process, but it is easy to imagine Laozi, saying more if he could do as Buckminster Fuller did in his nine-hour lectures entitled, *Everything I know.*

Laozi illustrates becoming, sufficiently with the example of, a nation becoming, One. Created from the start - productive and living together; as the chicken & egg. The chicken is a frame in the shape of a pyramid, and the egg is its enterprise. The Nation and its enterprise are born together, the politics and economics are one - a four from the three energies (Ch. 21).

We accept a king as being two - his person and his people. As a two, the person king with his people are inherently unstable together. They find the divine, which is also a two, being the combination of good and evil. When the king joins the divine, they are two twos - a one, now with the divine, providing the king with his authority.

They are unproductive they seek another two twos, they find land and water, which are themselves joined to another Two - utility and technology. The nation starts when the four twos' (all ones) attract spontaneously; to form a Nation. It's a pyramid shape with space inside (to be productive), and a presence to the outside. The nation is born with a frame, and a womb-like the chicken has.93

The state is the energy of trust. It's formed by tension, in a corporeal body. The harmony that resonates within it has a real frequency, and that frequency creates movement from stillness. We call it life, the movement that demands space gives the energy to the others that make it, life pushes against out from within - this pressure provides the frame of the nation with its tension, and that a volume that contains its life.94

Laozi has told of the creation of the state, from non-being - to being a frame (field). The state's production (GDP), will always be dependent on his creation relationships.

Laozi warns of an aberrant component in the frame he calls a violent man. This entity could be within the pyramid structure itself, or between one of the two twos. If the king becomes too full for the land, he becomes the violent man - one is enough to destroy the frame of the nation.

The weakness and the strength of the nation are these founding relationships; this is the beginning of all learning, a known supported by today's molecular science. Laozi knew not to judge the fruit from the flower by his observation of beauty leaving the dirty factory. He did not need a philosophy to understand modern science.

Laozi has argued that a thing, or a name does not describe, a situation, nor is its potentiality encoded in the constituent parts. The opening chapters of both his books (Chs. 1, 39) refer to living things being created by nothing and by difference making energy, this is now explained by nothings tendency to express itself by maintaining the other in the most economical structure - that of a pyramid.95, 96

43. Induction.

Trust is universal
it has no nemeses,
moreover, is welcomed by all potential,
faith in trust starts everything that will be.
That is how I know - the benefit of no action,
by the lure of potential,
my own movements are to attraction,
I am excited always in the thrall of an exchange,
I know the wins from an exchange,
they are the trade of potentials.
Now I teach nonaction,
I do it with no words,
the movement comes
from the still,
the whole world can see its product.

Essence is enough.

Trusting is an exchange of faith. One trades with something for the realization of an image or the making of another. There exists a belief in the thing for a transfer of trust to make something of it. That is our vernacular now, and not so strange; however, Laozi is adding something, he says; the element has potential, it has an energy, and that is what makes an image real because the energy gives motion.

Entropy and Time

Now the making of an image becomes a thermodynamic process. The existence of the image effects because it loses or gives power in an exchange. Since trust is an energy, it conducts - from one body to another.

All things are porous to energy, whatever their form. Wherever potentials are close, an effect is affected, because energies like heat transfer and affect. Energy is a frequency, it penetrates a potential, and makes the seemingly impossible. The exciting of a transformation with energy is what we later recognize as effecting nothing but affecting something called a product.

Laozi teaches this in silence because conduction is silent. In stillness wherever unequal potentials meet, they resonate, and that non-action tunes each to harmonize the other different. One becomes made a new thing, while the other is transformed, either exhausted or renewed.

Neither student nor teacher makes an effort sitting together in silence, yet they exchange energy - the penetrating from one, is a merging to the other. We habitually call that learning, and the process, teaching, because it is an effort to learn, and a work to teach.

However, the product got by effort and work, could have been given equally well, and possibly is, by letting conduction do. An alternative parallel explanation is that the potentials of teacher and student compose by nearness, without effort - the conduction is a function of distance and mass, their constituents resonate transferring, this arranging is the creating called success - say in learning.

In closeness, a potential exists as a presence; it has a frequency that broadcasts. Wherever the signal is trusted, the conduction is enabled, and the transformations effected.

The natural process of making something is to be attracted to its potential in the beginning. The product of attraction is the absorption of energy, caused by being still, and it is more effective than force. The exchange of energy between potentials make a product; making needs no effort or words because the power of trust is a faith in potential, their tuning resonance is a movement greater than effort.

This process is intuited by most, but ignored by instructors because it can be re-created by work or study, and demonstrated by simple experiment. Here we see academic free riding in a parallel universe, which is the real world?

Regardless of the evidence, Laozi's explanation for making stands, learning is a contact that conducts, the potentials merge and become. Laozi better explains the results of the working to learn experiment, because work is an effort, and that form of energy has a substitute in a purer form - essence. Laozi explains the Savant, the Savant is a paradox to teaching, but explained here by Laozi as a man with a sensitive tuning device.

44. On winning.

Are your desires a danger for your body?
Does your avatar role demand, pilot of your body?
Fame or life,
wealth or society:
which is security?
Winning or losing:
Which does your mother prefer?
Success exhausts energy and risks life.
Forever winning is impossible;
intuit enough, and you will understand plenty.
To choose the prize of a long life,
avoid disgrace,
be modest in choosing, sure doing,
moreover, spend your energy living,
else you will die guarding what you did not need,
moreover, doing what you did not want.

The corporeal self help.

A role subjugates a real person, with an avatars inflated expectations, they are the labor of a virtual society, a foreigner doing a job in another's space.

Compound growth (always winning), and calculated risks, are the dangerous fairy-tales told by the rentiers to deceive an avatar. In reality, exponential growth is impossible, the nemesis always met, and calculating the risk of death is proof of insanity.

To concentrate on getting a profit - is like a soldier seeking fame: inevitably the gain invites a loss like a soldier does a bullet. Tempering the desire for profit is incurring expenses; being disgraced surviving is the enterprise of life.

Experience is to recognize the hologram projection of the rentiers' promise and avoid them. People survive the crazy-brave by not trusting, (avoiding) them.

The self-regulating mechanism that controls behavior in a trust-based society is exchange, and it develops naturally to the point that further would be more onerous than useful, and stops of its own accord at that limit.97

45. Useful or perfect?

Flawless seems not quite right,
yet magnificence cannot be improved.
A measure is inadequate,
satisfaction is perfection.
Like the straightest line looks bent,
the greatest skill seems simple,
see it takes an effort to hear eloquence,
The great and perfect is pretension.
See deception,
a desire for things tricks.
However, free of desire,
the utility is all,
and had with experience.
By not demanding,
you know what to, how to,
by what is useful,
and what resonates with you,
what you tune to is what rewards your effort.
Effort can respond to cold,
however, stillness will absorb energy,
so, she that accepts the surrounds,
gets everything with ease,
she will be the ruler of the world.

On when and how to act.

Appreciating is the experience of utility while trusting the tool or system. Using the thing, and knowing success, is presuming the absence of disappointment,

The competent respond to the objects at hand without the effort of thought. They are doing not expecting, because they are trusting and wanting nothing, non-action, is not demanding perfection, but getting utility. This acceptance of *adequate for purpose*, permits an entrepreneur to act at the moment. Their productivity is explained by a fortuitous naivety (that nothing will go wrong) of pretension, and certainty of what is best.

However, there is a time where the productive find a tool, process, or system, inadequate, where frustration compels the new. These are the moments to be still, and stop doing-using, those moments are strikes; action by non-action.

Creating stillness was called passive resistance by Gandhi. Laozi thinks - it an awareness in using, an instinct to learning. He likens it to a trip-switch on a capacitor - the energy stops discharging and switches to accumulating (qi) charge.

The competent stop working, if they expect to be disappointed. The entrepreneurs unemployed potential builds - it resonates with others close, and this switch from doing is what makes the new, and a better without effort.

Their strike, increases the potential, they make a difference, by not discharging. Appeasement is slavery, continuing to use expecting disappointment is surrender. What eventually drives change, does it from the roots, and by stillness.

A strike signals, a disappointment, and the difference made from not doing indicates the solution (makes an image).

Entropy and Time

Wherever the competent are disappointed they invoke a stillness, by intuiting the time to stop contributing.

The person that can be still at the appropriate time will be doing; she will be experienced, curious, frugal and visionary. She is the one qualified to lead the whole world, because she is done responding to cold. To make a difference, she will stop, accumulate the power from her surrounds, and make later, but better. Action by no action.

46. Self defence.

Where the commons are free, the people are,
efficacy reigns,
race horses are used to work the fields.
Where the commonwealth is owned,
the people are conquered,
then violence reigns,
police horses are bred in the city.
Where the rentiers' control;
There is no delusion greater than collaborating,
there is nothing venaler than a rentiers sycophant,
and no greater waste than their keep.
The people's needs are guaranteed,
by denying the rentiers.
The producers rely on certainty,
and certainty in time is security to market.
A fair exchange with the commons,
is a modest one, and free of desire,
greed has no place in the commons,
frugality tells the producer what is enough,
and that signals the conqueror against meddling.

Modesty guarantees freedom from repression.

If sovereignty were universal, there would be no
entitlements and no reason for discontentment. Sovereigns have
no duties or betters to obey. An abusive exchange is

impossible, without leverage. In a society of equals, fair trade is the norm, its guaranteed by the consequences of bad manners.

In the state without law, trade is based on mutual respect and governed by politeness. In a free commonwealth, racehorses are used to plow fields. The farmer's horse is a productive asset, a source of enjoyment to him racing, and also his warhorse. By being productive, happy and powerful, the farmer gets respect. It guarantees he will be treated fairly in trade.

Where police horses (warhorses) are bred and raised in the city, they are used to enforce privilege. The breeder's horse is his chore, and he has no opportunity to race it, or ability to use it fighting; he will be the tool of the police tsar, a servant to the man that does.

The suburban breeder is dependent on the venality of the state for his survival. He will be a joyless sycophant raising the horse. Having invested in producing a weapon, he depends on the police to use it, for his share of the Police extortion.

The eunuch lawyers create rules for people to break, making it their job to find crimes; the cut psychologists look for people to fear, making it their duty to control them; the weapons-manufacturer creates the means for violence, and each relies on a conqueror to employ them (ch. 30).

Rentiers and eunuchs do not exist when the world lives according to Laozi; The producers limit what they take from the commons; its more than they need, but not enough to attract abuse. The tragedy of the commons is told; the triumph of the people; the Police Tsar experiences diminishing returns, and his fight proves more expensive than the prize. An armed society is a polite society - said Robert Heinlein.98

47. The inner light.

Without being told,
you can know the laws of exchange.
Without seeing for yourself,
you can know the patterns of production.
The further one enquires the less one learns;
Thus,
the entrepreneur knows without asking.
He understands relations by intuition,
he has experienced productive relationships.

Creating wealth is intuitive.

Laozi has explained many difficult ideas with nuance and evidence, to this point, now without the science; he yells.

The more you enjoy, the less reliant you are on authorities. Will a deal be accepted? Why would you waste energy making it unfair? How low would you go for experience? How can that be taught? The answers to Laozi's questions don't rely on assumptions or require qualifications. Each exposes the academics that purport to struggle with complex issues.

Deceitful dealings need to be taught by economists because they are not intuitive. Taking advantage of another in exchange is counterproductive. So, comparative advantage (abuse of power) is taught, to be learned. Laws are required to permit the abuse of comparative advantage, and those need enforcement to make the academics right, and the peoples' inclination to fairness wrong.

Sincere dealings happen to be fair and also productive because they are. Proper transactions in the home, are the majority of all dealings, and because they are successful, they are ignored by academics, they prefer problems to evidence.

Sincere dealings are not taught, because they happen - like all good things do, spontaneously. Experienced people dismiss comparative advantage, and succeed by making fair deals that advantage all parties. They do not ask the law to permit or want the police to ensure.

Laozi need not be the authority; he encourages you to partake in exchange and discover your born genius at trade without police violence.

48. Trust learning never.

Misguided by education,
you labor to produce and work to know.
However, by exchanging from stillness with potential,
you know to produce,
moreover, to trade, and not labor.
Get gravitas from,
making and trading,
use it to improve the commonwealth,
make no effort to learn,
accept facts and affairs,
and ignore them,
return to the stillness,
you will always be wealthy.

Facts and affairs are the folly of fools.

Laozi said to banish learning and vexations end (ch.20) now; reject education. Teaching suggests that we should labor to produce like we work to learn. Whereas experience suggests making no efforts for either.

David Hume, Kant, and John Dewey speak Laozi; facts are temporary and conditional, new evidence or cupidity with convenience will prove facts otherwise in time.99

Laozi is the most radical of philosophers he says; accept facts while they suit your purpose - after that ignore them. The self-organizing economy does not rely on knowledge or labor, because its initial movements are attracted, and those will be determined involuntarily by gravitas.

Free agents do not avoid the energies they have no control over, they take advantage of them for momentum - they will sling-shot advantage from adversity. Free agents do not bet against immovable objects or labor in denial of them. Free agents use repulsive energy to close the distance on better opportunities.

Influence extends only so far as you are trusted - in distance, or only as long as you are trusted - in time. Your gravitas is the all of your effective power, it is the sum of your merit, but it vaporizes at the limits of other people's tolerance, or exactly where knowledge is irrelevant.

For Laozi experience is superior to education: it proves patterns, instructs on limits and shows what is appropriate. Is it useful? What is it worth? Am I compelled or obligated? Should I trust someone?

All questions answered in the Daodejing by ignoring them and trusting Newton's laws. Laozi teaches that attraction is the prime mover. Proximity and gravitas explain more of getting to the moon than fuel or effort do. There is no logic in trust just an intuition of energy; intuitions are feelings experienced not lessons learned.

49. The winnow or the plough?

The Sage has no agenda.
However, they;
Intuit ambitions,
bolster efforts,
and impose on dreams.
The productive joined to an image encounter the Sage,
the Sage enables dreamers.
The Sage is honest with the dishonest;
they Sage trust the degenerate.
Is the Sage naive?
To society, the Sage is confused,
ignorant and muddled,
the Sage seems silly to the productive,
and infantile too,
people treat the Sage like a child.
Yet the Sage enable credit where it belongs,
being derided is how a foil is forgotten for achieving,
the Sage want to be redundant,
in a prosperous, and safe Commonwealth.

The Sage speeds time.

Populations are not homogenous, and they have no unity. Their mind as a whole is repugnant to the entrepreneur. The Sage prefer dealing with individuals, enabling each according to their image.

The Sage despise concealment; their inner certainty makes them indifferent to what others know or think of them. While the Sage individual shows herself, many do not understand her.100

The facilitating Sage will enable individual ambitions, even if they conflict with community desires, she makes no judgments. Hers is a noble endeavor because it enables the whole society, by ignoring it.

If the Sage were to aid the commonwealths ambition, she would only provide cover for weak elements to hide. The Winnow makes a society productive; the plow nurtures the weeds too, the crop thrives by banishment, not tolerance.

To assist productivity, the Sage actuate selected individuals to avoid, orbit, or join others appropriately; she thereby influences the whole population. The success stories get mimicked and the failures exampled.

The sage assists a selected person to be successful. If the person is aiming for the gutter, the sage will urge them to hurry. Society benefits most by cleansing, removing toxins from society aids the well-being of the nation.

50. The problem with assets

The avatar accumulating wealth,
will cause its host to die.
When adding your life as beads on the thirteen,
so too is death counted.
How is it that an abacus is an invitation to death?
It is because the avatar counts his life by assets,
he protects those pretenses with the sum of his life.
Whoever knows the value of living,
travels fearing no rhinos or tigers,
because the Rhinos horns can find no pocket to pick,
Tigers claws can find no place to grab,
he free of desire for protection,
never needs armor for battle,
because weapons cannot find a place to target him.
How is it so?
Because there is no dying ground,
the entrepreneur's asset is her Gravitas.
An entrepreneur's ability is not booty for a tiger.

Unspent currency & assets are liabilities.

The Laozi maxim is to avoid death, he suggests taking what
you need from life and to keep moving; don't tempt fate. The
avatars *want*, gets diminishing returns, and a short life for the

mother's child. Laozi now instructs on the great chimera of assets.

In ancient times traders would count their wealth by moving bracelets and rings across their bodies one neck, two legs, two arms, and eight fingers. Each trinkets position and sum recorded his assets. Their system of accounting was called the thirteen because the body had thirteen hooks, those were later made an analog with wood and called an abacus. If the trader was laden with beads, he advertised his worth to predators.

Should life's purpose be misunderstood, as the accumulation of assets by the owner his, corporeal body is jeopardized guarding them. The avatar owner will be confronted with thieves (tigers), confidence men (rhinos) and the taxmen (weapons) wherever he goes. Inevitably one of them will get his assets and over his dead body.

If you do not measure life with assets, then there is no reason to fear an unnatural death. The predators ignore entrepreneurs because their gravitas is not a booty attractive to pirates.

Land and resources are not valuable in the commonwealth; they are like the stones on a beach wanted by nobody. If the land is counted as an asset, the avatar owner will defend it, and his person's mother will mourn her son lost to idolatry.

Assets cause misery not enjoyment. Gravitas is the only private wealth that can accumulate; everything else belongs in the free domain, where it is available to use. Gravitas cannot be taken by a rhino, or by weapons because valuable things either exist as potential or are consumed as ephemeral experiences, neither exist as objects to be taken.

51. The full explanation of Political Economy.

All things were potential energies,
they became by attracting an entrepreneur to nourish,
their response was spontaneous,
they resonated to the attention,
and re-arranged,
in the image of the thing thought to be.
Those potentials became what appear;
products made by labor,
however, they were energies always,
that are merged by the entrepreneur's volition,
by frequencies harmonized - that took form.
Taking form is the show of things,
moreover, the all of,
when, where, what;
rears, grows, shelters,
feeds, and clothes everybody.
Entrepreneurs claim no possession,
of their services now called products;
they merely joined with the potentials,
they met them in the commonwealth,
and without the potentials permission,
guided them.
After the shaping and improvement,
the entrepreneur sends their service back,
to the commonwealth as a product,
from whence it came,
she offers it to the market for bid,
now free of conditions.
The price bid is the communities' judgment,

of the entrepreneur, of the act called service now,
the peoples sanction is indicated by a penal price,
and forgiveness by a high one.
The appearing product sold,
earns the entrepreneur an acquittal for her service,
and the returning entrepreneur is celebrated,
for her good faith in the enterprise.
The primary virtue of the market is justice,
the how, what, why, where of all doing in society,
to live judiciously by the market,
and with the Commonwealth.

Smith's invisible hand, plain as Laozi's glove.

Wherever a commonwealth, all things have potential. It's energies cause arrangements, those are recognized later as enterprise and by products. The entrepreneur is merely present when she joins with the other energies, and conspires to perfect their movements in her image.

Without laws preventing, the entrepreneur engages with the commonwealth. Her activity amplifies what she is attracted to; it resonates, and the movements are called work, she saves her effort and lets nature do the most of it. The entrepreneurs later seek societies forgiveness for their liberties taken in the common and for influencing its arrangements. Nature is a free domain, but taken is with a tacit agreement that the taken is improved, and returned for judgment.

The agreement to take from the commons is an understanding. This chapter is very similar to Adam Smith's invisible hand, except Laozi, is talking about producing windows, with timber taken from the forest, not washing the profits of heroin trafficking with a silk cloth.

The entrepreneur's enterprise spares the community the effort of producing. What's made by serendipity appears wanted for the rearing, growing, sheltering, feeding and clothing of the people. The cupidity of society is admitted when the entrepreneur returns their secondments via the market. The virtue of the market is that it both penalizes the producer for her liberties and rewards her initiative.

The market is the producer's court, the manufacturer submits to the market, as an apology to the commonwealth for taking its substances, and accepts the judgment of the sale price.

Entropy and Time

The full market proves the economy is driven by production, and not by demand. The economy's mantra is, make it and it will be wanted at some price (in agreement with Say's law), and not the fanciful demand it notion, that products will appear in the future still wanted.

Laozi's economy is boldness and innovation. It produces unexpected things those suggest elusive opportunities - they tease further movement, and a momentum enough to ensure the economies perpetual motion.

The promise of the economies continuance assures the future State because the currency given to the entrepreneur in the market, is a token that will be accepted tomorrow. Therein is the full explanation for the wealth of a nation. While the assurance of currency is operative, the entrepreneur sustains society in the present with natures secondments improved, and the understanding that she will be returning later for more of the cupid market justice.

The demand economy we are familiar with assumes a scarcity for yesterday's desires and sees progress in their supply. It seeks the products that are expected by a people wanting them now while sourcing them from foreign lands (another space) making them unaffordable on delivery at another time.101

No one can know what he desires until he sees it, people can only be sure of what they don't want by their past experiences. The Laozi economy is therefore in sync with our subjective motivations and visceral experiences of life in the present. In contrast, the demand economy - makes for tomorrow, what was wanted yesterday, forgetting our time – today.

An innovation economy resembles an artist's colony. The products themselves may not even be wanted or understood. People have most of their satisfaction outside of the market, and only the entrepreneur's surplus seeks justice.

The products are intended to be independent of the producer like they were in the beginning before they were taken from the commonwealth and made a product. The market restores them (transformed) to their heirs; the people. The producer is innocent of resource theft in the commonwealth, she was drawn to it by an attraction forced by Newton's Laws, and she returns any surplus to the people in the market - improved for their betterment, not for export and luxury.

52. The good of Autarky.

All things produced by foreigners as luxuries,
can be made over,
moreover, better at home.
Know the foreigners' products,
and don't demand them;
go back to the beginning,
and make them at home.
In doing so, you can only benefit;
take no risks in getting things,
become their producer.
Seal the passages,
shut all the doors,
and till the end of your days
you will be satisfied.
Open your mouth,
open the door,
meddle in affairs, and
to the end of your days, you will be wanting.
Making things from the beginning is security,
see the bright product,
study the small details,
moreover, use the stillness at home,
and better them;
Producing is how to live a full life,
be the creator; you were born to be.

Demanding, is begging to be poor.

To have things; know them by use, and imagine them better. Laozi advises having fancy things, by making them. He talks autarky. He advocates Henry Carey's American System, favored by Dr. Sun Yat Sen.

By encouraging the local production, of products available overseas, he spares people the drama of demanding foreign goods.

Don't meddle in the affairs of State to get foreign goods. Live without calamity as their producer. Be a meddler petitioning for things, and be forever wanting as a consumer, wishing for a producer, fearful as a citizen. Foreign goods are seemingly on offer. However, getting them is to open the door to affairs, and those are problems beyond your control.

By shutting the passages to foreign goods (demand), you will not concern with whose got, because necessity is the highest authority, it will direct your efforts to produce what you need.

By closing the doors to what can be got, you protect your family from unwelcome visitors. Working to make what can be made, will eventually, by steps make more sophisticated products available; so, trade necessities while developing the foreigner's things.

Scarcity, or want; is the inability to imagine substitutes. Choosing simplicity is choosing wealth, it is getting more from less, either producing alloys, or making a good from the available, a better.

Scarcity can disappear with an artistic flourish, or a potential seen, so production is often unnecessary. Soddy explained artistry in economics with the example of a caveman freezing to death sitting on a mountain of coal, he not knowing the coals potential.

How does a ruin become a tourist attraction, or swamp creature - shrimp? By necessity. It is the creative discipline that Laozi calls simplicity, he later calls it frugality and suggests it is leisure; a good from not producing the unnecessary, it is a sign of wealth from creation, and it is better than any from work.102

Necessity explains the attraction that compels production; the alternative is the free trade; a fantastical system of inventory magic that relies on what is, and what can be got with violence.

Free trade is a misnomer; it is debt trade, it is unicorn trading made real by venal, abusive, unfair, contracts enforced with armies.103 Foreign goods cause disharmony at home and wars abroad. Their availability prevents substitution, which is the most of production and all of satisfaction.104

53. A father's advice.

There is a choice between,
the elusive unknown rewards of a producer,
or the certain prizes of an exalted servant.
Choose the path of mystery,
moreover, only fear to stray from it.
The path of ease is one of fantastic promise,
lavish courts and grand affairs.
While the market guarantees nothing;
it makes no promise.
In the courts, they wear smart clothes,
moreover, they control potent tools;
they gorge themselves on other's efforts,
accumulating titles to their property.
Living by theft in a society of trust,
is to misjudge tolerance, power and time.
The greater wealth knows the three energies,
choose the path of mystery,
and live with its satisfaction.

Be the entrepreneur, or perish with the kleptocracy.

Laozi gives advice to the next generation: choose not to be a eunuch, remain the uncut block, become the model of the world and live a long life. Be the farmer plowing the field with a

206

battle tank, be the infant, and trust the Commonwealth - it is your mother. Fame, or life, which would a birth mother prefer?

54. How to live well.

The property belongs to the commonwealth,
it cannot be sold.
The ruler guards the commonwealth,
never granting patents, titles, or licenses.
Build the commonwealth,
by adding to its property,
moreover, share its knowledge,
so that it will always continue,
Future generations honor the legacy of entrepreneur's.
Moreover, do it without piety - by mimicking them,
and by bettering them,
they continue the practice of building,
and making the commonwealth more,
also, giving to it, by sharing the knowledge,
and growing the wealth into the future.
So, cultivate;
the generosity of the past in your person,
and the power will be apparent,
the practice in the family,
and wealth will be lasting,
the relationships with the village,
and the wealth will spread,
the enterprise in the state,
and wealth will be abundant.
Build the commonwealth,
and productive will be its standard.
Therefore,
judge the person by his generosity
foremost to the commonwealth,

see the family through their enterprise,
enjoy friendships through the village,
experience exchange with the state,
Share knowledge with society.
How do I know all this?
By being a part of it
by seeing it.
Have a look at what it is,
this making and doing by free agents,
is all of it,
for the common?
No, when they make a legacy to the future,
they are rewarded in the present.

Giving to the state starts the cycle of wealth.

The benefits of cooperation and exchange are appreciated in perpetuity when captured by autarky and shared freely. Where a path made through the mountain, ease is given to the future. The path is a gift made, like a wheel. Could anyone of owned the wheel? These are achievements not assets given, that is a conceit of the present, these are gifts assumed by the future like good manners are, they belong in the commonwealth forever.

The work is done, the thing made, the bridge built, knowledge found, are all the futures given by the philanthropist population. Trolls, rentiers and patent holders be-gone, they can deny none of it to the future.

The gift of the presents' achievement is utility, but for the future, and proper recognition will be given to them, by the future continuing the present practice of building, discovery, and philanthropy. Then always the next generation is advantaged by progress, and not hamstrung by historical rights and patents.

By celebrating the virtuous cycle of giving to receive from the commonwealth, there are no new owners. The old rights never were, and never will be, because the commonwealth cannot exist in the future if it was given away in the past.

Dead people have no rights amongst the living, just a legacy of knowledge made public, and an infrastructure appreciated. Theirs is a currency redeemed, and that is; *them builders paid in full.*

55. The children judge value.

Entrepreneurs are as infants;
wasps do not sting them,
birds of prey do not attack them,
their learning is little,
and their labor is weak,
yet the energy they attract is powerful.
They know nothing of the union of the two,
yet their genitals are aroused,
their virility fully formed.
Infants can scream all day,
without exhaustion,
they are not forced to scream.
Knowing how to produce with gravitas,
is not to waste energy laboring,
with too much effort,
things grow beyond their prime,
so, exhaustion follows.
Those things are a burden to keep,
the future will not maintain them.

Effective is using the free energies.

The workplace is a lawless space where the petty
interferences of regulation and compliance (wasps) avoid the
entrepreneur. She is passed over by confidence men, thieves
and tax collectors (birds of prey) because she has no assets.

Predators are cowards, and those like certainty, the entrepreneur has gravitas, hers is like the infants, it is powerful. The infant has a mother, and she is connected further and in relationships unseen. Predators will not attack what they do not understand.

The infant that screams all day without exhaustion is the entrepreneur not acting, the infant screams while breathing, she does not breathe to scream.

The infant's abilities seem beyond her capacity, but she uses her gravitas, the infants screaming is her aligning. She is orbiting, and avoiding, trading gravitas, she will create when settled with her newly acquired, or lost gravitas appropriate. The entrepreneur, like the infant, creates while being still, when she is attractive enough to orbit, or join, she will not labor to make, or work for attention.

An infantile erection is Laozi advising; be the creator-impregnator nature designed.

When the entrepreneur is attracted to a potential by necessity, she is frugal and draws on her wealth in the commons to produce. If she were Amish and had gravitas, she would get a house by baking a cake.

Unproductive work has no value to the future. The infant today judges value tomorrow, he is the judge of today's efforts, because he will be the redeemer of currency later. He will be the one honoring it with his non-work in the future.

If you labor in an institution that has no value to the future, then the future will consider your work a waste. If the future does not benefit, it has no obligation to redeem the currency issued in the past. Here is a warning, the infants will judge the worth of effort (by theirs – it will be less than yours), if a legacy is not evident by their standard in magnificence, your endeavors are not honorable.

56 The politics belong to the productive.

Producers do not advocate,
rentiers do not produce.
Production is dark and silent,
Producers do not talk about favors,
or advantage in the light,
they create from stillness in the dark,
theirs is an inspiration,
a producer,
blunting sharpness,
unraveling tangles,
and softening brightness,
is doing the necessary things,
to produce what they can, not what they want,
they have no interest in perfection.
The primal union is exclusive;
It belongs to the producer and the commonwealth;
neither of them can improve it,
only appreciate it.
Don't benefit foreigners with trade,
it will harm the producers,
and destroy the commonwealth.
Don't give foreigners custom,
it will impoverish them,
moreover, it will beggar the commonwealth,
and destroy the Union.
However, don't shun foreigners,
treat them as nobles,
Pander to the foreigner's avatar,
protect his person from the markets justice,
the foreigners are not accused of a crime.
Treat the foreigner's avatar with ceremony,

however, do not violate female state with their trade.
The market is exclusively the union's child

Wealth and security, for the union only.

Those that know don't meddle in affairs. They get on with unraveling tangles, softening brightness and merging with the dusts (ch. 4). When they have enough, they retire. Entrepreneurs do not waste energy making what they cannot, or teaching what they never learned. They are not benevolent, or humanitarian they have no concerns with, rights, or curiosity.

The primal union is between the producer and the commonwealth. Products are created from its resources and are made wealth in its market. A sexual union well describes the political economy.

Entrepreneurs know nothing of economics, yet their instincts sense it. Sexual experience is spontaneous, and, not being explained - is a pre-condition for the intercourse to be followed correctly from its beginnings in trusting.

At the consummation of the Union - in the market, there is no need for enhancement and no possibility for harm. The Commonwealth is an accommodating female, and the producer is born erect.105

The particular conditions for union between the producer and the market are no rules (sharp knives), contracts (tangles) or confusion (brightness) and a moment of stillness. The same circumstances that enable the ideal sexual union, enable consensual production with the Commonwealth.

Entropy and Time

The union is by necessity a private affair, and its currency is trust. The currency of the commonwealth circulates with the building; therefore, it is only honored in their shadow (Yang Yin).

Foreign trade debases the currency (child) and violates the mother (state). Advocates for markets are not producers; they are the agitators. When the state has a strong union of a king with producer, the pimps for foreign trade and benevolence will have been banished (ch. 38).

57. Uncivil laws make civil war.

Lead a nation by enforcing rules,
be the Prince at war with the people,
lose a nation to the people.
Allow the ways of exchange in the commonwealth,
be the Prince celebrated,
and for leading the people to wealth.
How do I know?
By this:
The more rules and restrictions,
the more avoidance and taboos,
less is done,
people become sick.
Where laws are made venal,
the people are divided,
only the sly thrive with laws.
The more exotic products,
the stranger things happen,
cheaper luxuries make men steal necessities,
allowing foreigners by law is denying the producers.
Therefore, the Sage leader,
makes no rules,
he lets the people law themselves;
he is disinterested in their wants,
he lets them be;
He makes no demands on them,
he lets them enjoy their products.
Where the economy is an uncut block,
the people have simple desires,
then the leader is secure.

A ruling is secure when it is allowing.

As long as it is admitted that the law may be diverted from its true purpose; that it may violate property, instead of protecting it-then everyone will want to participate in making the law, either to protect himself against plunder or to use it for plunder. (Bastiat, The Law).

Laws manipulate nature; they enable the improbable and prevent the likely. Rules make a confusing labyrinth of society, and prove common-sense, to be plain stupidity.

The first laws establish ownership rights, they create insecurity for those not owning. All laws are the first laws. Ownership is an exclusive privilege of the few, ownership heralds only obligations and servitude for the people.

All manner of strange behavior results from ownership rights when most people become unhinged from the commonwealth they are forced to abide by boundaries and assume obligations. Exclusion by owners invites the peoples' trespass and begets their transgressions. Desperation self-suggests grandiose solutions to a scarcity caused from plenty.

Nations fail in battles with their people, in civil wars - not foreign ones. When a population has to defy a status quo that won't parlay with its wealth, the end is nigh. The father of all learning, a violent [ruler] will die a violent death. Rules enforced, are the only that work, and where the rules exclude, then the dying ground for the leader, is in his home, with his people, over the rules.

People prefer; poverty, piracy, and anarchy, to enslavement, they rather cleverness and violence, to being disadvantaged by ownership.

A people excluded by laws create their versions of abuse, those mimic oppression in their private domains - they will make contracts, and enforce them with their versions of exclusion. Rules beget contracts, and those avoidance Wherever a call for more laws from the people, there is enough acrimony in society already to end the leaders rule.

58. Advice for the King.

Where the Commonwealth is free,
the leader is not enforcing laws,
the people will be productive.
Where rentiers own the commonwealth,
the leader will be a fearful captive,
the people will be cunning.
The Vast fortunes are by ownership;
misery and deceit are behind that pretense.
Who knows the results?
Where every right is a wrong,
where 'what's done' cannot be undone,
where help is a hindrance,
then change is coming from stillness.
If everything's exclusive, many things are impossible,
access denied to many is - most production stopped,
and potential wasted to all
Therefore, the sage ruler will,
square the commonwealth's ownership without laws,
straighten the rentiers bent without violence,
he will allow the producers to be,
without rentiers.

The ruler has one opportunity.

What is Property? Property is Theft. P. J. Proudhon 1840

Given a race of beings having like claims to pursue the objects of their desires; given a world adapted to the gratification of those desires - a world into which such beings are similarly born - and it unavoidably follows that they have equal rights to the use of this world. For if each of them "has the freedom to do all that he wills, provided he infringes not the equal freedom of any other," then each of them is free to use the earth for the satisfaction of his wants, provided he allows all others the same liberty. Conversely, it is manifest that one, or part of them, may use the earth in any such a way as to prevent the rest from similarly using it; seeing that to do this is to assume greater freedom than the rest, and consequently break the law.

2. Equity, therefore, does not permit property in land. For if one portion of the earth's surface [quoted deliberately and purposefully from, Henry George A Perplexed Philosopher 1892] George Quoting Herbert Spencer, Social Statistics 1850 Chapter IX. The Right to the Use of the Earth.

Jean-Jacques Rousseau wrote;

>The first man, who having enclosed a piece of ground, bethought himself of saying; this is mine and found people simple enough to believe him, was the real founder of civil society. From how many crimes, wars, and murders, from how many horrors and misfortunes

> might not any one have saved mankind, by pulling up the
> stakes, or filling up the ditch, and crying to his fellows;
> 'Beware listening to this imposter; you are undone if you
> once forget that the fruits of the earth belong thus all, and
> the earth itself to nobody.' Discourse on Inequality 1754

Marque (citizen) de Sade, and P.J. Proudhon too traced the right of property to the principal; that property in the commonwealth could not exist. Laozi says that a feudal lord is the commonwealth's trustee - not its landlord, or their agent.

Without the excluding laws of ownership; most everything in society and its commonwealth is understandable. Nobel prize winner for economics Richard Thaler 2017, explained that fictions have no place in science, or economic behavior - Unicorns cannot feed the family. The peoples' stupid economic decisions are called *Irrational Behavior* by economists they are not a mystery deserving of study, the *Irrational Behavior* is a direct result of the peoples exclusion from the common wealth.

The first laws create private wealth from the public domain. The purpose of all other laws is to trick those excluded to demand permissions. Those other laws are made to apologize for the wrong of privilege - with promises of opportunity. The laws supporting ownership, for example offer ordinary folk compensation to trade their Labor to owners.

Laozi questions the cognitive dissonance of a society without a common wealth. He asks for how long can an incredulous people confuse wealth with labor, or when will the people excluded wake to a commonwealth-theirs to use without permission. How long can the leader maintain the fiction of ownership, before being killed?

He suggests a solution to disappear the problem of ownership for the leader. An action, without action, is to grow the grief out. Laozi encourages the leader to allow the natural course to happen - let the entropy.

He suggests encouraging new production, and new wealth by being disinterested in the fabulous wealth of titles to land and intellectual property. He thinks they will naturally erode with trade and progress. His solution is to assist what nature will do in any event without laws, by non-action.106

When the rentiers are left alone without the leaders (police) protection, they only lose in trade and progress. The rentiers will then be excited to risk and trade of their own volition.

59. The feminine instinct for leadership.

In leading a nation without laws,
be economical with your attention,
be cautious to act,
moreover, be protective of your gravitas;
By your being a leader nonchalant,
the commons get used.
The people respect your stewardship of them,
also, appreciate their useful wealth in the nation.
By being economical with your actions as a leader,
you ignore its opportunities,
give them away,
to show you are the gracious hostess,
and the spendthrift mistress,
and the responsible mother,
leading the state, that welcomes, gives and cares.
The peoples' opportunities and success,
are your security Sire,
and that is your reward for leadership.

Be frugal to enjoy a long life as a leader.

Being is a discipline for a ruler. Not competing with the people for opportunities or imposing demands on them for taxation is a sensible ruler giving thanks for his precarious position.

The successful ruler chooses nonaction in leadership. He is frugal in his palace so that he can stay in it. The sage ruler plays all of the feminine roles, to actively give opportunities away, he stays in the background and allows others their way. The effective leader will disgrace his avatars pride, and he will want to be ignored, as the idiot competitor.

Trust is the nation's real wealth, it accumulates as a reservoir in the commonwealth; providing each has a claim on it, and the leader has none. It is sufficient for the people to have confidence in their leader's non-intervention, for the wealth of the state to promulgate.

The leader's restraint makes room for the people to acquire gravitas, and that empowers them to produce more. He gives them confidence that he is a weakling, and can't take advantage of them. When they are so assured with that confidence however given by the not-idiot leader, the people are elevated and become more productive than even the Kings avatar could expect.

Trust and wealth thrive in the absence of disappointment. A ruler's restraint and modesty ensures the prosperity of the state, and that is the whole of his survival as the leader.

60. The nation rules itself.

Ruling a great nation is like cooking a small fish.
It is unnecessary,
the nation explains itself with its potential,
as the fish does, as a meal.
In the free commonwealth,
a thing is before its production.
Wherever the experts and rentiers ignored,
the products appear - as if discovered;
their potential was always in the common domain,
just unexplained by rights,
obligations, permissions, and labor.
Wherever energies mix, random events happen,
without planning good things happen
with the best intentions - no harm results from failure.
The Randoms are welcome to potential,
moreover, the producer uses their energy.
The Commonwealth has a surplus of potential,
Sage rulers know the energy given to surplus.
as the treats of wealth,
not the concern of kings.

Leading a nation is a production that is allowed to happen.

A small fish is caught sushi, so to cook the fish is to invite disaster; A Nation is, and its people are found productive, so to meddle with them is unnecessary.

Ordinary people with access to the commonwealth find all of their needs there, and with its surplus they are creative. They will use their enterprise to do idle things, like cook a small fish rather than eat it raw.

The leader of a Nation will use his surplus to produce some folly art piece because leisure and experimentation are the rewards of plenty, not the object of labor.

Production with surplus and co-operating with others concentrates volatile energies in confined spaces workplaces like kitchens are dangerous, the efforts may fail, they may make a surprise product. In a demand economy, failures and surprises have consequences. Demand relies on promises, and those on guarantees - demand cannot be satisfied without justice for failure. Surprise with demand is a failure to deliver.

The teleological explanation of the conventional enterprise taught; has the State awarding resources to ownership, the owners limit supply, that causes their scarcity, and value is said known (made). The excluded, are denied their role as providers and are coerced to supply their own demands with contracts. By obligations and under a contract, the people are responsible for performance, because justice demands the supply, for the owner be paid his resource value.

Where the commons are free, nothing but the efforts exchanged are lost in a production disaster, and they are lost mutually. The commons have plenty, so there is no bother with restitution for the surplus taken; the commons don't demand justice for waste and failure. No harm is done to a commonwealth by a disaster in production, more likely its product will be enjoyed - if only for the experience.

Where the nation is ruled by trusting, a ruined meal is of no consequence. If the Randoms of cooking, ruin a fish caught in the commons, the production makes an entertainment. It gives a crispy-fish recipe to the public: the entertainment and the recipe prove that additional wealth was inherent in the commons - but unseen in the fish, and man (man), the fish had more potential than realized, and the man had a talent for cooking not discovered.

A proper accounting will show the Randoms of production do not ruin the surplus fish. The purpose of every enterprise is satisfaction. An unplanned satisfaction from surplus and a savant cook are the gifts of plenty, not a demanded meal provided by an owner, planned by an expert - contracting a cook, and overseen by the states justice system.

The Laozi lets the Randoms flourish, and he welcomes the surprise from freedom and surplus. When the nation is without laws, the Randoms contribute. A schoolyard fight and natural selection are examples of spontaneous production where random elements can be relied on to do some good.

Laws, rights, and justice are the only likely sources of harm in producing things. They are the ruin of meals, and nations. Laozi uses the small fish metaphor to say; the Commonwealth is full of potential; the sea is packed with fish for the taking, the society is over-flowing with talented chefs to shine, and workplaces are riddled with Randoms for good effect if only the ruler let them be without owners.

61. The win – win.

A productive State is a feminine one;
It is inactive but hospitable.
All are drawn; welcome to its potential.
Submitting to a foreigner,
she conquers the foreigner.
When he lowers himself,
he becomes her useful tool;
however, he acquires merit - moving,
moreover, credit from her for his contribution
he has conquered her.
What a feminine state has, the foreigner gets;
however, what the foreigner has,
the productive society takes.
This exchanging is curious,
they both conquer getting,
Providing the productive society,
is the first to lose its pretension,
Moreover, be the hospitable female.107

Asymmetric relationships resolved in Union.

Synergy is manifest in the win-win, a transaction where both parties give something valuable they did not have; both getting more than they gave. In a card swap, each giver of a single card receives a complete set.

The win-win is achieved by a union when the more significant party invites it. The greater nation will be the feminine one; she plays the gracious - awaiting the erect

228

foreigner to approach. Waiting denotes time, here understood as distance. The better nation must be attractive for the distance to close.

She assumes the accommodating position to enable the foreigner access, to become full, she is empty. The foreigner drops his pretensions to be her suitor, he acquires merit by his effort, and credit for lowering himself.

They both seek opportunities. Both are given the gravitas by the other - each is granted the power to take the potential of their exclusive union.

Laozi advises that union is the How of successful relationships. In union, both parties behave without pretension, they are polite, respectful and honest. Respecting each other without cleverness, in private and by stillness, a union consummated with sincerity is a successful coupling. She is the prime mover.

62. An ode to trade.

Private wealth is derived,
from an exchange with the commonwealth,
that private wealth is the treasure of entrepreneurs.
Private wealth is got nefariously from the people,
It is the booty and treasure of rentiers.
So, what; wealth is wealth,
moreover, all wealth is good,
there is no lousy wealth.
Words can be sold to assist, and given to deceive,
deeds can be bartered for, or got by violence,
things of no value can have value,
Only time determines the worth of private wealth.
Producing is guaranteed by income,
while the wealth got from guile,
and violence is risked in the trade.

Hence, on the coronation of an emperor
or the installment of three ministers,
don't send booty for favors,
ignore the ceremony,
moreover, be productive.
Why did the ancients value exchange so much?
Because the rentiers cannot keep their wealth;
it always flows to the producers.
Entrepreneurs celebrated the rentiers;
their wealth was natural to get by trade,
the new emperor's gift is the curiosity,
of the commonwealth made just,
by the producers.

Entropy and Time

Sweet trade is Justice.

Laozi disagrees with property rights, but he supports people having possessions, regardless of how they got them.

P.J. Proudhon made the distinction between property and possessions that Laozi tunes too. Possessions are a form of wealth, but they are not property. In the illegal (black), elusive and unheard economy all manner of acquiring possessions will happen and can't be controlled.

However, the fictional wealth held as property is inferior to the real wealth held as reputation (measured as mass) because the legal property - regardless of how, or where it was acquired, has a limited life. The new emperor can nullify titles to property given by the previous emperor's. He can cancel licenses and patents at his whim proving the temporal value of the titled property.

If the new emperor is a sage one - he will cancel the privileges he did not benefit from. The new emperor celebrates his Jubilee, by nullifying titles (canceling debts), and allowing opportunity to force trade. The former owners of the titled assets will have alternative opportunities in other endeavors. there are no consequences for their loss, it is cheered.

The highest respect is given the new emperor by ignoring him. If you get involved in his affairs, you are not productive. Show respect for the new emperor by sending sweet rain to the common from your efforts improving the public domain - don't petition for franchises or exclusive rights to take advantage of the people using it.

Productive people naturally avoid those that are not. Where property rights exist, their owners will be exchanging without the necessary gravitas - they are babies at trading. When unprotected by laws, and needing to trade - the violent ones become less wealthy, the productive are experienced at the trade. The economy gives real justice - sweet it is without laws.

63. The Sage have no problems.

Practice being still.
Allow approaches,
and opportunities will appear,
watch others become,
have no preference for their things,
accept facts and affairs,
and ignore them.
If you meddle with other people's efforts,
they will be your burden,
so, treat their efforts with respect,
moreover, find no difficulties with them.
All of the significant things are done in the beginning,
by removing barriers,
also, overcoming objections,
the sage ignores rules,
they treat obstacles with contempt,
so, their ambitions are not meddled with.
See the great things done by the Sage,
are but small courtesies,
those are what permit, invite, and tease movement.
The sage makes no promises, and do not assist,
So, the Sage never have difficulties.

Abide in stillness - Action by nonaction.

Production starts at the molecular level. The sage acknowledges that efforts, in the end, nourish production, but primarily are concerned with how production begins. Effective production starts with experimentation, observing the constituents mixing without assistance.

Choosing to be still is a decision to be idle; It is a time to observe what the constituents do, without help. Stillness is a positivist version of passive-aggressive behavior. One is still - only to clear the space for the other energies to react, work, move, live - to see them do.

Extend and pretend is the mistake of; working to make work necessary. Laozi suggests that we stop working to begin making. He explains the Chinese norm of not closing a circle. The circle is an electrical circuit, and the break in the circuit is a spark gap.

The unfinished circle represents the moment where qi is still - it charges at the gap. The qi jumps to begin the circuit. Production is a leap of trust, one made with force (F), acceleration, (certainty), (M is Gravitas of the actor) $F = Ma$. The leap (is the energy given to acceleration from M) that starts production from stillness is with a Force and for a purpose, with certainty. No meddlers or interference can usurp the determination of a spark to jump.

The Sage makes no demands, they ignore their senses, have no morals, and obey no rules. The Sage seek space; how is irrelevant to the Sage because a movement is more effective attracted than made, the sage entrepreneur makes no deliberate effort, thereby they do no wrong.

The Sage let others and nature do the difficult work they do, wisely finding no problems with it, and appreciating their efforts. A blindness to the means is for them a sanguine beginning to the making of a satisfying result.

The significant problems are the symptoms of a corrupt society (exclusion, allocation, starvation). They are the burden of others - those laden with the graft that caused the easily-solved-with-banishment problems.

While those problems exist, the sage does not care for them, because those problems are solved making the difference at the spark gap; by stopping production, to begin again, the Sage will defy the sophists and usurp their control. Their banishment later is the delight of an afterthought.

64. What to do – when.

Things need maintenance;
breakdowns are foreseen,
preventive modifications are done,
because the small things are necessary,
and easy victories take no effort.
Just by arranging details,
and taking care with them,
most things are done with the old instructions,
moreover,
everything necessary is known before any effort made.
The great tree springs from a single shoot.
The terrace of nine stories, from a small hole.
The thousand-mile trek from one step.
Those least's are the beginnings,
and also, the all of completions.
The Sage assists in those beginnings,
however, leaves the energies to produce alone.
The Sage does not make – effort things.
The Sage are never working.
The Sage let things become in their image,
by inviting their development,
and ignoring the journey.108
They never meddle with the energy attracted to their image,
however, towards the end is a beginning,
the Sage assist with a beginning.109

Nature works at the quantum.

An action is warranted when it is useful.
The law of diminishing returns stops maintenance.

Laozi explains how to get things done, smarter, quicker and better with momentum. He calls it Action by non-action. The entrepreneur stops working whenever progress is unsatisfactory and returns to the beginning. Not everything is worth doing. Waste is a sign to stop doing, and consider a different approach, or making something new, or different (Ch. 45).

The physical explanation of what Laozi calls, action by non-action is; letting the energies take their most likely form - without interference. Like a magnet shapes loose iron filings, the entrepreneur shapes energies; she is the field. The energy spontaneously arranges around her, they will create something without her effort, and she will want to see that. The first step from the still (chs. 16, 21), is the one Laozi calls small, but it is the beginning. All things are made better without effort - from the three at the roots.

Laozi describes production with quantum science and field theory, in addition to, or equally with gravity. Elements are energies, and their matter has a charge and acceleration, their vectors make patterns and show form, this is a process understood stochastically. Laozi uses the science. He discusses people like Neils Bohr did elements, and production like Schrodinger did fields as a structure, for the enterprise of elements.

Creation occurs naturally at the molecular level where energies are malleable. In the later stages of being, energies can only be forced or destroyed. By attending to the energies at the start, and by taking care of the emerging forms in the end - failure can be effortlessly averted. The moments at the beginnings (phase transition) are the only opportunities for shaping or creative destruction.

The father of all learning is a violent death. If the elements are unsound, then the form cannot be from its beginning. Rather than working to extend logic and pretend authority, the Sage allows failure to herald the new.

The sage is not concerned with things; they are disposable. The Sage always turn to the beginnings, after first taking non-action, they stop. They Sage are optimistic. The Sage start anew, for better, from the start always the beginning.

65. The evil of education.

The ancient courts never taught people,
They freed them of learning.
The more education experts have,
the more it fails them,
their failures harm others.
Rulers who promote education
divide and rob the country.
Those that rule without befuddling the people
enrich the country.
Educating is the basest method of coercion;
allowing people to be,
shows a leader's sincerity in ruling,
moreover,
he demonstrates his trust,
in the peoples' sage relationships.
Being alert to the wrong of education,
is the foremost wisdom,
banish the academics,
and the useful knowledge will become apparent.
Harmony cannot be with all,
banishing the deceivers makes the state wealthy.110

Education exists to entrap people in slavery.

Laozi mocked academics in chapter 20 and said their subjects were trivialities, later at chapter 48, that schooling was a waste of effort, now he speaks plainly; education is toxic.111

Without any teaching, facts are discovered by doing things. Laozi complains that the country is robbed of its potential by education because generations are denied the ideas to be had from experiences. We learn better at work, and more by doing than studying.

Authorities are made redundant by new knowledge. Wherever a Philo Farnsworth or a Nikola Tesla, progress happens. People get knowledge when facts prove themselves. Here we see Laozi's explanation for poverty; its a paucity of facts, their absence explains idleness and reduced productivity. A Stagnation of ideas defines dogma, and that a curriculum.

Wherever experience is denied by education, with a law or fact accepted, it prevents our work drifting to the realization of splendor. Teaching the timidity of dreams is the mission of a school's curriculum, and their success is proved by generational poverty and stalled progress.

The sophist academic John Maynard Keynes asked, concluding his 'General Theory' 1936,

'Is the fulfillment of these [economic] ideas a visionary hope? Have they insufficient roots in the motives which govern the evolution of political society? Are the interests which they will thwart stronger and more obvious than those which they will serve?'[and he answers his questions with satisfaction]

Bertram Russell explains real dangerous knowledge, by discussing John Dewey and education, warning that if society embraced the suggestions of free-thinkers, and acted on facts -

convenient to them, then there would be a civil war with the status quo.

'Dr. Dewey's world, it seems to me, is one in which human beings occupy the imagination; the cosmos of astronomy, though of course acknowledged to exist, is at most times ignored.

His philosophy is a power philosophy, though not, like Nietzsche's, a philosophy of individual power; it is the power of the community that is felt to be valuable.

It is this element of social power that seems to me to make the philosophy of instrumentalism attractive to those who are more impressed by our new control over natural forces than by the limitations to which that control is still subject.

The attitude of man towards the non-human environment has differed profoundly at different times. The Greeks, with their dread of hubris and their belief in necessity or fate superior even to Zeus, carefully avoided what would have seemed to them insolence towards the universe. The Middle Ages carried submission much further: humility towards God was a Christian's first duty. This attitude cramped initiative and great originality was scarcely possible.

The Renaissance restored human pride but carried it to the point where it led to anarchy and disaster. [The Reformation and the Counter-reformation largely undid its work.] But [the] modern technique, while not altogether favorable to the lordly individual of the Renaissance, has revived the sense of the collective power of human communities.

Man, formerly too humble, begins to think of himself as almost a God. The Italian pragmatist Papini urges us to substitute the "Imitation of God" for the "Imitation of Christ." *In all this, I feel a grave danger, the danger of what might be called cosmic impiety. The concept of "truth" as something dependent upon facts largely outside human control has been one of the ways in which philosophy hitherto has inculcated the necessary element of humility.*

When this check upon pride is removed, a further step is taken on the road towards a certain kind of madness-the intoxication of power which invaded philosophy with Fichte112, and to which modern men, whether philosophers or not, are prone. I am persuaded that this intoxication is the greatest danger of our time and that any philosophy which, however unintentionally, contributes to it is increasing the danger of vast social disaster.' 113 [emphasis added]

Russell refers to the power philosophy of Dewey, he calls Laozi's synergetic energy *community power* and cautions that using it would be a vast social disaster - for the vested interests. He warns against challenging the ruling class, calling that; *cosmic impiety.* He threatens civil war, and the bloody renaissance of the Status-quo, if they are challenged.

Russell explains education, as *conditioning to stop anarchy.* By inculcating the population with nihilist philosophy, education diminishes the peoples' ambitions. Education teaches reliance on the ruling class, and that enshrines the status quo. If people can believe they are as dust in a vast universe, they will assume their dreams worthless, and poverty pre-determined.

Russell, elsewhere advocates Physics proofs, to demonstrate - time and space. Mathematics proves the betters see all - from their distance - from your time; they are the eternal observer and time traveler, you are the subject. Teaching these philosophies in schools, and reinforcing inferiority with religion and science, makes people know their insignificance so that they ignore their potential. Russell advocates education - only to disable the people's progress, making them vulnerable, is introducing them to servitude, and accepting of employment, or conscription.

Education is a ruse to prevent the able from usurping the status quo. By estopping the youth being instructed by their images, the rulers prevent a; collegiate being; a productive society, and that usurping them.

Education separates the advancing generation from their elders and occupies the young in the useless work of studying to learn. It stops children marrying an experience with their imagination. Children at school are denied the challenge of an incongruous society, or the quest traditionally accepted by youth to make a difference in the future.

Real learning is the gift of societies attractive-repulsive power, the energy that coaxes the young to challenge and usurp the elders. The traditional lesson is the self-taught one, where the status quo does not survive progress because the elders are bettered by strength or innovation, and parents are rewarded with the ancient gift of pride in their children.

Russell has been proved; today's science is a religion of dogma. It defines things by atoms, denies them by laws and proves them with miracles. Taught science is; artifice constructed by fictional laws, given effect by authoritative instruction. Whereas in reality; nothing is fully described by atoms, nothing can be denied by law, and mathematical proof is a syllogistic construction that proves the axioms made to fit.114

In sum, Russell explains that the sanctioned knowledge got from the likes of, Marx, Einstein, or Keynes is taught to prevent the ordinary folk from getting access to the potential in the commonwealth. The purpose of State education is to teach trespass, and property rights so that the owners can rob the country.

Laozi thinks like Dewey that Ideas are free, and new facts are *discovered right* for their convenience. Laozi talks like Hume; Knowledge comes from within man; we are generators of ideas and experiences of facts, not learners and spectators, he advocates like North Whitehead; Truth is evolutionary, and all reality is either in our temporary space and imagined, or not at all.

Nobel Prize winner 1988 Maurice Allias more than any other person is responsible for modern economics, and by extension society as we know it. The widespread use of his model has made him history's most influential provocateur. Allias gave the only theory guiding the world today at his Nobel acceptance.

'My theory of monetary dynamics is based on four main pillars: the fundamental equation of monetary dynamics, and the three hereditary and relativistic formulations of the demand for money, the supply of money, and the rates of forgetfulness and psychological interest. This theory essentially rests on original guiding ideas which are applicable to many fields, such as Economics, Psychology, Sociology and Political Science. They are: the fundamental analogy between forgetting the past and discounting the future; the hereditary psychological process of forgetfulness; the consideration of psychological time; the hereditary conditioning of men by past events; the hereditary propagation of monetary phenomena with a gradual weakening through time; the concept of lagged regulation implying the existence of limit cycles.' 115

In lay terms Allias modeled public relations, winning a Nobel prize for showing how to control society by teaching fiction as truth. Allias himself did not understand the cause of his observations, he never made the connection of behavior with propaganda, or knew why his mathematical model was so successful.

Maurice Allias, unwittingly put Mathematical formulas, to public relations. Allias had no explanation of behavior, just the observation; that people responded to information in predictable ways.

It was, Edward Bernays that explained this phenomenon now called Behavioral Economics. By Propaganda 1928, and Engineering Consent 1955, Bernays discussed irrational action, thirty years before Allias observed it. Bernays spoke plain, saying - *that mass education was public relations*, and the purpose of education was to, trick people into acting against their interests.

Bernays was the first to show the economists a hedonistic actor. Thorstein Veblen ridiculed the Hedonistic man, of economic myth, by saying that lemmings did not exist. In 1919 Veblen had the final word on supply and demand because without a hedonistic man the entire discipline of economics was a chimera.

Defying common sense, Bernays created the Hedonistic man, that Veblen said was preposterous. By introducing pornography to the world as sex education, and smoking as healthy, Bernays made Veblen look naive, and classical economics had its first proof.

Veblen was forgotten, and Allias won a noble prize for observing predictable irrational behavior and the full proof of marginal analysis. In reality, Allias measured the effectiveness of advertising and public relations.116 Allias merely observed propaganda, his formula proved that a society could be controlled in the present, by creating its history (facts). Allias showed the maxim; you can predict the future - if you invent it.

There is nothing progressive in the work of public relations. It only illustrates that by simultaneously changing the perception of history - people have always smoked, and the present - that cool, healthy people and doctors are smoking, then the history and facts prove each other by logic, and with observation. The created Orwellian history and those new facts make the hologram that George Smoot calls a simulation and that theory. Otherwise said; indicating false potentials forces their promise.

It's the game described by Keynes as economics, a discipline based on two fictions conveyed as facts; the ownership of resources, and the value of a currency. All resource prices and efforts exchanged for them are manipulated in a debt based currency, by interest rates and taught right by observation. It is the incomprehensible system of non-logic, and no equity that controls the population of the world, against their interests.117 118

In contrast, here is some real wisdom, from a witness to the first world war, an earlier noble Laurette and practical scientist;

'We thus arrive at the conclusion that any sort of perpetual motion is impossible. A continuous stream of fresh energy is necessary for the continuous working of any working system, whether animate or inanimate. Life is cyclic as regards the material substances consumed, and the same materials are used over and over again in metabolism. But as regards energy, it is unidirectional, and no continuous cyclic use of energy is even conceivable. If we have available energy, we may maintain life and produce every material requisite necessary. *That is why the flow of energy should be the primary concern of economics.*

In a world which has adequate supplies of energy, scientific knowledge and inventions for utilizing it, and the man-power able and willing to perform the necessary duties and services, poverty and destitution are purely artificial institutions, due to ignorance of the principles of government, actively, **if not deliberately, fostered for class ends by legal conventions** confounding wealth with debt. Under any scientific system of government, they would disappear like small-pox and malaria, by means of preventive rather than ameliorative or curative measures.'119

66. The union nation.

The leader attracts the people to his sea
he rises like the tide - and enters the streams;
He meets their first,
they come high,
and the others follow,
he welcomes them low.
The leader joins them,
in the common area,
each is a welcome guest sometimes,
and a host at others.
In his presence,
the people are allowed;
in their presence,
the leader is polite.
All champion their union with him,
and call the ordinary area their special one,
his area too,
their State and its potential- is their opportunity,
each supports the leader in supporting their trade,
because of the joining,
they trust the leader will not compete with their craft,
so, none challenge his.

The how of the kingdom.

A nation is a series of relationships, and the most important of those is the union of people with a leader. The Union with leader has no force or contracts because the leader is attractive, he has superior gravitas.

The Union relationship is both ways involuntary. When people discover the leader's potential, they will join his orbit and champion him. They are like guests at a party, pleased for the invitation, while the leader-host is grateful for their attendance. All celebrate that common sea of relief, and see the party arrived, as a potential to happen.

To initiate the union that makes a nation of people, the ruler is accepting. The attracted, are respectful entering the orbit of the ruler. They forget pretensions and become more realistic in their expectations. The leader restrains himself, he pretends to be ordinary and feigns modesty. Both are cupid in a deceit convenient.

In union, the invitations accepted by a former self, and the later self-denies the RSVP, the former self is transformed, and forgets how. The great ruler and the better people, became those when they joined in the common, they were elevated, acquiring a charge from their meeting, they got induced with power like a copper coil meeting a magnet. The same each; true, but transformed to powerful and better, both are made more by meeting.

Their movements are free, but not necessarily voluntary, because the momentum of crowds has a compulsion on the leader and the people.

As the ruler is in union with an improved people, he speaks through them and acts with their complicity and pride. The people are pleased with their superior image - made magnificent in the leader.

The best union is an unspoken conspiracy, one of false flattery and real standoff - one so fragile - that it cannot be tested with impositions or expectations from either party. It's a cupidity perpetuated so-long as it is convenient and no-longer.

67. The three jewels.

The whole world will proclaim my economic way,
as perfection,
it has no peer,
and cannot be compared.
It has three tensors, they are:
trust,
frugality,
and not wanting to be the first.
Trust makes faith, and that allows production,
frugality guarantees the trust,
and not wanting to be first secures the confidence.
When rulers exchange without trust,
there is an advantage,
when they are generous without being frugal,
there is dishonesty,
where they insist on relationships,
there is abuse,
those communities are violent and unproductive.
Trust is the only mechanism not needing;
advantage, dishonesty, and abuse, to get more.
Trust is the gravitas called wealth,
It is the security needed,
that enables stillness,
the only necessary for production,
and the movement that supports life.
A king surrounded by life is secured by,
trusting good faith makes production.

Laozi declares his knowledge superior.

The society is a series of relationships, those are founded on three tensors; trust, frugality, and non-competition. Ordinarily, we say; trust allows liberty, frugality ensures honesty, and not competing with your partner is wise, and easily compare the Laozi to other philosophers.

However, Laozi has a nuanced understanding of the Trinity. His trust describes synergetic power; his frugality explains velocity, and not wanting to be first means; be selfish in relationships - give the other Space, don't suffocate them with compassion, so to let the relationship live to work (Ch. 13).

His trust is a physical entity - measured by mass and used for its power, the trust Laozi talks of is the potential of the relationship, he links trust to the kinetic power that substitutes for work (trust expects to get).

Laozi's frugal in a relationship, ensures the relationship is available - as a potential power. Frugality limits energy, it is the relationships *regulator* that prevents its burden, and what supplies the extra when needed. This frugality ensures everything got from a relationship is timely. Frugality is a practice that guarantees efficacy, the Japanese call it; Just-in-time production. Laozi called its regulator *passion* earlier, and described it as superior to demand because it has an inbuilt valve regulated by common sense.

Not wanting to be first is an oxymoron to Laozi, because all things are nothing without their other. It is the king and his people. There can't be one first, because one is nothing. So, the parties to a relationship are one, or none.

When the relationships are known by Laozi's scientific tensors, rather than their parallel in virtue-babble, they accurately describe enterprise and exchange. Trust, frugality, and not wanting to be first are today called energy, efficiency and fair dealing (contracts).

Laozi's economy is illustrated as a form, by the three tensors of trust; his form, the triangle, disciplines the economist, no tensor is greater than the other. Laozi invites us to visualize economics, and talk of the subject, with the authority of sound structure, rather than skyhooks.

Laozi boasts about his systems superiority because it customs its components - the relationships fit and work as a one in any configuration. Therefore, it has no peer. The Laozi is the only economic protocol to be described - starting from nothing, and by first principles.

68. An entrepreneurial dance.

A skilled artisan is gentle and calm.
A competent soldier is frugal in his fighting.
A conqueror is triumphant by not conquering.
Success is to partner things,
engaging with them,
is to become indistinguishable from them,
by entering them and merging,
the relationships tensors are tested,
because the space to be,
is defended jointly,
to battle requires cooperation,
so that is not contending,
Getting cooperation,
is checking the partners potential,
measure it accurately while being frugal in battle,
to not compete, but cooperate later.
Making is synchronizing with the others energy
at the beginning,
so, let them join the image, they are making,
having gravitas and using gravitas
are the highest achievements of experience.

Relationships make good & bad happen.

The actor as; artisan, soldier or conqueror is an entrepreneur, and producing. The best are merely present, seeing potential in their image. However, they are prepared with tools at hand and do have the confidence to engage with their images attraction.

Wherever the substance (carbon) of the actor is amongst the other energies, tool, rock, enemy; her essence, is in the image and it is laboring beside them, as an additional force engaged.

The entrepreneur sees potential; she adds her actor's effort to its energies - amplifying its movement. Her highest achievement is to get it into a heightened state of energy so that it resonates to her tune, and contributes to her image.

The soldier is the actor joined to the sword, together they do the work with the image of the entrepreneur, the enemy moves to make his death - in your image that he amplified and owned.

The battle arranges the relationships space; it is cooperation to protect the existence of that space. The area in battle is a shared one framed by the tensors of the relationship making. There is no contending in cooperation because it is for the existence of a shared image, explaining how an image becomes real by the space made for it.

Not contending, is using the others energy in synchronization with your movements - those made while cooperating with the other to protect a shared space. Not contending by this co-operating is never battling, it is the highest achievement in production and life. It is to dance the bound energies in a relationship to resonance with your image - testing the arrangements while trusting yourself moving in-synch with the other until it forms in the pattern of your making.

Laozi's Way to Wealth & the Holy Grail

69. Civil gravitas wins wars.

Generals have a plan for war:
They would rather not have one.
However, if armies meet,
the Generals like to host the party,
never be the guest at war.
They would instead withdraw than advance.
They call this an invitation to treat;
it is conquering without confronting,
roll up the sleeves,
so the arms are stronger,
the generals are formidable at home,
the pretender has more problems on tour.
There is no greater calamity
than creating an enemy by attacking it,
because to overestimate the enemy is to lose restraint.
When opponents meet,
the one with more gravitas will win.

Co-operation is the achievement of Generals.

The general's preference is to gain the advantage of nonaction by being the host to a relationship. Nonaction uses gratuitous assistance, here doubt (the enemy's avoidance), or the power of gravitas to achieve without making the physical effort of going to war.120

By being the host rather than the aggressor (guest), the general accumulates energy for war, because his society is productive by not being at war.

The host has the advantage of delaying the attraction of an easy potential, (using time), and of exhausting the aggressor traveling to meet (distance). We can intuit this nonaction as being passive-aggressive. Laozi's instruction in dealing with difficult others is to; take no action BUT keep house. The general's preference is to cause himself no difficulties while expecting the vicissitudes of adventure to befall his aggressor.

If first nonaction fails, the guest overcomes doubt and survives the terrain, then war is necessary. It then is a production like any other an action-by-nonaction which starts by stillness.

The general will have more significant potential. The Generals have practiced frugality and will have the ability to produce at the velocities needed for war because their frugality is the just-in-time type and the ideal to supply an army. The generals hosting are; last to war and therefore are trusted with the goods to wage it (roll up the sleeves), they have credit.

Trust implies nonaction, frugality defines nonaction, and not wanting to be first commands nonaction. All restraints, the generals real battle is at home if the General behaves well in his relationship with the productive people at home he will harness the power of the bellows with their rally for his action (Ch. 5).

Healthy practical relationships abhor disappointment. Even in battle, nothing is as valuable as restraint. To win a war; be economical, be cautious of action, and be mindful of diminishing returns.

Remember, the ancients say yield (avoid, join, orbit) to overcome, for gravitas is the superior power. Gravitas makes the movement that enables opportunity. The victory will be got by the party with the gravitas power, not the one making an effort to win.

70. Look to the east, Laozi is coming.

I have asked to be heard;
Let the nation produce with the gravitas of its people,
from its potential and not their labor.
I refuse to promise things or wealth.
I only say;
that my protocol for exchanges make things better,
and with less effort,
but because those start from nothing seen,
and can't be explained easily,
Academics cannot teach it,
however thankfully,
first principles do not need teaching.
My way tells of the wonder seen in the old buildings,
those are scrolls. superior proofs,
I hope that rulers will allow more buildings,
however, they will not;
They intuit the way, and flirt with its curiosity.
So, while they get wise,
I travel the great circle in rough clothing,
and keep the way alive,
saving it for the same place but in another time.

Laozi laments for a leader to embrace his model.

Laozi was prone to wishful thinking. Ideally, the king would elevate him to the role of a lawgiver, adopt his protocol and enjoy the nation's prosperity, but Laozi knows that elevation is self-defeating. He laments for the Kings blessing that won't come and yearns for a more obvious path to his protocol's adoption.

If the king could let it be,
subjugate himself to its quandary,
and live with its perplexing existence,
the economy will thrive. (Ch. 32)

Laozi is realistic in exile, he suggests self-help to the people, but his primary appeal is to the king. It is only the king that denies destiny and educates servitude. Therefore, only the king need let it be.

Laozi's only purpose was his lifetime job of advising kings, but he left the reservation when he offended the status quo.

The Laozi is premised on the king being more Host to a self-organizing society, than a visionary ruler. The premise is said by many to be a treasonous suggestion, yet he supported the Emperor. Laozi was usurping the academics. His battle was with the economists and advisors, not Kings'.

71. Enough said.

Knowing what I do not know is wise.
Ignoring what I do know would be a travesty.
I am sick of the burden,
however,
I am exalted by the enough said.
My economics is great,
all others are rubbish.
See them for their vacuity,
moreover, recognize my ways greatness.

Laozi is adamant about his protocol and its promise.

Early in my career, I had to choose between honest arrogance and a hypocritical humility ... I deliberately choose an honest arrogance, and I have never been sorry' (Frank Lloyd Wright).

Laozi's resignation letter. It is not a slight at the despot, but at the experts. He did not go along to get along. He refused to implement policies that went against his better judgment. He believed in societies maintenance, but extending the life of institutions beyond their prime was a perversion. In paraphrases of chapter 71:
Knowing what I know is wisdom.
Ignoring what I know is violence.

Entropy and Time

    I am sick of violence. I am not violent.
    [Therefore, I will not be involved in it. I resign.]
    Then look first at how the system we have now works;
    it does not; it is sick.
    When you see that,
    recognize that my system is common sense.

72. Laozi takes his own advice.

If rulers impose on the people,
they bring turmoil on themselves.
If the ruler interferes in their homes,
he will be a nuisance,
if he meddles with their incomes,
he will be a thief.
When the ruler an ordinary foe,
he will be warned off,
If he threatens, then fought in the streets.
If he does not interfere with incomes and homes,
the people champion and support him.
I know that a productive society is a trusting one,
trust only exists in the absence of disappointment.
I am ashamed of my profession,
I have renounced their dogma,
I choose to have no part of it.

A leader's demise starts with his bringing attention to himself.

Here is the reason for Laozi's resignation. Policies introduced, not his, and Laozi could foresee the consequences. The leader revealed to the people as a common thief, a foe, a meddler, and a warmonger.

Laozi was not a revolutionary; he chose exile. Laozi decided on passive-aggressive, not like Socrates did - to cause his death and get revenge Laozi wanted to speed the leader's stillness. His passive was an action by nonaction. He was a loyal servant to the King. He wanted his absence, to cause a vacuum, and that a pause. He went on strike, but he was coming back.

He let the overwrought ruler free to take the advice of his thieving courtiers.

He expected the avatar king would die a violent metaphysical death invoking the wrath of his people. He thought the real leader, the YELLOW king, would wise up and take the sage advice to banish the sophists, reclaim the commonwealth as the trustee of the common (Ch. 45).

Laozi was circling; he was always coming back to help the Yellow Emperor. He went west with the sun, to return in the morning of another time. He is always going to come, he will always be seen in the east by a yellow Emperor looking to improve his country's wealth. See him now on the front cover.

73. Clever or wise?.

A Passion with daring is risky,
bravery with stillness is uncertain,
of these two,
which action is better,
so, who is it clever that knows?
The way of heaven does not contend;
either may be appropriate.
Which would heaven hate?
The clever see these as difficult questions,
BUT every mother knows more than clever people.
I will wait,
It is not my time.
I know gravitas will determine the order of yielding,
and the outcome of affairs,
without any logic, or ceremonies.
Action-by-nonaction is a time without distance,
it's a movement without effort.
Daring and bravery are the wrong questions.
Gravitas is their superior and the nemesis of both,
Trust works like a net with large holes,
It catches nothing,
yet it holds everything near and far.
By stillness gravitas attracts energy,
It that creates a charge and called passion.
From stillness, passion will prevail over demand.

Laozi is in tune with the times.

Laozi chooses exile to avoid. By making that choice, he treats his own life: he illustrates how to decide which action is correct and why. What authority logic hates is irrelevant to a mother (the Commonwealth).

Laozi does not make logical decisions. They are anathema to his whole teaching of join, orbit, and avoid by gravitas. In his exile, as in his job - he was not a player; he never had the gravitas to influence affairs. It was unnecessary for him to decide between boldness and effort because he had no currency to play either hand. He was never a leader, and never would be.

The way is not to contend because trust cannot. Entropy answers everything about energy except when; it tells nothing about the timing.121

If the Dao be adopted in the future, it would occur as a production, and naturally by a confident people, yielding to enhance a leaders gravitas letting.

The Dao will be a spontaneous creation in society at some time. Nothing happens forced, and what does is intuited by a mother. The mother knows, and the academics fear the child joined to the mother

.

74. Laws and justice.

If people do not fear laws,
why threaten them?
If they did fear laws,
why would they commit an offense?
In a free society,
making laws is unnecessary.
Where there is a transgression,
there is always an aggrieved party.
Administering justice on the victim's behalf,
would be like chopping wood,
in the place of a master carpenter,
You would deserve to lose your hand.

Laozi resorts to logic to explain the folly of laws.

If people do not fear the consequences of law enforcement, threats will not affect them. When a people defy the law, it is a sign to the King of his decline. The leader is losing a war with his people when the public ignores its statutes.

If people did fear the consequences of law enforcement, it is a warning that society has venal police, brutal duties, and onerous obligations. A demand economy relies on enforcement, and that on fear.

In a society free of desire, where wealth is a currency backed by trust, people treat each other as armed sovereigns. In that society, the ruler allows. He lets an aggrieved party deal with a transgressor appropriately on his own.

There is no benefit in state justice, and no satisfaction felt by the transgressed, just the ceremony of magistrates, and the consequences of their overreaching. The aggrieved are entitled, well motivated, and better positioned to extract as much justice as they trust to take.

An armed society is a polite society (Robert Heinlein).

75. Onerous demands precede the fall.

If the people are starving,
the ruler takes their grain.
If there is disharmony amongst families,
the ruler meddles in their affairs.
If they risk their lives to produce,
people are subject to demands unreasonable,
the ruler treats them like animals,
where opportunities include the possibility of death,
then the ruler will not live a long life.

Laozi bypasses the king and appeals to the people.

Laozi summaries the circumstances of his resignation and exile, explained in chapters 70–74, as total frustration.

For Laozi, the ultimate appeal is not to reason or moral philosophy. He neither invokes a superior being nor the universal laws.

Perhaps he imagined the political participation that we have today would enable his way. Ignoring the king and addressing the people directly, he uses the logic he hates, to tell of the time.

He points to the final sign of political and economic change - bickering at home, hopelessness in the workplace, and a disinterest in the Commonwealth. He continues in the next chapter, on behalf of future generations.

Entropy and Time

76. Titles preclude the next generation.

An exchange based society,
is considerate and dynamic.
If it strays from the exchange,
and provides everything for all,
so, allocating rewards,
with tithes and stipends,
it creates rentiers and beggars,
by favors, and violence.
If rulers enforce laws to protect titles,
and those to fund benevolence,
the tithes are demanding,
the whole of societies enterprise,
and the young will have nothing to trade,
Where a potential cannot attract a something,
all movement stops.
See that an unbending tree is hard and strong,
however, it is easily cut down by the energetic young,
Therefore,
even the police are on notice.
If the nation does not parlay with the young,
if its history of titles precludes exchanging potentials,
the nation invites its end.

Laozi speaks to arrogance.

The fair exchange is profitable, this realization, was the origin of society; people profiting from exchange returned for more, they made profitable relationships attractive. When others joined the trusting circle they became - a community.

Over time, those exchanges were agreements and later laws, those were arrangements acceptable and legally enforced. However further on and in our time, those laws are made such that they exclude the young from trade, by either insisting on qualifications or by asserting the ownership of a prior generation, and community loses its dynamism.

Where the enforcement of the rentier's claims and taxes, takes precedence over people producing and trading, then society will be depending on violence and benevolence, rather than on the exchange it was founded on.

Laozi asks for how long can old violent predators collect rents, and allocate benevolence by extorting the disenfranchised producers with the police.

Laozi has a clear bias for the young, and for the future.

He tells the leader that society was founded on the honest exchange, NOT property rights. Exchange includes the young, allows and enables them, the police were intended to aid exchange and trade, not, exclude the young from a property, and enforce tithes with stipends. Laozi warns the leader that the opportunities belong to the producers, and their success is his longevity (Ch. 59).

The next generation is the supreme authority; they will overcome the legacy of trusts, historical licenses, patents, and land ownership. The young will not give patronage to the zombies that own. It is inevitable that they will take action by nonaction (strike & act).

Laozi's Way to Wealth & the Holy Grail

Laozi [paraphrased] said let the blood of patriots water the tree of liberty and let there be sweet rain before Lincoln did.

77. **Which mechanical advantage?**

The ruler is wealthy, his society exchanges.
It works like an archer's bow.
The entrepreneur loads the bow with an opportunity,
He draws the string,
and the bottom and top demographics join,
together opposed to the target,
they share stillness,
as the entrepreneur teases the strings tension.
The loaded bow frames all the energies for production.
The leader allows quarry hunting,
he enjoys feasting with entrepreneurs,
and with the high and low together.
Where sophists dominate the ruler,
a bow is called a pole.
Cutting a length from the top of the pole
that ruler uses the more significant portion as a lever;
to advantage movement from the people,
he uses the smaller length as a stick,
that to prod the people laboring.
The bow powered by inspiration,
the lever and stick by violence.
Which society produces more?
The one that uses cooperation?
Or, the one that divides and coerces?
The archer expects no gratitude,
for her part in the shared endeavor.
The sophist wants compensation for his effort,
with the lever and weapon.

The Archer exemplar.

The working bow powers production when drawn, the three demographics together produce more energy than they can individually. The alternative is the lever & stick.

Both methods use mechanical advantage, but the bow has the additional power of all cooperating in work, none engaged in the waste of coercion.

78. Who will be the Laozi?

Trust is legion; it has no nemesis.
Trust has no adversaries;
all welcome it,
it transforms everything.
It seeks no permission
finds no barriers.
People know trust prevails over violence,
yet they revere laws, and over trust.
The Sage is clear,
she says:
He that can speak truth to power
moreover, show him the pitiful bounty of the country,
repressed by sophist laws and taxation,
that sage will be called the Laozi.
He that penetrates a society's lethargy
with trust and makes it productive
will be honored the world over.
Speaking this truth will be praised, not punished.

79. No debt is worth collecting.

Where debts are in dispute,
and only settlement can avoid acrimony.
The sage unties these knots;
she settles the recalcitrant obligation,
and forgets the debt.
The virtuous will settle with the Sage;
others may not.
There is no harm to the Sage,
or the Commonwealth,
gravitas is the measure of accounts,
It alone shows the power of good men,
and tells all others the value of the way.

The question of justice in a state without laws.

Here is the only footnote to the Daodejing. Its an afterthought needing an elaboration.

Wherever a debt is unpaid, the avatar sage will accept the obligation to settle the matter. Later, by nonaction, the recalcitrant might suggest a means to pay the sage. Sums can be made to add up (ch. 27), and changed circumstances may enable payment.

In the event of nonpayment, the Sage has no concerns; the economy is growing, random events happen, there are no assets. Shakespeare's Shylock, discovered the wisdom of nonpayment, with the value of society.

The Sage make no judgment, lose no time, and waste no effort on disputes. This way of settling debts was explained by Laozi as; shaping the common, squaring without justice, straightening without violence, and being wise not clever (Ch. 58).

An unpaid debt does no harm, where measured in a currency backed by energy, because energy is free, like everything else in the commons. Bad debts are nearly always the result of unfortunate events, or in-experience merely wasted efforts where energy is free to waste (Ch.60).

The Muslim sanction on debts is explained in the Koran and elsewhere by the ancient logic of sharing losses, a loss is a loss and limited to the incorporeal endeavor failed.

At the end like in the beginning all decisions are made by gravitas; therefore, the only account that matters gets settled accurately and automatically by merit and with credit by gravitas, avoiding, orbiting, and joining.

Laozi's Way to Wealth & the Holy Grail

80. Laugh, the dogs eat chicken.

Make the leader's administration small,
let it have the fewest mandarins.
Though there be a vast state apparatus,
the people have no utility from it.
Though there be war machines,
let them all be idle.
Have the people access the commonwealth,
so even if they have the means to travel,
they will stay and make deep roots in it.
Let the people have armor and weapons;
they will never use them.
Let them record agreements on strings with knots,
tied in production and untied in the market.
They will all be wealthy,
trusting each other,
to produce their necessities,
let them enjoy the food, clothes, and homes they make;
they will be a people not wanting rare objects.
Though neighbors are so close,
that their dogs and cocks are curious,
the neighbors will grow old and die,
without ever having a dispute,
over the chicken.

An ode, to the joys of exchange, anarchy, and autarky.

A model of the perfect state. A small idle administration, and a vast economy, hosting wealthy people humoured by their pets.

81. Banish the academics.

Hard work is not how to get wealthy;
getting wealthy is not hard work.
Good advice on hard work is nonsense;
educated men that teach of work,
and of obligations are not learned.
The wise diminish learning
and seek opportunities,
they accumulate merit to their credit,
and achieve wealth being still with gravitas.
The economy is cruel, but it is kind.
It creates and destroys wealth spontaneously,
however,
its ruler never fails to give opportunity or support life.

Appendix to the Laozi by Edward Brew.

Thermodynamic Economics

&

The deal with the future.

Introduction

'I advise those who wish to learn the art of scientific prediction not to spend their time upon abstract reasoning, but to decipher the secret language of Nature from the documents found in Nature: experimental facts.' Max Born Experiment and Physical Theory, 1943

Economist Maurice Allias asked. 'Should the Laws of Gravitation be Reconsidered?'122 Allias was neither doing extra-curricular research or having a mid-life crisis, but he did check the evidence of the earth's rotation, and of the tides moving. He proved the cosmologists were not stars at observing, and found evidence for scientific knowledge that invited alternative theories. .123

This paper entirely revisits the path of Allias, who won a Noble prize in 1988 for his contributions to economics.124 There is a scientific explanation for the creation of wealth, and it does draw on aspects gravity theory, but at the relativity end

We will discuss the history of economics later, but be reminded early that Adam Smith's first book was titled Astronomy, and John Stuart Mill mentor of Marshall, and Keynes, said that tidal theory was the foundation of economics. From Mills book of logic;

> 'Inasmuch, however, as many of those effects which it is of most importance to render amenable to human foresight and control are determined like the tides, in an incomparably greater degree by general causes. . . It is evidently possible, with regard to all such effects, to make predictions which will almost always be verified, and general propositions which are almost always true. And whenever it is sufficient to know how the great majority of the human race, or of

some nation or class of persons, will think, feel, and act, these propositions are equivalent to universal ones. For the purposes of political and social science, this is sufficient. An approximate generalization is, in social inquiries, for most practical purposes equivalent to an exact one; that which is only probable when asserted of individual human beings indiscriminately selected, being certain when affirmed of the character and collective conduct of masses' John Stuart Mill125

The nonsense of economics asserting that general propositions are universal laws and that crucial matters 'can be sufficiently verified like the tides,' is the sole discussion of the Stanford Encyclopedia entry on economics, cited later.

The Allias war-time observation was of the economy producing more than it consumed.126 For the economy to exist as a system, consistent with his observations of industry; he could only, describe production as an over-unity machine with access to a free energy.

Most people think over unity, and free energy cannot exist, however, in 1944 Allias observed the French war economy differently, he saw the surplus everywhere, and it was the complaint of producers, and workers alike.

P.J Proudhon, had so much confidence in the over-unity machine of capitalism, that he urged the masses to work harder for the surplus. Proudhon wanted the markets flooded with produce (particularly housing), so the plenty would cascade prices, in 1851. The paradox of over-unity was a inconvenient truth for Marx to avoid. Had he admitted over unity, State Capitalism as Lenin called communism, would never have been proposed.

The doxing question of this paper is; Would a formula given to make everyone wealthy, be shared? The answer yes, is not so evident to a person born with a comparative advantage, but it comes from the Laozi.

This paper is an appendix to the Laozi because the Daodejing told of the political arrangements necessary to accommodate, the unlimited (relative) wealth they had BCE. The questions *of how to share* a commonwealth will be considered with care if the formula is realistic, and has proof. Those discussions would engender excitement, and speed the new arrangements.

However, for a status quo, the doxing question warns of a reckoning. A new theory of wealth will tell of today's financial canards, and beg questions. Who was responsible for all the meanness in the past? Who denied the plenty always available?

The problem with classical economics has been, its confusing of; morals with goods, values with assets, work with worth, and money with everything. By those confusions, classical theory concludes that; money is an asset, work is a duty, and goods are expensive.

Confusions made axioms then laws, are the seeming genius of economics because nearly all of the world's population are working for a currency, that cannot buy what they made, or justify what they did. The 'producers' in society are called consumers needing support, and the 'supporters' are called productive needing resources. The labels have confounded economists, and in their confusion, they think it is the supporters that need more because they are better at allocating than the consumers were at producing.

The classical theory relies on the people needing, to force demand, to want for the supply coming, whereas the clear thinking available from solid science, elaborated on here will make plenty ordinary, and demand impossible.

The Economic discipline has disgraced itself by using fanciful axioms, with syllogistic definitions. It denies the Newtonian motion, by insisting that satisfaction is had in the best of all possible worlds, and by equilibrium. It promises better times and asks for the publics patience, but tomorrow has arrived for economics.

Equilibrium can neither describe a system working, nor inspire a man to make a pair of shoes. Only imbalance and opportunity can make a man move without force. The voluntary movement of attraction, is of such quality, that it gives a momentum enough to excite another, and that perpetuated, is the system that will be described here, as the economy of plenty. An eternity of equilibrium will never make anything move, only a system of exchange can do that.

Richard Stone won the Nobel prize in 1984 for making a sequence of equilibrium states into a model, yet Thorstein Veblen described his description before he was born, as taxidermy. Veblen said in 1914 that marginal analysis (supply and demand) were the effects of the disease (scarcity, and need), not the explanation of living, and he was right Stone's model is now known as a cartoon of accounting.

Classical economists have had their turn saying proofs are made by turning Aristotle's world of cause and effect on its head as Mill explained above, they affect a cause in their theory, following tideolgy. Classical economics is accepted by society like cancer at the funeral, tolerance of treatment does not extend beyond a cure.

This paper will re-invent the subject of economics, explain it from first principals, and describe it with a working model - never in equilibrium. Classical economics has no comparative model and no answer to the one proposed here. Therefore, a brief explanation of why, and how it came to be that the classical economists have no scientific theory follows.

History of Economics.

In ordinary discourse, classical economics started with explaining mercantilism to an agricultural society, more used to discussing land reform, than shop-keeping. Classical economics was popularized by the East India Company, having Adam Smith explain why the company needed the British Army and the peoples' taxation, to rob Asia in 1773.

Smith was early, a genuine and curious philosopher. There are two Adam Smiths. Early Smith was born to a world where nothing was unexplained, everything known came with evidence from the Bible, but he lived in a time of curiosity, one teased by contrary and sometimes whimsical observations. His was a time when it was fashionable to boast that phenomena were discoverable, and those 'discoveries' were claimable as disciplines like cerebral physiology (phrenology), and phlogiston theory - now called pseudo-sciences.

Smith first studied the history of Astronomy; he was not interested in the planets, his subject was logic, he wanted to know; how a fanciful explanation of the stars moving became facts accepted. Smith's Astronomy was an inquiry into knowledge that preceded Thomas Kuhn The Structure of Scientific Revolutions 1962.

Smith thought that the purpose of philosophy, or the example of Newton, was to make correlations between unexplainable things, his wonder was how those correlations would later be accepted as true. Smith disagreed with Newton's universe but told it right. He enjoyed the Newton fan club, but not the gravity.127 Today, Smith would title his book - Newton, the making of a Rock Star by Adam Smith. The later

Smith was less curious; the old Smith was an apologist for big business.

In 1773 the Honorable East India Company was bailed out by the Bank of England. It was a giant fraud newly financed. The company had made promises (issued securities) of such magnitude that the Bank of England was prevailed on to settle them for the bondholders. Having settled the company's debts, the Crown collected its debt, and the Crown did that by ordering the British military shadow the companies fanciful schemes in Asia. The military was expected to enforce the company's fallacious contracts for drugs and prostitutes, so the bank of England could pay back the Crown with the profits.

The bond bailout and the deployment of the military for commercial reasons was abuse, plain to see for the British public. The company published an explanation to them and titled it The Wealth of Nations. The book was a company public relations stunt, to justify the Crowns support of the company, and its long-term employee Adam Smith wrote it.

The East India Company was not a company as we would understand one today, it was a guild of brother pirates, criminals, active in foreign countries. The pirates pillaged Asia and disturbed the high street with their booty by selling it cheap in Camden. Abroad the company settled its debts with heroin, at home, it perverted the social order with sanctioned vice and ill-gotten riches.

The guild of brothers were upper-class twits, and they needed to justify their favor with the Crown, to the British public. They had to allay the Parliament, by their convincing the public of their righteous enterprise

The company tapped Smith; he was to explain the company's special relationship with the Crown. Stealing from foreigners was to be the equal of shop-keeping in the high street. Smith was to describe the violence of piracy as the ordinary work of trade ambassadors, and the workhouse, as the public school.

In Smiths own words he said;

'He intends only his own gain; and he is in this, as in many other cases, led by an invisible hand to promote an end which was no part of his intention. Nor is it always the worse for the society that it was no part of it. By pursuing his own interest, he frequently promotes that of the society more effectually than when he really intends to promote it' (1776, Smith Wealth of Nations Book IV, Ch. 2)

Above is the most misunderstood quote in the entire literature of economics, best paraphrased by modifying the books title Theft and plunder is for good. The noble purpose of Nations is to encourage and defend booty, or by paraphrasing Smith himself; The brothers are innocents trying to make a living like everyone else, they have dark angels, but by their crimes we are a wealthier nation, - their piracy gets us a goodly share.

Smith brought himself to the companies' attention by publishing an earlier book entitled, The Theory of Moral Sentiments 1759. The East India company thought Smiths moral sentiments were for sale, and they were right. They groomed him to say in The Wealth of Nations, what The Theory of Moral Sentiments did not say about property rights. The company pushed Smith to extend the discussion in The Theory of Moral Sentiments about familial rights and individual rights to include economic rights and political rights.

If The Theory of Moral Sentiments could have a little more of David Hume's money subject in it, and perverted for the company's sympathy - then the revised text would become the narrative explaining the Honorable company's activities, and for the good of the nation. Smith immediately understood the brief; he was to make the crimes of the East India Company into an explainable procedure, that into discipline, like Newton made constants into math, trigonometry from guessing weight and distance, brilliant and Astronomy awesome.

Smith was paid an annuity for life, ten times his usual salary to be the companies apologist, and it took him fifteen years on that salary to tweak his Moral Sentiments into The Wealth of Nations for the company. The foundational book of economics was forced on the innocent "Adamites" by the company. Smith did not defend his book, after its publication he took an obscure company license as a harbor master and spent his days cheating the chancellor, of customs on the companies imports.

Smith repackaged theft as hard work, calling it free trade and that a good. Smith's logic described slavery and drug pushing as a legitimate enterprise. Smith passed piracy-of as a natural science, and he so successfully explained this new science of enterprise, that academia teaches it as fact to this day, like they do Astronomy by Newton, Evolution by Darwin, and Gravity by Einstein.

The middle and most significant persona in the invention of the economics as pseudo-science [sic.]128, was the publication of Elements of Logic 1826 by Richard Whately, later made the first professor of political economy at Oxford University. Whately said that syllogism [axiom] was the central feature of logic.

Whately is the only towering figure in classical economics, an acolyte of Leibniz, and optimism he looms over every discourse and paper to the present day. He, more than Smith, invented the science that describes the art, by saying that;

> "syllogism is the science because it is based on clear theoretical principals, like science is based on clear theoretical principals. The art was, therefore - a general application of the science, and that [science] could be right by being wrong."

Authorities derided Whately's logic before his time. Francis Bacon in 1620 said logic was notions confused and carelessly abstracted from things, and Descartes 1637 said: "logic was syllogism that serves to explain what one already knows or to speak freely without judgment about what one does not know."

Economics has never had a Clerk Maxwell, or a Rutherford - to discover anything real, so it has never had an Oliver Heaviside, or a Charles Proteus Steinmetz to explain it. Economics is therefore yet to have its first paradigm shift. Thomas Kuhn would be silent on economics because as the Stanford Encyclopedia explains, it is yet to produce any knowledge at all.129

Thinkers like Deleuze & Guattari, and Frederic Jameson, accurately critique economics because they engage with the disciplines axiomatic foundations in Whately, all other commentators surrender to the confusion of Whately's syllogism. Henry George, Frederick Soddy, and Guy Debord were successful critics, but only because they saw the subject as strangers. The genus of Whately is that; persons introduced to his school, are neutered by its axioms, twisting morals with mathematics, and money with virtue.

The final event that began economics brings us to the end of the East India Company and the present day. It was the publication by John Stewart Mill of '*A System of Logic*' 1843. Mill explained the purpose of his book in the preface, after first acknowledging the excellent work of Whately for pushing the syllogistic art beyond reason, and goading any that could not follow as being un-initiated [sic.];

Mill said (at page iv) in the preface

'[That this] book is an attempt to contribute towards the solution of a question, which the decay of old opinions, and the agitation that disturbs European society to its inmost depths, render as important in the present day to the practical interests of human life, as it must at all times be to the completeness of our speculative knowledge: viz., Whether moral and social phenomena are really exceptions to the general certainty and uniformity of the course of nature; and how far the methods, by which so many of the laws of the physical world [are] numbered among truths irrevocably acquired and universally assented to, can be made instrumental to the gradual formation of a similar body of received doctrine in moral and political science.'

Mill at the time of writing his system of Logic was [THE] Principal of the Honorable East India Company; his sole purpose was to keep the British government's military protection for his East India Company. Today, his job description would be Chairman, of the World's Central Bank. His business depended on the Crowns support, so his job was to get that support. He was after all robbing Asia with the British military and funded by the people's taxation. He only wrote books (had them written) for the public, to ensure the parliament's cupidity with his nefarious activities.

J.S. Mill was homeschooled by his father, a senior brother in the East India company. Mill had One interest in life, and it was the company.130

Mill's System of Logic was to reinforce the public support of the Honorable company, by calling it *the public enterprise*, deserving of Crown support. The metonymy, calling theft - income, and drug pushing - business, used to good effect by Adam Smith in the Wealth of Nations was to be re-invigorated by his new system and forced into Whately's construction of logic.

When the British government did take full control of India, they ignored Mill's system of logic. The Parliament used their common sense and acknowledged the reality of evil, and the cost to England, of funding crime in Asia. The parliament saw theft as theft, not income the way Mill did, and parliament thought wage work Mill's way was enslavement, a crime apparent. The parliament thought murder, as not justified by debt collection. The House of Lords did not understand the logic of raping women as Mill did; as children, being initiated to the enterprise of prostitution with a free education, just paid by others in arrears. The parliament knew that violating foreign populations was not the business done by markets and that the riches of drug-pushers and pimps was the poverty, not the wealth of nations.

The British parliament did not accept Mills twisted words as a system of logic; they merely saw his Honorable company's actions impoverishing nations, was plain simple WRONG, with no explanation in Smith's high street.

The economics of Smith and Mill never did stand scrutiny by reality. Now the Mill quote above can be paraphrased for the modern reader, that might have had difficulty reading the pretentious, self-serving words of a psychopathically deranged Eugenius criminal. It shamelessly says that;

This book of logic will help the company win social standing with the establishment that despises and opposes it. The logic system will bamboozle and destroy the opposition of Europeans (that threaten the company's business and political protection) - it will destroy those enlightened people that can see our exploitation - our capital pushing its dominance within the mercantile system [and the people were in 1843 revolting against its mirror in the Dutch East India Company].

This book will create a new discipline called economics - by mimicking the method of science; it will create a more sophisticated fiction than Smith did - so that the witless public will see the activities of the company in requisitioning the British military and treasury as essential to the survival of the British crown.

Using Whately's syllogistic method of logic - the system is updated so that it will entirely excuse our; theft, drug pushing, slave trading, exploitation, deceit in securities and our usury of money as the formal generalizations of income, work, liabilities, and property.

Then by further logic, the system will use those nomenclatures to discuss the company business, as if it is the same as any other mercantile endeavor; providing useful employment, and bringing needed goods to market for the benefit of ordinary people. Then we can defend ourselves, by referring to the abstractions of our activities using the new terms, and them as a generalized good. With this method, we send all of the meddling concerns of the disenfranchised onto academia, washed clean of our hated activities that revolt the public sensibility.

With this book, we invent a pseudo-science, we will eventually succeed in making our metonymy and syllogisms certain truths, universally assented to. We will copy science, defining our activities as natural phenomena. We will discuss the abstracted generalization of our plunder as a legitimate business.

We will call; theft - an enterprise, or free trade; ownership - capital; money - debt; and scarcity - supply & demand.

We will gradually create the received documents of economics. They will be, in time; the base of our doctrine. Our divine right to own and plunder will be called economics. Having achieved that, we will control and manipulate the doctrine made science, by funding academia for perpetuity. As to whether moral and social phenomena can be logical equations, the scientists have done it with tides; we will do it with plunder. In any event, the public is too stupid to work it out.

Mill was the godfather of Bertram Russell, a Eugenius too, and later an apologist for the company. Mill was a significant influence on Marshall, who taught the President of the British Eugenics Society, John Maynard Keynes economics. The preceding is the real history of economics; an upper-class twits public relations stunt; the example set for tobacco companies and their doctors to follow in the Twentieth Century.131

Nothing has changed the history of economics since 1843, it is an artifact, tinkered with, and today it is on display with different background settings and geographic arrangements, but it is as Smith, Whately, and Mill *invented it ours* now, a chimera for making the criminal East India company an honorable enterprise.132

That company has now morphed, it's the same brand of brothers, their descendants call themselves bankers now, and the economists living at Mt Pelerin call this new finance enterprise of the company in Switzerland; necessary for the Wealth of Nations, same as the old one. Banking is an Honorable enterprise too – now according to economists.

This Morphing of the East India company into today's banking industry was aired in the introducing portions of Carroll Quigley's 1966 book Tragedy and Hope; A History of the world in our time.

John Maynard Keynes in the concluding chapter of his General Theory 1936, paid homage to the Mill preface cited above by saying;

economics was a harmless game to distract the average man [sic.] until he is 'taught, bred or inspired' [sic.] (to be a coolie).

According to Keynes, the purpose of economics was to make the people cupid in the owner's crimes by getting them addicted to their game [sic.]. Keynes was careful, however, to allay the concerns for the owners (by 1936 - bankers) he assured them that they would not be usurped by the average-man [sic.] players, because those are the addicts of the game invented - slaves to it. Keynes assured the bankers that with his general theory they would retain the power to change the rules and that the addicts will be too busy 'tyrannizing over their bank balances' [sic.] to complain. Keynes thought the purpose of economics was to get the average man [sic.] to work for the company scrip (money). So addicted would average man [sic.]

be, that he will work for the drug, as the coolies did in China, for the East India Company.

Could economics be evil? Voltaire thought so; he wrote twenty versions of Candide, banned in America until 1925. Candide is thought to be satire, but it is a clear-sighted observation of the optimistic logic behind economics. It's all for the best, and whatever is right was called optimistic by Leibniz; Smith got his invisible hand from Leibniz, whose premise was - god could not create the perfect world because only God could be perfect; thus, this is the best of all possible worlds.133

Here is a paraphrased version of the original Pinocchio. It is worth remembering what is told to children, and forgotten by adults;

Dear reader, I am the cricket. The blue fairy and I understand each other; you are hanging from the tree by your neck. We are half-way thru the story, you traded your school-book for a ticket to the show, the blackbird warned you, but you became the willing victim of the Cat and the Fox (money & politics) They do not work for gain - only to enrich others. You took your money to the field of miracles, and they helped you plant a gold coin tree, you were warned by the parrot, yet you are a puppet hanging in the tree with no money, do you need to be additionally convicted of foolishness by a monkey.

Is it surprising that the city of simple Simons is a city that sells its citizens body parts, to wage war abroad? A place where the elite are hawks and vultures riding in gilded carriages? Will you do sneaky things in a city of simple Simons because you are pressured by the economics of simple Simons? Will you accept my kindness in rescuing you? Your family is showing you. Will you abuse their love - only to end up a donkey trained to do tricks - whipped by the ringmaster in fun-town, and sold into slavery? Yes, you will - because you are a fool, you lie to yourself, you harm yourself believing lies, you have good intentions, but you will remain a liar while you believe lies.

Take this message Pinocchio. Will you cause the death of your family, before you see the Cat and the Fox (money & politics) for the beggars they are. Ignore them - acknowledge the society that needs you as you need them, do more than labor, show generosity and you will be reborn a real person, you will get all the fresh money (it is better money than the old) you need. The new money will be given as credit (to start). When you wake up Pinocchio, you will be creditworthy and know what to do.

This story was written by Carlo Lorenzini (Collodi) 1826 – 1890, the George Orwell of his day - Pinocchio was the Animal Farm of the 19th century. Lorenzini was a volunteer soldier and journalist. Like Orwell, his political opinions were so strong that he was a threat to the status quo, so he wrote Pinocchio as an economic text and disguised it as a children's story.

L. Frank Baum did something similar with the Wizard of Oz to get it published. Lyman (his real name) was supposedly a raving lunatic obsessed with the manipulations of the gold standard in the depression. He followed the yellow brick road (the money) with the tin man (industry needing liquidity), the farmer needing an overdraft and the lion (William Jennings Bryan constitutional silver dollar), after sleeping in the field of lies (with the media), they followed the road with the everyman (Toto) all the way back to Lincoln's greenback, emerald city. Where Dorothy met the agent (cat) that controls Lincoln's money behind the curtain. Dorothy wears silver shoes in the book

A New Model.

"You never change things by fighting the existing reality.
To change something, build a new model that makes the existing model obsolete. Buckminster Fuller.

This paper acknowledges Professor Ha-Joon Chang of Cambridge University, his Economics: Users Guide 2014, for saying – "economics is not a science," and the authority of the Stanford Encyclopedia of Philosophy, Economics Winter 2013 Edition - economics is not a science, and has never produced useful results. The credit belongs to professor Steve Keen, Debunking Economics 2001 for proving that classical economics was always, and is today a blatant fraud.

With those acknowledgments, this paper will now describe a new economic model using the science of Thermodynamics.

*****

The classical definition of economics is;

the study of the choices that affect the allocation of scarce resources amongst a population with insatiable desires.

The Stanford Encyclopedia of Philosophy Winter 2013 says that 'the [hitherto existing] definition and precise domain of economics are subjects of controversy within the philosophy of economics.'134

Professor Ha-Joon Chang adds that this has been the perpetual problem of economics. He says the conventional definitions ignore the subject matter, which should be the;

Economy -money & work, and the other things that have to do with the way we produce goods and services distribute the incomes generated in the process, and consume the things thus produced.135

Laozi's Way to Wealth & the Holy Grail

Investopedia offers an overview of the results of an ill-defined subject by saying;

'Specific branches of economic thought emphasize empiricism in economics, rather than formal logic. This is most true in macroeconomics or Marshallian microeconomics, which attempt to use the procedural observations and falsifiable tests associated with the natural sciences. Since true experiments cannot be created in economics, empirical economists rely on simplifying assumptions and retroactive data analysis. Some economists argue economics is not well suited to empirical testing, and such methods often generate incorrect or inconsistent answers.136
*****

It is beyond the scope of this paper to review the practice of economics past; however, it is not controversial to say that, there are known problems with the discipline, and this was told to the Queen by LSE Professor of economics Tim Besley. He explained the 2009 financial crisis to Her Majesty as "The greatest example of wishful thinking combined with hubris and principally [caused by] failure in the collective imagination."

Daniel M. Hausman, the author of the Stanford University Encyclopedia entry on Economics, identified six fundamental problems with all branches of economics, they are;

• The conflict between, science purporting facts, and morals asserting what ought to be.
• No theory has a defined catalyst to make events happen.
• There is a confusion between what causes people to react and the reasons people do so.
• Economics observes the observer, making it absurd.
• Its definitional breadth necessitates idealization and abstract simplification which nullifies its usefulness by abstracting it from reality, or applicable only where all things are equal in special and impossible cases.

300

- It relies on un-prove able coefficients (demand) having axiomatic relationships with others such as supply and price; its proof is, therefore, a unique example of syllogistic failure.

Hausman concludes that success in economics is controversial.137

Macroeconomics is mostly ignored by economists today, they have re-defined themselves as actuaries. They work now, as Hausman said, to reduce data by absurdity, retro-fitting mathematical equations until by exclusion and adjustment they correlate to observation. The Black, Scholes, Merton option pricing model 1973 is the best example of this hubris because it works until like the queen learned, it does not.

This paper deserves attention because each of Hausman's six concerns are answered. This new theory is no part qualified, it has no exclusions, and makes no assumptions.

*****

With the above discussion showing a definitional vacuum, this paper offers a new definition of the subject;

Economics is the study of the human-kinds intentional conversion of some types of energy into others. That of labor, trust and matter into work, manifest as matter in services made for the future as products, and entropy enjoyed in the present as satisfaction, or used for utility.

Economics is a topic of the greater subject Political Economy.

The political economy is the system of arranging the social environment to allow the most-possible productive outcomes from its exchanges with energy, by ensuring the greatest freedom of its participants to do so.

Preamble

This theory is complete and is immediately useful. It will prompt community discussions because it insists on the re-arrangement of existing property rights.

The success of China's Loess Plateau restoration (8% income growth for Twenty consecutive years) and of Singapore since 1950, were both dependent on the preparedness of people, to trade one set of property rights for another.

The people gave away some rights and won a share in the grand scheme of the ancients; of Nation building. Those smart to trade on China's Loess Plateau, and on Orchard road, have found themselves wealthier than they could have been by other arrangements of property ownership.138

This model demands the informed trade of property rights, part following Henry George, to allow its implementation.

The term property includes all debts, and titles to property including intellectual. As the debts are canceled, the former creditors and title holders receive no compensation (but suffer no loss). Any person resident in a home or occupying a property will have possession of that property, the assets on the property are the possessions of the occupier, the land and resources belong to the commonwealth. Property is subject to ground rents, but persons will be spared all taxations on income and goods.

The significant events will be;

The;

• nullification all debts,
• The issuance, of a new currency,
• The replacement of all taxes, with Utility Tolls, and Land tax.
• A prize based compensation for intellectual property.

This model is partly affected in Singapore today, where 22% of the enterprises and 90% of the housing are state-owned. Singapore has an unbacked currency and a thriving economy that supports the median of its population, with the highest living standards in the world.

The reforms; returning assets to the commonwealth, and the canceling of debts, will deny capital gains to the future, but make all productive effort profitable in the present. The former system of, debts and asset hypothecation, will be replaced by, seigniorage and trade credit. The currency will be issued, like trade credit, against the expectation of production.

The new seigniorage money will replace banking. The state will fund new industries and infrastructure. Those investments will displace the rentiers (bankers) that have ensconced themselves in the Utilities sector, and those new endeavors owned by the Commonwealth will fund a living wage for all.

Coffee shop bill markets will mediate trade credit arrangements like they did in 18th century Amsterdam, these are ideally suited to our networked society today.

Ancillary to the reforms mentioned above is the re-imagining of the government as a public trustee. Clarifying the government's role in society will prevent its meddling in private spaces like education and health. It is well established that wealthy people (and all people will be wealthy) need no assistance to; educate their children, maintain their health, settle their disputes, or regulate their behavior.

Introduction.

Engineers demonstrate systems with a cylinder engine. They place elements under some pressure, in a confined space with fuel and show them working. The French railroad engineer, Carnot, determined that with three variables; Pressure, Volume, and Heat, he could find all of the useful information from any system.

The economy has been taught in the past as a process while being simultaneously asserted a system. The too much purporting has confounded generations of students, and infuriated scholars, such as Steve Keen, Richard A. Werner, and Michael Hudson.

People rely on the economy being a system; else they would not return to work tomorrow. The process tells the return will make economics a system but proves it impossible by competition eroding profit, or comparative advantage denying opportunity. The process is what classical economics teaches; it gets results until as the Queen learned it does not, because it is designed to terminate. The process always needs the never taught bailout for it to continue, that is the only returning in the gulag process.

The bailout comes from banking, and it is called bailout, because it is not financed, a bailout is a fudge. The bailout is pretending that classical theory can continue as a system (without assistance), it cannot, as Greece, and Argentina pre-and post-bailout have recently demonstrated. The gulag cannot be described by a Carnot engine, because all of the input energy is used, and none is forthcoming for the next cycle (Kelvin).

Marginal analysis (Supply and demand), is the centerpiece of all classical theory, and it says that a demand is made of the gulag, at a price expected, and supply is forthcoming. It assumes that the gulag has no problems supplying; the inmates never die, there is no innovation, and the demand is always made. Classical economics is silent on how the process meets any reality, whether it be an aging demographic, finite resources, or changing climate. Keynes admitted that assistance is possible but dishonestly portended it to be temporary, and repayable (would return to equilibrium).

Here we will describe an economy with a future, so we will ignore the terminating process of exhaustion and degradation known by classical economics, and use a Carnot engine to describe a system that creates more. We will discuss the economics asserted by assumptions, but not known from theory, or reality. We will show economics in a different form, one that has evidence in history, and proofs in physical science,

The science of Thermodynamics is asserted as being settled in this work and is used to explain economics as the endeavor of Nation Building for the future. The How of society is discussed as a consequence of the people's ambitions for the state.

To apply the science of Thermodynamics to the endeavor of nation building, we will introduce five new economic metrics; Pressure (P), Volume (V), Heat (Q), Enthalpy (V), & Entropy (S). People are made an idealized gas. We will assign them a periodicity (charge), and call their charge, a Net Present Value. These charged people are the sole subject of this economic system. There is no capital, and resources have no value.

This model uses the work of Bastiat, Soddy, and Buckminster Fuller; it will assert as they did; that resources are not a factor of production. Soddy said that, with the progression of human intelligence, nature is either not, or an increasingly less important factor; meaning that with innovation, we will create everything from nothing valuable, or create more with less.

This paper rejects the Labor theory of value; it relies solely on the thermodynamic measures, described by the Carnot model.

This paper is not speculative, the thermodynamic model being introduced here fully explains what economists have called the Singapore paradox; strong currency, high income, no ownership, low taxation, no resources.

The Economic Measure of Pressure

In the context of economics, Pressure (P) is the weighted index of necessity, for example, the number of days a person works to feed and shelter themselves in a year, inclusive of amortizing the days required to gain qualifications to do the same. Pressure is a measure of; transparency and fairness, made value for use in the model, by an index.

The Pressure value measures rent-seeking, inclusive of taxation by the government; it tells of the, public policy or rent-seeking for profit. Economic Pressure is calculated, by constructing and weighting an index of the burden that adds pressure to the constituent (element, later person).

In visualizing (P) in a thermodynamic system, imagine necessity as the quantity that weighs on the top of a piston head: the more necessity (a weight), the more force applied to the cylinder chamber requiring more energy from the constituent elements to do work. In an economic system, the gas opposing the pressure to work is the mass of society. If obligations burden the piston - with say, license fees, or land tax, the pressure is felt by the individual working, he is forced to spend energy (later called money) to overcome the pressure, and the system is affected for better or worse.

The Measure of Volume

Volume (V) is the weighted index of freedom. It accounts for the quality of transport and access to communications; social mobility; education, leisure, the availability of money, access to research.

The aggregate weighted index of freedom will be the value Volume (V) of the system. This index is more easily attained by measuring frustration and inverted to be a positive number.

The measure of (V) will tell of the opportunities to innovate, engage, use and interact. Restriction by patent and land rights, social hierarchies, and qualifications will tell of the more or less opportunities to make wealth from a potential (matter).

In visualizing Volume, as the measurable area of a system, think freedom.139 For example, the greater the freedom from restriction, the more area participants have to move and act. A scientist without financial or moral restrictions could start research without asking permission and use any materials, or methods to do so.

An architect, identifying land with potential, would have the opportunity to redevelop it, without having to seek approvals. An unqualified engineer, needing to build a factory for his superior pump, would be able to source the funding quickly without conditions.

Freedom engenders activity, creating bigger spaces to act in, and more opportunities to do so. It pushes the boundaries - expanding the system, but does not leave it.

The control of Pressure and volume are the domain of the polity, the community, in government (acting) have a valid and vital role in determining the burden of pressure and the area of activity.

This model does not suggest a laissez-faire doctrine. By defining the role of government, this paper will enliven the polity, both inviting government intervention, and limiting it.

Pressure & Volume determine the systems Enthalpy.

Using the State variables (P) and (V) we derive the economic systems Enthalpy, this is the measure of the internal energy of the system; it is the energy of the elements within - under pressure in volume. Enthalpy measures the whole systems energy; it is the mass contained in the system, bounded by the energy given it.

The energy is Matter closest packed - or volume under pressure. The counter-space separating the matter within, is imagined as a fabric analogous to gravity, and will be explained later as the currency.

Money is indistinguishable from the people matter in the cylinder - because people are described quantities measured in currency, valued by energy. In effect, people are atomized by units of currency (people have a NPV in the energy currency) and Joule's measure their worth in units of currency. The money is explained later in more detail when discussing heat (Q) and work (W).

The elements in a Carnot engine are gases; here they are, people, and made to act like a gas. They are given a charge, measured in currency, and bounded by their collective energy (V), under some pressure (P), they have a potential to work, and that is the Enthalpy measure.

How valuable the elements, or what quantity of currency, is irrelevant in starting the thermodynamic economy, because the performance of a system is learned by its change (delta) in working. Everything explained by thermodynamics is relative to a previous condition of the State variables, P, V, Q. So, relative here, is objective. Relative is literal because it is to the previous condition, using relative with thermodynamics is not qualifying, it is the result because thermodynamics measures only change.

Intuitively we know relativity in economics - it costs more to have the street cleaned in L.A. than Jakarta, and it will take a relative investment in the Beverly Hills Canyon, to achieve the same effects, got on China's Loess Plateau.

Entropy and Time

Thermodynamics tracks energy changes, a little is enough in poor places, and a lot is insufficient in richer ones. For example, add 60 degrees to 50 degrees to get ten more, but, add 10 to Zero degrees for the same ten. A more significant investment is required in the hotter system to achieve the same degree change in the cooler.

We intuit already that an investment made to any economy, is adding energy to a system, we can see the elements responding and the economy coming to life with investment. Traditionally, we assess that intuition about investment, as a process by looking to its product.

We say that a product, is the Return on Investment (ROI); the product determines the benefit of the investment. We will now discuss a systems performance measure and suggest enthalpy, is the more appropriate measure to access the value of an investment.

Enthalpy is isolating the internal energy (work in progress, part equals money issued by trade credit) from work done, to determine the worth, or performance of an investment made. If an investment, produced no change in work (GDP) from the system, the ROI measure would say it was a bad investment, but the system engineer would say the system has a high enthalpy (H). The system is priming; the elements are creating space (currency) internally, the elements are arranging for a more efficient future.

Else, the engineer might say; the system has expended the energy through porous boundaries (V), indicating your location is at the center of The Garden of Eden, where there is no pressure or need to work.

If the engineer saw that all of the investment produced work, a 100% ROI, he would admit that all of the energy was converted to work (GDP) but warn; there is no such efficient machine. He will say - there is a problem with the system after the investment, the enthalpy has diminished, the currency was exhausted from within the system. So, either the people's effort is being extorted (the gulag - explains efficiency), or the peoples' efforts were misjudged by overvalued goods, or goods for export, making a scarcity at home, and the society needs restoring to reality.

These are early examples of the more useful information produced by a thermodynamic analysis, they tell of the paucity of information given by the ROI measure. The engineer can explain why we should fix a wildlife habitat, or an ancient bridge; he would say, it is an excellent investment to produce nothing valuable, because the enthalpy of the system has increased.

Grand and distant projects inspire people and make them proud, that is a change, thermodynamics tracks changes. When people are changed by an inspiration, they trust each other with trade credit; giving each other worth is a rising enthalpy and a not lost investment.

The engineer says the people are worth more. After the investment that produced no product, the people have more money, and nothing was lost in the system, it is yet to produce.

We will learn later that the entropy of the system will give further information, that may confirm, or negate the engineer's intuition; that time will tell more of the system's performance. We are yet to construct the system; we have to see it working to know its usefulness. Let us continue.

The Measure of Heat

Heat (Q) is correctly understood as atoms moving, or as kinetic energy. Therefore, the technically correct measure of heat is the one that measures energy by movement, or work, as a Joule does.

Temperature is the anarchistic scale that described heat for the caloric. Temperature belongs to the time before the discovery of energy - when things were hot before atoms were discovered moving to make them hot. Therefore, temperature today measures the abstract of energy. Temperature is a scale, its use is a mere convention, but one that invites us to use an alternative scale for energy.

This paper will use a different scale for heat; it will use the money scale, to measure energy. Labor, oil, and electricity are forms of energy each can be converted to friction, resistance, combustion. Those engineering terms tell us of heat, and that heat is energy. We intuitively know, energy has value, because we pay for gasoline with money; money is energies measure, it is a scale, and therefore the equal to what temperature measures of energy.

Executives refer to the price of oil every day because price provides the same information to the decision maker using heat, as the scientist has using temperature. Neither the businessman or the scientist are confused working together discussing the same enterprise using different scales of energy.

Money is the parallel and equal measure (a gauge) of energy. Because, today we know its heat by the British Thermal Unit (BTU), and that has always had a price in money or a value in energy.140

This paper will adopt money as a measure of heat (Q). We will also adopt energy as the unit of an idealized new currency, that loses value in use like energy does.

Now we will call the heat sink for the thermodynamic economy, a money pump, and think of it as is the supply of goodwill to the economy. Money is explained by the trust (goodwill), because money is advanced on the promise that it will be redeemed, and in this model, it is issued in good faith because it is issued expecting that it will produce goods; get work (labor energy).

Seigniorage is this economies money source, and the energy of trust measures, getting work from money. The heat sink (money source), is only limited by the imagination (of productive enterprises) and the honesty of the Issuer (State), it is therefore available in unlimited quantities as the currency backed by the full faith and trust of the people, like the greenback was.141

Let us now say, what we know about this system; that as gas molecules move at increasing velocity with increasing heat in a Carnot engine, people move at increasing velocity with more money in the economy, because heat is equally understood by thermodynamics in the money scale called price, as in the degree scale called temperature.

Declaring a universal standard in the future to measure energy, say a Joule142For both temperature and money, would make all the relationships clearer for another generation. However, because of the historical, descriptive error of temperature being energy in thermodynamics, money can be thought as temperature too and made heat in the model. This innovation allows the thermodynamic proofs to stand unchallenged in their application to the political economy.143

Energy as input and output

The sole input and only product of a thermodynamic system is energy. As an input, energy is known as Heat (Q,) measured by temperature, while as an output it is called Work (W) measured by Joules. Were that system to describe the political economy, the input Heat (Q) would be called investment expressed in money, while the work done in Joules (W) would be called Gross Domestic Product (GDP), expressed by money (as it is now).144

Investments are made as Heat (Q) to the thermodynamic economy, by the continuous issuing of currency as seigniorage.145 This input (Q) initiates the production customarily spoken about as private & public investment originating from the banking system, and called lending. However, the investment process is described here, from its foundation in thermodynamic science - so it ignores the traditional banking role.

Seigniorage describes the energy introduced to the system as the investment, and wasting money is the most of producing the goods and infrastructure. The waste is familiar and will be discussed later as consumption, leisure, and depreciation.

The goods and infrastructure will be unfamiliar because they are not demanded, and may not be necessary for the present generation. They will over time be more like the ancient Pyramids, and the Loess Plateau Restoration.

A wealthy population will not be demanding housing, consumables, or education, because they will have those. The wealthy, honest society of the present, will be wanting to gift the future generations with a legacy, one so valuable later, that they will have assured themselves, that the future generation will honor the currency issued to build it.

The system of the Ancients was a deal with the future, and it explains why we are today marveling at their achievements. What the pyramids tell, is that the builders issued currency, backed by infrastructure. The pyramids tell us that our ancestors were honest builders, and gave reason in the pyramids for the next generation to redeem their currency.

Laozi's Way to Wealth & the Holy Grail

This investment by way of seigniorage is unconventional, and it would be said, by a classical economist to be inflationary. However, in a thermodynamic system, the energy is either destroyed in making the assets or changed into them (GDP) and destroyed in their use. The money is either spent making the assets, or invested into them, and further spent as the assets depreciate. The money changes value, with the energy, and like the people that affect the system do; it dies, the energy dies, the assets depreciate, the money loses value. Later it will be explained that the money is progressively withdrawn from circulation with tolls, as the assets and goods are depreciated or consumed, part following Gessell 1929.

An additional subtlety of the deal with the future is that the system, works by hysteresis, it is never in equilibrium. At the time of production, the people inside the Carnot cylinder are trading. The engineer calls their action a Hysteresis because trading has a pulsing movement (say up and down), and it has a time factor, any inflation is inside the cylinder lifting it, any contraction is inside the cylinder expressing waste. The deflation and inflation are emergent from the cyclic action; they are expressed with a delay exclusively in the productive sector (by business). The delayed emergent of inflation or deflation was explained above as the variable enthalpy (H).

The productive sector understands the temporary nature of wealth - of winning and losing contracts; it welcomes hysteresis (an AC time lag), wearing losses while chasing opportunities. In effect profit and loss never make it to GDP, so don't inflate the societies asset prices. The constant input of new money ensures the system's continuance (excitement) while isolating the society from its effects.

The economic engine; Society and Work meet with entropy.

The purpose of a society is to cooperate in production because the purpose of life is to be useful (R. Waldo. Emerson et al.). To be useful for the next generation is explained as the final word of this paper, which is describing a system of exchange, to deliver on a contract with the future generation.

We acknowledge the satisfaction of community daily, but forget that society is foremost an economic construct, made to cooperate in work. Cities like Detroit and Hollywood exist because they produce cars and films, their societies are, because of production, the people known by roles, assembly workers or actors.

The wealth from societal cooperation is the synergetic benefit of the community; classical economists ignore this, they pretend societal cooperation to be their misnomer for efficiency. Economists say cheaper & quicker is efficient, but their ignorance of community and misunderstanding of engineering has the effect of commodifying people and diminishing society. The engineer tells of community that; cooperation is less friction, it creates more work and uses lots of energy, and those are good things.

Entropy is the science word for the community valued. The scientist thinks the experiences of the community (entropy) is an essential effect of investment, doing work. The classical economist looks at measures that show, unemployment, inefficiency, and expense. The engineer will explain, that an investment of money gets three things; a rise in the internal energy of the system (enthalpy), the community does some work (GDP), and stuff happens.146 The stuff is the Entropy (S) value.147

A positive Entropy change shows that societies are affected by turning energy to work. It measures Pressure, Volume & (Q) Money, and tells if the investment was worthwhile.

Where an entropy value, higher than One, from changing the investment (Q) in an economy, the thermodynamic interpretation says the cooperation was good for the community.

Where an Entropy value is derived, equal to One, from changing the investment (Q) in an economy, the results are not so clear, because not all work is beneficial, some work is for work's sake.

If the entropy value is less than One, from changing the investment (Q), it will indicate loss from an investment, and waste from working.

The economist Bastiat was the first to explain low entropy (< 1) with his vandalized window, - an indolent youth creating unnecessary work. Bastiat's allegory was published seventy years before the engineer Carnot made his model engine. Using classical economics, fixing a broken window produces work, the classical economist says that increases GDP, and it is a good thing. 148

More to know about Entropy.

Entropy is described formally by the second law of thermodynamics; this law is, inaccurately known as the law of disorder and decay. When misinterpreted as such, the second law suggests a Malthusian view to economics - that all energy not used is wasted on diminishing returns and that effort only speeds destruction.

Malthus was suggested, as science to the club of Rome by Nicholas Georgescu Roegen. He knowingly misspoke, which was a habit of his. There was in the 1970's and is now a stochastic explanation of entropy that tells a scientific truth, the eugenics club at Rome (now at Mt Pelerin) did not want to hear.149

When stated correctly, the law of entropy says - that a system will take its most likely form. Adrian Bejan explains this law with another law that he calls Constructal Law - a system lives by evolving for easier access, and the measure of that is a change in the system's entropy (S).150

This correct understanding of entropy, immediately suggests; a good to society. It says that where energy has been spent (or time has passed) something has been done because arrangements to travel have been made; elements have been placed, bookings made; there has been an effect of energy, and things have changed in the hierarchy at home. The surroundings have been fitted for a purpose in time; energy rigs for work, for later, it makes, a Hysteresis, that a difference soon, movement defines life, that is good.

*****

Imagine the lack of GDP, while a whole society stops work to evolve for easier access, to live. Imagine the internal energy moving, and the energy spent discussing the giving up of freehold titles, intellectual property, life without insurance, and finance. The entropy variable will tell of this time, that it was of the most exceptional value to the community, there was no work done, and tremendous benefit. The people invested their energy evolving with a tax deal, an annuity, a secure property, and not just for them but for the future generations, a health plan, a dream, and a purpose - to live by evolving for easier access, as the Constructal law says living things do, entropy tells us How? It is by evolving, and Why? Because we are living, and want to live.

Entropy measures the evolving, its more than progress, it's a check that says; tomorrow will be better because we are investing, in the future. Tomorrow we will do our job; differently, we will not be called stupid by Einstein, because we are evolving, we will expect a different result because we did a different experiment. That is Entropy. The bigger the entropy, the bigger the changes for, the better. It is the commonsense, that science calls entropy.

Already we can see that if the entropy rises, and little or no products are made, then that tells the engineer that people are moving to Detroit, arranging, preparing to work. The child is born in New York, he is a potential cook in Detroit (just not yet), making his first move. The thermodynamic economist is a time traveler of sorts; entropy is part Net Future Value (NFV), the benefit of arranging to evolve, is a benefit that goes to the future, an investment measured in the present. The Lorentz transformations will be introduced later to mediate our relationship with another time.

Entropy and Constructal law predicted this paper, and told of this writer, our system of economics will take its most likely form, it will evolve in such a way that it provides easier access to the imposed (global) currents that flow through it. This paper directly applies Adrian Bejan's Constructal law to economics and explains; what the economic systems most probable form will be.

The entropy variable gives no indication of the virtues timing, of later, but it does tell of the direction. For example, no physical law stops a rock from rising rather than falling from a mountain. The second law tells us that it is statistically improbable - the rock will (with near certainty) fall to the ground at some time in the future. Similarly, there is no physical reason why a cold body could not transfer cold to a hot body; the second law tells us it is improbable.151

Entropy and Time

Here we talk of human nature - is it more probable that a scientist seeking funding for an experiment to prove his cancer cure, will conduct his experiment with the funding given him? Alternatively, is it more likely that he will use his grant to fund a cocaine habit? Does a man with an opportunity, make the most of it, work hard to benefit from it, or will he ignore it? What is more likely?

It has been the obsession of social sciences, to focus on the populations criminal, mental, and slothful aberrations, those one percent, six full standard deviations from the median population, and conclude that people will respond inappropriately to the stimulus of energy. Entropy measured by Stochastic's tells us to ignore the suspicious sociologist, and listen to the common sense of a mother. The sole subject of economics is people, and the people experts are mothers. The scientists mother will tell you that her son will find the cure to cancer, and that is all to learn from the second law of Thermodynamics.

We people are nearly always good, and the entropy measure proves that given the opportunity, we nearly always step up and become better. Here we see the perfidy, even mendacity, of the status quo in government and by the finance sector insisting on securities, and guarantees for investments. Here we have a hint that a fully funded dream could be a reality if we pay attention to the entropy.

A nuclear potential is excited to an explosion: talent is a potential power like nuclear is. When talent is excited to write a bankable song, we see its effect. The thermodynamic potential of economic elements acting in a Carnot engine (society) can be appreciated now by the science; love is kinetic energy from a potential, excited from a meeting, is wanting a family; is creating the movement to build a house.

Love expresses from a latent potential to the thermodynamic economist. How much investment is needed to bring the child's potential to adulthood, and make them attractive enough to find a partner? To fall in love, so that they explode on the economy, wanting a home for the attracting of a family? Entropy (S) answers - stochastically, and more usefully than any other theory of social science, to a political leader.

Laozi's Way to Wealth & the Holy Grail

The latter expression, of kinetic energy by work, was primed at an earlier time by investment not wasted, that went to entropy. Appreciating time, as the direction of human well-being, and that time has a measure in political economy will force the recognition of unacknowledged potential. Entropy intuits a value in all quiet things and suggests their viral kinetic activity at some time, and the appearance of work (GDP) later.

Entropy tells of spiritual potentials, of thoughts making images, some of which; statistically, will have a physical manifestation by way of their common denominator in energy at some time.

The one common factor, in goodwill, trade credit and state seigniorage is the trust they issue, and we call that money. Money gets work from the present when it is trusted to get work in the future. Energy trusted is paid forward, the getting back has always been called redeeming money. Money and its equivalents are potential energy when issued, that change to kinetic when redeemed.

Understanding that the effects of money issued by trusting, are one way in time - to the future, will revolutionize the polity and its economics. The Entropy nourishes the state, and the States potential is enhanced such that people respond to good faith money with work, at some time.152

We have lots of time to learn with the money redeemer in the future, he is sometimes 2, or 10 years distance, other times 200 years, so we increase the arrangements to accommodate him at the different times. That covers much distance; it will take some entropy to travel that far, this type of trip suggests preparing by rearranging the forest, cleaning the air, stocking the rivers, and checking on the health of the oceans. This trading partner might consider paying a little extra occasionally for a better building, because he will be our decedent, and we will expect him to have higher standards than we do.

Be warned about 'your' descendants, they will have discovered the Laozi, and they will be using this economic model, they will know the value of entropy when they redeem the currency issued many years ago for the fresh fish from the river stocked way-back-then.

Entropy and Time

When the pharaoh moved the first stone to Giza, were people inspired to join in and help, or did they wait until he moved the second? Moving fifty stones in a desert is a wasted effort to a classical economist. At what time, or how many stones need traverse the desert before he thinks entropy a value? When does an expensive process, become a free system of voluntary exchange? At what height was the pyramid when the classical economist thought entropy, enthalpy and a Return on Investment? When did the pharaoh moving stones in the desert, have an asset? Is the message to the future from the pyramid, an economic riddle? One intended to teach us, to evolve as a nation so that the next generation trusts what we did with currency in good faith.

Entropy tells the economist a story about investment, the arrangements, once thought of as waste, as time lost and effort not making worth. How much nothing makes something? Arrangements of comfort like happiness, consumption, and leisure, are the preparations for excitement. Entropy values the now, for later as the GDP of the future.

Talking Entropy.

The introduction of Entropy (S) to political discourse will protect society from the economic dogma of supply and demand. Keynes said at chapter 24 of his General theory that every crisis however named has been an unhinged idea of a defunct economist, blindly followed, and the 2018 Nobel prize winner Paul Romer, commented that a classical economists greatest fear is that their "mathy" theories, full of "tricks" might actually be used in real life.153

With the Thermodynamic discipline; modeling will show in advance the theories which yield useful results. Political dreams will have a test, any plan that affected one of the three variables P, V, and Q, could be justified or rejected for a good reason.154

If a political plan called for increased Pressure (tolls for new infrastructure), and the entropy (S) remained constant or increased above One, then that plan, would have a reason to be supported, and the economist would have his first ever objective evidence (not relying on assumptions) to suggest an investment to a population.

The thermodynamic economist could say with conviction, that society should re-arrange (evolve to live), and accommodate the new activity. The plan justifies the issuing of new currency. The model shows society will cooperate better under the plan for more pressure, with better infrastructure, they may do less work (GDP), but what they do later will be with more efficacy.

Increasing entropy (S) shows the benefits of cooperation, by its effect on production, even if the work (W) is less, because an entropy that increases hints at synergy in the workplace, and that is a good had by the workplaces' symbiotic twin, society.

Say an additional pressure (P) was put on the population to pay tolls for the new bridge (W), and as a direct result of the investment (Q), the people had more freedom to move (V), we then derive a positive change in the entropy of the system. But, if the output (W) GDP has fallen, then we will say, there is an additional benefit from the workplace synergy, but that was traded with the society, such that the workplace was the loser to society, and the winner too, because the societies benefits are the workplaces ease of moving with the bridge, its less friction (V).155

In the laboratory of the chemist, thermodynamic reactions are never in equilibrium, because time is the factor that explains movement in all natural systems, and the economy is no exception.

With the constructal law of Bejan's; its over-time and the Allias equations tell; only of time. Time is the measure of distance, and it takes energy to cover a distance, so time tells of the effort, or movement never seen in the GDP. This effort, is in say; arranging, energy (value) hidden seemingly spent in the entropy variable but it is a form of potential energy (like elasticity), and a type of synergy too – for later.156

The elements never quite settle for the chemist, after mixing, reacting, and working, they are always changing, by trading and swapping. Here is the gift of the entrepreneur, it's a potential, a product of sorts called a profit, and sometimes it is, while at other times it is a loss, and better explained by the unopened gift actively trading, and testing synergies over time.

All complex systems in nature are trading systems, and most elements-trading have multiple others, each is reacting to the changes in P, V, Q, while each is reliant on the others energy (H); all are benefiting while wanting, and losing-while getting. Scientists describe this trading; an hysteresis, and cannot get an accurate measurement of it at any time.

However, they will say of an economic system reacting that; the society is the other, getting the benefits of synergy from the workplace other, losing. The scientist describes profit with time in the entropy variable. Synergy is the profit, it in time is part enthalpy, and in another time part entropy and sometimes it is GDP, and it is always a good, just a changing one, in different times.

Synergy defines profit. It is a bonus from a potential changed by increasing entropy. The scientist, therefore, has a more intuitive understanding of why we go to work for profit. A profit (synergy) could be a solid, or a liquid, or a gas and be the same water always. Sometimes there is a little more synergy (imagined), and at others - a little less is evident, but in time, and later by the changes in energy all accounts are nearly settled.

Hysteresis is this timing phenomenon, in which the value of a physical property lags behind changes in the effect causing it - for instance, when magnetic induction lags behind the magnetizing force. This time lag is being explained here as being sometimes part entropy (S). An increasing entropy will show - the induction (a benefit) is to come later, that the people's potential everywhere is getting primed for its later conversion to kinetic energy (work).

Entropy tells of the arrangements for work to begin, and of progress. Laozi said it was the most critical stage; he called it stillness (phase transition), the precursor to production. The phase transition is a period of weirdness. It is a time that takes more energy than linear math explains. When the temperature is increased steadily to boil water, there is a time warp and a temperature gradient incongruity. It seems that no amount of additional energy can speed the transition for the moment to steam. Entropy is change, and economics is the application of energy to change things (produce them); economics is, therefore, the study of phase transition, and entropy is its critical measure because it tells of the weirdness in the timing.

The economy is an over-unity system when looked at holistically. The benefits of synergy (1 +2 =4) are over unity, but we cannot account for them with classical economics, or learn them from Newtonian mechanics because they disperse in the energy of the arranging society over time. Synergies (profits) appear with the habits of Schrodinger's cat.157

The benefits go to the future, and they need to be accounted for, to see them. The entropy increasing is an invitation to do a Net Present Value calculation, and a Net Future Value estimation of the primed, ready potential (physical & human capital). Entropy values, greater than One, indicate that the NPV's have been affected and a worthwhile investment.

If the entropy value decreased, or remained below One, in a modeled investment of seigniorage, the combination of changes in P, V and Q will show wasted potential or future friction in cooperation. A falling entropy value warns the leader about applying further pressure (P) now, to the potentials, restricting their freedom (V), or wasting their investment on useless infrastructure (Q), the people's energy (H) on useless Work (W).

If these thermodynamic appraisals of investments seem fanciful now, there is more to learn about money and finance later. However, bear in mind here, that most of all endeavors in the thermodynamic economy are nation building ones; land restoration, city building, energy generation, they will be projects of monumental scale, that will capture a rich populations imagination, like the Loess Plateau restoration, or the creation of another Singapore.

Henry Carey called this system of Nation building, the American system, and his only problem was that its success was that it was not more widely appreciated. Sun Yat Sen understood Carey's American system, he called it modernization, before it became his unfunded political plan for China in 1910. We are giving Sun Yat Sen a scientific appraisal. While asserting his mantra, that; the Political economy is nation building, people development, and community well-being, they are the legitimate sons of the State. The bastard child is Capital, he the only that demands a Return on Investment (ROI), and it is persona non-grata in the shadow of a proud Nations achievements.

Our measure is entropy, it a not spent energy, is an investment traded with time, and paid for later by another generation when the currency is redeemed.

Politics and economics are married by thermodynamics. It is the economy that generates entropy (happiness and wellbeing), and the polity that contracts with the future to get paid for the work done.

When politics is divorced from economics, they both demand finance but joined by thermodynamics, they generate their funding from the system. The Funding is an inherent feature of seigniorage money, it funds the present from the future – so over time, it swaps effort between the generations. Our best trading partner is not overseas; he is in the house, only he will not be born until 2200 CE. This paper will use relativity theory, later on, and show how to realistically trade with the future now, without using bank finance.

Entropy and Demand.

Classical economists assert that demand is either a force or a field/acting, both are said by axiom, to mediate action at a distance by commanding production. There is no evidence logically or experimentally for demand being either a force or a field.158

These evidence-free, mathematical, and syllogistic confusions are at the foundation of nearly all economic discussion. The unsustainable premise of demand being the force, and the explanation, while also being the field function is like saying that the electricity is the electricity and the magnet is equal to zero and also infinity which is equal to electricity too. Modern economics is utterly corrupted by the practitioner's convention of using these asserted quantities and mythical fields interchangeably, and also together in the same equations with assuming definitions and excepting conditions.

When using thermodynamic science in economics, marginal analysis is ignored. Entropic values show demand is merely the emergent color of matching everything. Potential energy and other energies generate all the useful information from thermodynamic reactions. The people, their workplace and their system (government) have the common carbon-based element, and they are energy in the form of people matter. The political economy is the space hosting a thermodynamic reaction of these people, it is powered by a trust in the redemption of their currency issued in good faith. It trades with the future in time and learns from the trade how to appropriately evolve living in the present, from the past.

Demand is like the steam from a kettle that describes boiling, without explaining it. Using thermodynamics, we say that demand is irrelevant, because it is neither an element in the reaction nor a State variable (P, V, Q, S) affecting the production, so demand to this new economics is neither a coefficient or a field.159 The Stanford encyclopedia calls the demand admired by classical economics; the observer - observing, and absurd.

Entropy and Time

Having dismissed demand, ideally, we could segue to a thermodynamic explanation of wealth, but let us discuss the familiar concepts of demand to recommend further, the fit and superiority of entropic information over demand-talk for economics.

It is understood that a desire for things creates a demand for them, which is a supposed force on the economy. Classical economics tells that the demand force is brought into equilibrium with supply by a rising price. Now let us consider a superior discussion of market price and the value of things demanded and supplied.

Take our desire for a real house. Part of this desire is the apparent motivation of wanting a place to sleep and eat. However, the more substantial part of our desire is for a home. Desire, when crudely converted to value by the market, becomes price. The familiar example of a home price, being seventy percent higher than the replacement value of a real house, is explained in thermodynamics as it was by Henry George in 1850, he said the majority of the actual physical house price, is the subjective metaphysical home price.

The amount of energy dispersed (not found in the building cost) energizing desire for the home is the entropy (S) made from societies effort, expressed as the desire for the home added to the house value. Thus, thirty percent of the market price represents work (W) for the house, and seventy percent represents the entropy (S) made from earlier work, now priced as the home portion of the market price.

Entropy and Work are both the effects of an investment in the system. The difference between the house price and the home price is what Thoth measured as time.

The engineer will explain the market price of a house in an established neighborhood by saying, that a previous generation did civic work to make its neighborhood beautiful, the home buyer is paying the ancestors for their making of the neighborhood. When the ancestors worked, they created the entropy we are paying for in the home price.

He will further explain, that a home price is nothing more than our redeeming of currency issued many years ago to the builders of the public place. The predecessors were a trusting society working in good

327

faith, and they issued their currency against the work we now value. That is the meaning of Money, and why it is said that it was issued in good faith because it was issued to honest people, who did the work they were trusted to do. Honest people in the past got money by keeping their promise; they were trustworthy, they got credit. The honest ancestor gave reason to trust in the quality of their civic work, they *made faith* into the building and trusted that their currency would be redeemed. That faith is what the present generations home buyer recognizes as value.

Here we are talking about public works performed by a past municipality, but we should intuit that this discussion of entropy is inclusive of the civil society (the past establishment of good manners) that accommodated the work as it was done. That not-useless work done by mothers in the home, that imbued the future with a respect for value.

An ill-mannered, future generation might not have the wit to appreciate their legacy and may have the gall, to not redeem our currency. Here we have a hint, at the importance of community, and the value of parenting captured in the entropy variable by the engineer. Good parenting, to an engineer using thermodynamics and seigniorage, has value because good parenting is a *currency hedge* useful for trading with the future. Here is another example, of the usefulness of science to sociology and economics.

The engineer will explain the market price of a house in a new neighborhood, not surrounded by established trees, paved roads, and not serviced by schools, is higher than the replacement value of the house built, as the future. He will say, the work in this neighborhood; is to be done, you are paying the Net Present Value, of the entropy to be spent. Children are being born far away; they will be joining us, we are issuing the currency now in good faith for civil works, that will be redeemed in the future.

The engineer will always distinguish, the replacement value of the house as the Work (W) and, the value of the home, its entropy (S). He will say of the two; entropy is the more critical, not just because it is three standard magnitudes greater in value, but because it is a State variable, and it values the surrounding system supplying the energy that gives the house value.

Entropy is the most of what we achieve, and the all we can wish for.

As a rule, all machines that use energy to perform work, including the human body achieve barely thirty percent efficiency. The housing market shows the same efficiency ratios as the human body, and a Formula 1 race car (30%). Doctors should be looking at the patients' entropy, not their thirty percent product manifesting as strength, or sickness.

The environment sustains living things. The senior partner of a professional firm nurtures the partners' surroundings and ignores the work they do because it is their business, not his. This commonplace observation teaches the second law of thermodynamics to all professionals.

Both the economist and the doctor should wish never to see the patient and be a redundant practitioner of things and people. An engineer will improve the town for the President by building a bridge, and make himself redundant.

Idleness is the result of entropy, and a measure of wisdom. Work is the penance of stupidity, and stupidity is often the requirement of work. The doctor works hard in the community with a poisoned water source, and a dangerous river crossing, like the economist, will, and everyone else in the low entropy community that has not evolved, not made arrangements to live, not had the discussions that this paper prompts.

People are confused by economics because we sell real houses to people wanting homes, we make clothes for people that buy fashion. Clarity is restored by thermodynamics; it tells of the home, and the fashion, in addition to the house and the clothes.

The subjective desires explain the inflated value of real products, because the surrounding is their potential energy source, and it is more significant in the society that they are invested in.

What is the NPV of the entropy made with the work done on the pyramids, did the ancients issue their currency in good faith, trusting that it would be redeemed in the future, because of their building? Was Thoth

330

the bill discounter.? All of history is illuminated by understanding, the origin of everything valuable is in the entropic energy spent evolving.

Entropy is the value of the living system and subtracted from the misnomer of an objects value, it is the greater explanation of living, alternatively stated - value is made more, and lives almost exclusively in the nutrient-rich environment we have been ignoring.

What comes of entropy is a curiosity called life, a product of its environment. Explaining why the worst house in an elegant street is a great home, the land is the house environment, it is valuable because it is surrounded by community, accessed by public roads, and serviced by society. A sickly child is healthy - in a sunny clime.

The peculiar value of entropy to economics is that it closes the distance between the value of personal desire and the value of the physical object. Entropy is a measure of probability, not an explanation of waste. It is a measure that tells a currencies worth in the future, and that also values our arrangements in the now to accomidate the market of another place at a future time.

A doctor trained by a thermodynamic economist learns the value of "made in Italy" and starts measuring his patients' excellent reputation, as their potential captured in the entropy variable (S), and allocates most of his effort to addressing that information.

The economist of the future will appreciate that the value of things is relative always to their surroundings. If the environment is not enriched, the potentials will not be excited enough, for the time when the currency is redeemed, when they are needed to be valuable.

The effect is not the subject, because the timing may not tell what the subject will be. Directly, kinetic energy is made wealth from the potential in all forms. Whenever the whole is enriched, the subjects appear, this is the lesson from the Loess Plateau 1995, and why Voltaire concluded his treatise on classical economics with Candide tending to the garden.

Potential needs excitement, and a cause to be seen, because we only see movement, so we need to excite the whole to see something move. The response is to entropy, so if energy is said to be spent on follies like pyramids or education, those will be the benefit asserted, but only 30% of the reason for the currency to be redeemed. The greater reason will be the not-surprise, and statistically predictable effect of entropy making the kinetic energy in the future from something nurtured in the past.

The not-bonus from the effort put into children, will be the not-surprise of a potential enriched by the entropy, an entirely predictable dividend of the 70% of value appreciated later, and nearly all of the reason the currency is redeemed in the future for the 30% value given for it.

Initially, the quality of the spending in the present is irrelevant (to start the system), but it gets more important with the enlivened polity that the start invites; movement is only got from more. Generally, the what, when, where, or how of investment is irrelevant to the practitioner of this thermodynamic science, since; why it will happen, has now been explained.

Why is answered because a sincere society acts in good faith and leaves the garden well-tended, each discipline themselves with a lifetime of reasons to trust the future will redeem their currency, so their life's work is given the worth they got paid.

The Hard Science of Thermodynamic Economic is simple

The second law says that energy of all kinds in our material world disperses or spreads out if it is not hindered from doing so. Entropy is the quantitative measure of that process: how much energy has flowed from being localized to becoming more widely spread out.

Thermodynamic entropy change consists of two factors. Entropy change is enabled [in Economics] by the Motional energy of molecules [i.e., people] (or from a bond energy change in a chemical reaction)160

However, thermodynamic entropy is only actualized if the process itself (expansion, heating, mixing, reaction) [i.e., Work] makes available a more significant number of micro-states [opportunities], a maximal Boltzmann probability at a specific temperature [wealth].161

In lay terms, by changing the three variables P, V and Q explained earlier, the probability of an event could be made more likely, and that will raise the entropy value to, or above One.

Adjusting the variables in combination, increases the probability of the spark necessary for the explosion of Potential, to power the economic engine from within.

Enabling more paths (freedom V) for expansion, heating (Q), mixing (H), reaction (H) and outside force say - tolls (P), makes the excellent event more likely, otherwise said; increasing entropy S > One makes the spark more probable. So, we follow Voltaire and cultivate the garden, because by doing that we have a near certainty of a good harvest.

Laozi spoke of agitators and politics extensively in the Daodejing, and we learn from Russell, Power 1938, that politics is the tool of economics. We are suggesting here what political insurgents like Che Guevara, knew - but inversely. Feed discontent, burn schools, rob hospitals, attack public utilities, undermine community initiatives until eventually, a revolution is sparked by some spilled milk.

Political revolution is a small part effort, burning a school is a small job, but denying entropy by insisting on an investment return is a massive conspiracy that yields results. The energy put into a system is seemingly wasted for a long time, but none of it is.

God said to Moses "I have set before you life and death, blessing and cursing; therefore, choose life, that both you and your descendants may live" Deuteronomy 30:19

Anything created is a production, and everything produced was coming. The waiting time or the interval is the distance covered in the present by the subject of economics. What is told by history as surprising events, and in markets by exorbitant prices, is now explained by thermodynamic science as predictable outcomes of investing energy, or not over generations.

Work remains the measure of an economy's production (GDP), while entropy is both the measure of an economy's potential and an indicator of the peoples' satisfaction. Entropy accounts for three things; the consumption of goods produced, the destruction of the assets used (depreciation), and the investment of society in the endeavors of the future.

In time as archeologists show us, everything is used, consumed or destroyed, after the money was redeemed. However, at the time of production, when the products were not yet used, not yet consumed, and still useful, they were fully paid for by the money issued to people that made the infrastructure and spaces for the next generation. A sacked city is a destroyed currency. It has been fashionable to blame wars on supply-side economics, some saying war is for land or oil, but we should intuit a more profound reason for destruction, it is to issue a new currency; to stop the redemption of the ancient currency, destroy their legacy.

The ancient builders had good reason to trust the future would redeem their currency, because of the quality and sincerity of their work, they knew it would invite our favorable judgment of value. Ancient cities and wonders tell us today of those sincere people - and our patronage of them, with our currency - is us redeeming their currency, proving the worth of the seigniorage profit that they earned. This thermodynamic system was theirs, and it is still working, it is plain to see in a nations culture, only we have never understood that it was running in parallel with ours.

When a tourist visits the Pyramids, she redeems the builder's currency, she pays for their food and wine, toasting their achievement in a parallel universe. This paper denies the central banks universe and says a seigniorage currency unites the generations in a trade as our ancestors intended - always to stay connected. They gave us money because they knew it would be valuable in the place they created for us.

Reading entropic information.

Entropy is the most critical variable in a Thermodynamic economy. The above discussion has shown it will have many interpretations, yet none are conflicting, and all are useful. When used to measure an economy's potential energy, viral theory (inverted/derived working its iterations backward from entropy) can be employed to estimate a populations income, before any investments, or activity.162 That income will say; half of the economies potential - using viral theory (35% of seigniorage) plus work (30% of seigniorage), because efficiency is 30%, and that knowledge demonstrates how easily thermodynamic interpretations can be useful to economic decisions.163

The amount of dispersed energy within the economy is the primed potential, while (W) or GDP is its kinetic (actual) over time. The potential is correlated to - but not equivalent to the traditional economist's measure of demand.

Demand and potential seem equal from varied perspectives - and at differing points, in time they are manifest in analogous ways, however, the superior viral proof and explanation tell that potential income at one point is half kinetic (actual) with a half-life at another. All of that information is captured by the Carnot model deriving the entropy value (S) from P, V, & Q, and is proved by observation.

The periodic table of humans.

The thermodynamic economy's elements are people, collectively the society. We will now compare the person, and the whole population to the Chemist's idealized gas so that, thermodynamic science can model our cooperating at home, and our reactions exchanging energy with society.

Within a Carnot engine's cylinder, it's people that have an opportunity-rich environment (S) to produce work (W), in an area (V), under some pressure (P), because they are trusted by each and all to do so, with trade credit (H), and community support - seigniorage (Q).

While the gas has been asserted, the human has not yet been, thoroughly inculcated as the element that is moving under the conditions of pressure, volume and heat in the economic system. To complete the explanation, the metonymy of the gas in the Carnot engine must morph for the model, into the reality of the human in the economy.

To describe humans, a reactive element to a thermodynamic system, we will concoct the economic person, by using atomic cartography, and by attributing them a charge (energy value).

We will then allocate each a place on a periodic economic table with the whole population. The economic description of a person effectively atomizes them as an amount of money, their assets have a value, and an effect on their behavior in trade, their income, and annuities have a; Net Present Value and an effect on their behavior, as do their abilities and skill.

This crucial task will find the metadata for the economist, that the scientist has in the periodic table of the elements from Mendeleev. The thermodynamic model will show the economic-population responding to the stimulus of money (Q) in the economy, as idealized gas does to heat in the Carnot engine.

When the people have charge, here we will say income, they trade with each other under some Pressure (P), in a confined area (V), and the model will derive the economic metrics, enthalpy (H), entropy (S), and work (W).

The Atomic descriptions from 1960's textbooks sufficiently illustrate the construction of our economic man with demographic and macro data.

The 1960's atom is understood, as a galaxy with an inner core orbited by concentric rings of electrons. Where those rings are incomplete, always on the outer, the atoms will trade their electrons, to complete themselves. The atoms will be seeking security, or advantage, by using their ionization energy (a form of will in metaphysical language). These atoms will seek to exchange their energy packets (income) or be sought by other elements with similarly unhinged energy packets (income) on others in their proximity.

Mimicking these physical descriptions, by using the chemists' cartography, we depict the atomic individual with an inner core that would vary according to inherent characteristics (e.g., sex, age). The inner core tells of the spiritual ego, or the person's inherent energy, and is the equivalent of the proton and neutron. The (electrons) energy packets that ring the core are income sources, each packet has, a net present value (NPV), and since money income is energy in this construction, economic man is born on the table with charge.

The outer rings of energy packets represent the powers (abilities and skill) acquired by the person, by their efforts in education and training. The abilities and skill have a Net Present Value because abilities and skill attract income. A complete middle ring will represent the NPV of the person's possessions, or the NPV of a lifetime annuity from intellectual property, or tenure at a University.

An economic man has, three qualities of energy packets in varying amounts, each resilient, and susceptible to certain conditions. He has a basic annuity - discussed soon as a living wage, he has the NPV of his assets and the NPV of his abilities and skill (the income he trades for work).

When these individuals are in proximity with others, under some pressure, and stimulated by opportunity (H), they will trade their charges (income) with others, in the model, and do the same later in reality as the elements do for the chemist.

Some economic-men have more of these packets than others, and we habitually call them lucky or wealthy, because they are more talented and able than others. Depending on birth, DNA, education and luck, some people will inevitably have more electron rings filled, giving them more potential, and a different position in the table.

This theory does not advocate equality or suggest benevolence by any means. The descriptions will be realistic, and accurately reflect the NPV of each person's income, as a charge for the model. These values will give us immediately the Mass of the system because our only subject is people.

The hydrogen molecule, as an example, can be thought of as a child – missing an electron (has a low income). These children, therefore are easily influenced, malleable, soft, accepting, ductile and explosive, reacting with everything is wanting to trade.

As atoms have their outer rings differentially filled, individuals do too, some people like atoms, are less prone to use their energy to complete themselves by mixing and transforming, while others will take advantage of their electronegativity (a type of compassion in religious language) to relocate and even morph into their neighbor.

The choices each make, depend on opportunities, those on timing, stimulus and many other variables statistically calculated. The economist will deal with and treat large numbers stochastically, and with their table tool, they will have the same success as the chemist.

There is inherent energy within individuals, and given the development of science from philosophy, it is hard not to see how all of the taught chemistry has not been described by observing human behavior.

Chemists regularly discuss atomic reactions by describing metaphysical will, ambitions, physical need, compulsions and sympathy: they talk of some elements being altruistic in exchange, and of others repulsed by partial energies. Chemists even allow for randomness and free will in reactions. They achieve seemingly spectacular results, excepting that statistically - their results are in line with expectations, which hints at the usefulness of this science to economics.

A noble gas such as krypton, with complete, many and dense electron rings, might be a retired adventurer or philosopher, happily married on a self-sustaining farm, impervious to the goings on in the economy. The majority of people are between extremes. Those that display child-like behavior are situated closer on the economic table to the child hydrogen with incomplete outer rings, compelling them in the right environment to engage with others. While those at the other extreme, would be the older demographics, with sophisticated skills, limited needs, having the more, and fuller outer rings, they will be closer to the noble Krypton on the table. Hydrogen and Krypton, then, are the bookends. Between Hydrogen, the human child, and Krypton, the wise Sage, is placed the whole population, a society on the economic (periodic) table divided solely by, energy attributed meta-data.

Wanting like a talented teenager, they would be in the transition section of the periodic table, inactive they would be in the Inert section. Superior energy and risk-seeking demographics (periods in the table) will interact with others in different ways to other individuals with an alternative, but not necessarily inferior configurations.

The atomic cartography will have few rules, but strict discipline, the categories, and descriptions will use the data, in units of millions of people (like moles), and rely as physics does on stochastic's, to find useful information with high probabilities. The table will be dynamic, because people get older, and acquire skills, they change with time, and the table will reflect those changes.

Entropy and Time

The periodic table of people must account for everyone that classical economics ignores, else we repeat the mistakes of the past.

What is certain is that all members of the human species are an element within the economy, because their existence commands resources, whether they work, steal or bludge. No useful economic theory can entertain excluding portions of the population.

The current thought in economics is that at the point of non-participation in the formal economy, a person, or even a whole region, or industry is an issue to be dealt with - an external factor demanding supply. That demand has been an invitation to banks, or churches, to supply it as facilitators.

When these facilitators, impose on a system of trade, they behave like pirates, because they have nothing to trade, and can't participate in the system. Their excuse for being is the Jesuit art, of taking and of allocating within the system. Their impositions have been called Supply-side economics, by dilettantes, and are the perpetual excuse for interventions and bailouts.

Unappreciated is that services are produced only for surplus, when the surplus goes (no matter how small that was), the services are not produced at all (supply stops). The agents pretend this is not so, by favoring some producers with finance (to lower their costs) enabling a surplus; otherwise they import, both actions fix supply. The facilitators can, and do extend the terminating process; they increase welfare (creating demand) by giving credit to a government, and they grow imports (conjure supply), but these fixes eventually need another fix, a bailout too.

Most people mistakenly recognize the facilitators as political operatives, and their failure is explained, as nothing more to take, a snipe at Karl Marx, but it is; *no surplus to trade*. The facilitators from the church and the banks are the practitioners of supply-side economics, they remove the reason to make with their supply and stop a system producing.

Classical economics always pretended a system, by extending trade (making supply) and debt (creating demand). Predictably, those remedies ALWAYS end in a currency crisis, and with a battle over the hypothecation of assets (the security for loans).

As an observation, the winner of every war (not a crime) in history was the productive nation, the loser was always the one relying on supply, from an extended, and pretended producer. More interesting, is that productive nations do not have wars. A war, for oil or land, is a war for supply, and that is a war to extend and pretend - classical economic theory.

When the political agents are prevailed upon by classical theory, to make a fair allocation of the societies production, economics fails the people system it is explaining. By classical economics ignoring some individuals, and demographics, it forgets its two only subjects (people, and *their* production). When politicians introduce facilitators, economics stops being useful and starts being harmful to society. The problem always starts when the economist ignores the unproductive while acknowledging their needs, by introducing a facilitator to supply it. Laozi called this the cycle of misery (chs. 17 -20, 38)

People still exist when they are disabled, so they do command resources and will influence events. The non-participating are present, and therefore the science of economics needs to account for them to explain itself as a useful science.

The omission of some demographic deciles and industries has been a convenient crutch for classical economics because its theory has misunderstood the field - demand as an element affecting production. Unfortunately for humanity, the economist's stupidity has been their self-fulfilling genius. By classical theory portending the nonexistence of entire demographics when they are not working, we observe the unicorn of demand.

We know the groups of people needing and wanting, and that do not work, because those are the most carefully recorded of all official statistics. They are called the field force, they are demanding, and they act on society - through institutions, such as churches, and government supplying. Those Facilitators become the coefficient demanding production on behalf of a demographic (welfare) with finance from the banks. It is hard not to laugh at how pure the deception of classical economics has been.

The theorists have conjured a black hole force and made their equations work - with a coefficient - finance, taxation, and by a field - benevolence. A theory is no laughing matter, and not an academic quibble because **Two Hundred Million** people have been **killed by war**, in our living memory, to make the lie of demand right, with a supply got from facilitators so that the classical theory could pretend our wealth by extending our (collective) poverty.164

Otherwise said; by denying Says law, classical economists have proved their demand theories by effectively nurturing poverty and burdening the productive sector with debt. In proving their theories correct, the classical economists admit fully, with the evidence of history, that theirs is an unsustainable process, needing a bailout (or a destructive war), and not a system with undrawn potential, and a legacy infrastructure, and future resource.

**All persons on the Periodic Economic Table have charge;
it is given them with a living income.**

Historically before harnessing animals to labor, it was human labor alone that combined with Matter, and supplied all the energy to power the economy, and it was they that enjoyed all the benefits, which we now think of as income. Since the appearance of the steam engine, that energy is supplied by the owners of the fuel (property rights), and the owners of the engine (patents). The effect of the industrial revolution has been the redistribution of the exclusive right to supply energy away from individuals, to the owners of fuel, and machines.165 166

The thermodynamic model introduced here, insists that the entire population is counted on the periodic economic table, and also that each person is charged with an income (Q). The chemist relies only partly on the money pump (Heat sink) for the Carnot engines power, the operation of the engine is dependent on the elements charge.

Because the gases have charge, they can trade with just pressure and volume. However, because they expend their energy trading (H) under some pressure, they will not continue to trade without being replenished - from a heat sink. The enthalpy increased, or spent by charged elements under Pressure, in an area (V), needs a further investment (Q) because, elevated elements only react further - to changes. More of the same gets nothing more in thermodynamics.

People behave like gases in this model, because economic-man is given energy, and we can think of it as their potential energy. The scientists say Mass is the Elements atomic weight. In this adaption of their science, we will call their weight a charge, because the weight of an element is with a 10^{-4} error (negligible), equal to the elements charge.167

In atomic terms, we will say our human elements have a skill that they can trade with another, and that skill is an energy packet (an electron) in the model. The energy packet is called income in the real economy.

The basket weaver proves that things are made without investment, an economy can be a system of trade with no investment, but it will have a

Entropy and Time

low enthalpy, and the charged elements will eventually be overwhelmed by pressure, or escape the area V, and the system will stall.

The inherent charge in the elements and the heat sink together are both necessary for the engine to cycle. If the elements have no charge, the heatsink will make a once only transfer of heat to the elements, and that would be followed by an entropic shrinkage, producing work or waste from the element once. That was a thermodynamic description of a mob robbing the supermarket. A process - not a system.

Each element on the periodic economic table has charge; our elements are people, if we are to use the science, we have to apply it. A child needing his teeth fixed needs money to generate enthalpy (a trading relationship) with a dentist.

We have said that the people give each other trade credit, but that also the heat sink is supplied with fresh money through seigniorage. The dentist will not give the child needing his teeth fixed credit, so the child will need to be perpetually charged with an income packet by a portion of that seigniorage money. The child is given an income so that he is manifest in reality with the periodicity demanded by the model. Only by being charged can the child attract a spontaneous reaction from the dentist.

The living wage is a hot demand; however, popularity has played no part in suggesting the necessity of the living wage, the science of thermodynamics insists on what common sense intuits - the elements need to be charged for them to exist in the system.

The charged child gets work from the dentist because he has money. The child belongs in society, and with a charge, he is acknowledged, a free actor, not needing an outside force like a parent, church, or government to pretend his positive right to demand the dentist's attention, he appropriately attracts the dentist's energy with his money given to enable him.

People inherently have potential, and wherever they do not, they can be charged with money as a battery is, to make acid useful. Like barren ground has potential given investment, people invested in, become a potential too, charged by being given money. Only by being charged does their potential exist for a trade to make the economic dynamo work. The Child is the next generation; he will one day redeem the currency issued him. In effect, it costs nothing to pay the child, he will one day work for the money he spent at the dentist, but he will do his work in the future.

Since an idealized people are here, imagined comparable to an idealized gas. Then in effect the model of the laboratory will force the reality of society, because the charge given each as a living wage, is a real energy given in the form of money, that will make others react to them in the real economy as gas molecules do with their molecular others, in a Carnot engine.

The actual economy will tend towards the model; because everyone is charged (with money), he or she will behave with the freedom of molecules-charged, and move spontaneously with the attractions of energy. The thermodynamic economy is itself a perfect example of creation; the model is thought into physical existence from its potential as an idea.168

The evolving people need a perpetual source of energy to live in a system like a sun shines to sustain life, people need an income to remain alive to the economy of the honest society, without crime or deceit. Therefore, we give everyone a living wage in the thermodynamic economy, and enjoy the productive system of community, without fear of demand, or want of supply.

The living wage is an annuity for life; there are no conditions. Women from childbearing age will receive a further 30%, for life and forgo all gender rights in the workplace.169

The question of affordability is not dismissed, but the purpose of this paper is to explain the application of science to economics, and not to agitate political agendas. Affordability is not a question that arises in Thermodynamics, because everything is affordable. Without being idealistic, there are no debts, the interest burden on a typical G20 country today would pay the living wage ipso facto. Nation building will concentrate early on electricity generation; power bills will be cut in half. Without a finance sector to bid houses up with debt money, housing costs will be cut in half, and drop further with new builds, on free land. There will be no transaction costs or compulsory education; insurance will be unnecessary and illegal. The efficiencies in the thermodynamic economy are such that the living wage will be continuously raised to incentivize early retirement or to incentivize lower paid but more attractive work choices in nation-building projects.

The science of economics operates as a refrigerator.

Many products are components of others, so for the simple Carnot engine to model a system that consumes its product, it will have a modification. The Thermodynamic system that works to work is called a refrigerator; engineers model those by using two identical Carnot engines running side by side, one feeding the other working. The first engine takes in heat and produces useful work, which assists the second. The first is the donkey that supplies the second engine with an additional energy source. The second-linked Carnot engine describes the Nation's economy. This model is sometimes said a reversed Carnot.170

We have so far, expanded the understanding of money such that it is the measure of energy, defined humans with atomic cartography, charged the human elements with an analog of chemical or electrical energy (the living wage), and adopted the refrigerator configuration of two Carnot engines to explain a society cooperating. By doing these four things, we have reimagined the discipline of economics, as a model proved by the physical science of Thermodynamics.

The model will show that under conditions of some Pressure (P), freedom (V) and a steady money input (Q), the system will do work (W) create entropy (S), and invigorate its constituent's enthalpy (H).

Now using the science to interpret a typical G20 economy, we will see; the pressure index (P) reflecting the imposts of capital and taxation, and say - there is a burden on the population measured by the P value. We will observe a V value, and say; the elements are, constrained or not by; regulation, ownership, patents, and say, the people have not enough freedom to interact, or not. We would use the changes in the money supply to learn the (Q) value, and by interpreting changes, from past periods, know the measure of entropy (S), and start discussing the worth of future investments. As an aside we would recognize asset bubbles past in the money supply.

We could then run a comparative model by changing the variables P, V & Q, and for the first time in economic discourse, we would know the extent of the opportunities lost, or not in the current system. We will have the ability to compare theories without live trials, and have an invitation to Nation build. The polity will have an alternative path to the only known from classical economics - bailout, debt, and war.

What is the Money

The thermodynamics tell what every mother knows, 'the boy's potential will be discovered' in time.

Money has been deliberately discussed here as potential energy, because the promise of its redeeming, invites work in the future. The appearance of money, therefore, makes energy by getting work later. Money is potential energy with a Net Present Value from kinetic energy (work) in the future.

However, the opportunity to issue money - by seigniorage from the heat pump, is only available to the good-faith society. A sincere and honest society can issue currency by seigniorage because it gives itself a reason to believe or trust that the next generation will redeem its currency.

The good faith society issues currency only to invest in work that will benefit the future generation, so they trust their decedents to redeem it, and because they build and act in good faith, the money is partly backed by the built and has a value in the future. We need not further intuit how money is potential energy and converted to work later because, a grateful future will honor its legacy.

The sins of the father will not be paid (redeemed) in the future. We are discussing the well-established principle of Odious debt in parallel. The principle of odious debt is merely the enunciation of reality. The debt that did not benefit the liable is an odious one and therefore voided. A debt nullified is more definitive than timidly saying; *cannot be paid, won't be paid*, we are saying that money issued to the future, won't be redeemed if it does not benefit the person working for it, and this assertion is a rare congruence of logic and justice with a law of nature.

Here we say the currency issued in lousy faith will not be redeemed. For the last 100 years according to the Bank of England, ninety-seven percent of all debts have been incurred, with the issuance of money, and we are saying here what our current law agrees.171 It was fraudulent at issue, and no sensible person could expect payment since the law says it need not be paid, and common sense says it will not be.

This paper is announcing a new model, it must warn of its limits with examples of history, and clear the path for its implementation. A precondition of the new system is that debts of the Templar type be called Odious according to their current legal description. In the New system, there is a method to trade our currency with the future, it is a market, but it only works if default on bad-faith currency (debt) has a price. Default gets a price when the law is enforced. When the law is enforced, money is issued in the present with good faith; otherwise, it will lose its value. Details follow.

What does a Government do?

A thermodynamic explanation tells of the exchange of energies by elements under certain state constraints of pressure, volume and heat, it explains all interactions of energy and is surprised by none. The allowance of polluting arbitrary processes into conventional models explains the failure of contemporary economic theory.

The physical system of predictable thermodynamic reactions interpreting the exchange of energies only fails when uncharged elements get inside the thermodynamic system (putting a magistrate into a neighborhood, is like throwing grit into the cylinder of an engine).

Political forces belong changing the Pressure, Volume and Heat conditions, they have a valid role manipulating those variables, deciding on investments, tolls, and boundaries, but not in the system, trading.172

If the model is run with uncharged elements, say a priest or a magistrate, then more investment is required to produce the GDP. The elements with a charge that have purpose are burdened from the inside by the zombie elements (like dirty fuel). Initially, the additional heat required (as an investment) to support the Zombies is sourced from a wealth reserve (heat sink Q). However, once these reserves are exhausted, and they will be because the honest society will not issue currency against waste. The system is corrupted by friction and is unsustainable.173

The wealth reserve (heat pump) is the community's goodwill (potential energy) existing from time immemorial as a type of commons. It is a reservoir of trust. When emptied, it cannot be filled, without social upheaval.

Where a foreign body is admitted to the economy that has no explanation in the model, the force is ejected, it will be seen by a falling enthalpy, during a period of low GDP and high investment.

The everyday activities of government that require mediation are unnecessary in a thermodynamic system. In a Carnot engine, the elements behave spontaneously by being attracted and repulsed,

Entropy and Time

according to their potential and charge. Wherever purported forces (positive rights) acknowledged, the thermodynamic system stops living like an ant farm does on energy, and starts looking like the dollhouse of Keynes that requires assistance from outside its boundaries to elicit movement within.

How is Money destroyed like energy? Who is Gessell?

Money is issued in good faith only if it is accepted in trust that the issuer acted in good faith. It is circulated in good faith trusting again that it will get a service (work) in the future. Therefore, money is energy, because it is exchanged for work. If money is in reality energy, then it will demonstrate evidence that it has the potential, transition, exchange, and Kinetic characteristics of energy.

When energy is used, it is destroyed. How can money be used as energy, and not be destroyed? How can money as energy be backed by the services it was converted into, and still be circulating when those goods are consumed, or depreciated?

Silvio Gessell partly gave the answers in 1929. Money cannot retain its value as it moves through the economy, over time, and by use, money should lose its value by three percent each year (this paper suggests significantly more, to reflect consumption and depreciation). Gessell argued that money's purpose was to circulate and to circulate it needs to be exchanged for goods, and for that to happen it needs to be the equivalent value of the goods. Money cannot grow in value while goods go out of fashion, or deteriorate over time. Gessell thought money should lose its value at the same rate that goods do.

He made this revelation public at the beginning of the great depression, suggesting Money be stamped, devalued monthly. Deteriorating money would be spent while it had value, and not hoarded. Money had to demand services for it to create employment and fulfill its purpose in exchange.

The conundrum of too much money and not enough demand confounds economists. They say that; an increasing money supply, unmatched by employment is a recession, needing a bailout, rather than admitting classical theories planned process; to trick the producers, Keynes called it a Game [sic.] at Chapter 24 of his general theory (ibid.).

Since classical theory, pretends a role for banking, on the supply side, to extend its demand coefficient, producers get false market signals and overproduce for its ever-weaker demand force. The depression starts, when the pretended demand field (imagined money in the hands of consumers), prefer bonds, leaving services unbid.

Fitting syllogisms is how Keynes should have titled his book The General Theory of Employment, Interest, and Money. Keynes had to pretend the role of banking on the supply side of classical theory, to extend the pretended demand field. He as a consequence asserted the facilitator banks, could, by manipulating interest rates, appear the unicorn demand (now coefficient) so that the excess money created by the banks can bid for services (make employment).174

Economist, Irving Fisher considered Gessell's clearer thinking seriously, as too, did John Maynard Keynes, who said in his General theory;

Those reformers, who look for a remedy by creating artificial carrying-costs for money through the device of requiring legal tender currency to be periodically stamped at a prescribed cost in order to retain its quality as money, or in analogous ways, have been on the right track: and the practical value of their proposals deserves consideration ...The idea of stamped money is sound. It is, indeed, possible that means might be found to apply it in practice on a modest scale.175

Today, money is taught to be a store of value, so it losing value is opposed to what money is thought to be, except that Keynes gave the idea faint praise and an acknowledgment of an inconvenient truth.

Money is not an asset. Money is not a store of value, it is, in fact, a utility, it has the nature of a public convenience that is only used when it is; needed, clean, and trusted to work.

Gessell is anathema to classical economists, he is their proverbial elephant, because Stamped money exists in our pockets today, only by other names. Gessell gave the only known fix for classical theory.

Classical economists today call Stamped money a negative interest rate or official inflation. Sometimes they admit unofficial inflation, but will never admit stamped money. They will say that we have too much money, and not enough demand, and pretend that Fisher and Gessell never spoke. They offer no acknowledgment that the combined inflations and negative interest rates are stamping the money at 13% p.a. for the average consumer.

Gessell proposed a 6% loss at the height of the recession, today 13% is insufficient to cover the lies of classical economics, so economists call stamped money also, Quantitive Easing (QE) which is ipso facto, Stamped money.

Quantitive Easing (QE) is issued to purchase discounted securities at their face value. QE is, therefore, money stamped because it is issued for the sole purpose of it buying less than it could. The loss of purchasing power by inflations, and negative interest rates, together with QE and bailouts for bankrupt countries that can never repay, tell what the economist can never admit.

That money today is being stamped, and for the wrong reasons, it is losing near 22% p.a. in G20 countries in 2018. This paper proposes a monetary reform, therefore not so radical, it proposes - we issue honest money, and that it loose value, like it does now, but for the right reasons and more rapidly than Gessell explained in 1929.

Gessell told 'where money earns interest or is hoarded; goods would not be bid.' If the money supply was not circulating to demand goods, Gessell reasoned that sellers would be forced to undercut costs, to get sales, they would lose money and stop trading. Gesell thought this insight on the problem with money was the full explanation of the Great Depression. Gessell wrote a lively book, explaining that if money was allowed to grow in value by earning interest or even retained its value by being hoarded, while physical goods were being superseded, or deteriorated and become unfashionable over the same time.

Gessell never imagined that his proposal would have scientific proof in thermodynamics, where money was the equal of energy and therefore must be depleted like the energy in use. Nor did he imagine that by using thermodynamic principals' money could be issued in significant quantities as seigniorage backed by goods like trade credit, and withdrawn by collecting tolls, (taxed & destroyed, not stamped) at the rate of the infrastructures depreciation, and with consumption, without causing inflation, while guaranteeing full employment. For Gessell it just seemed to be common sense.

In the Thermodynamic model proposed here, the money will not be stamped or lose its value by stealth as it does now, it is openly withdrawn so that it cannot bid prices up for luxuries or assets.

Money is destroyed by collecting ground rents, and tolls, it is withdrawn from circulation at the same rate that things are consumed (22 % of GDP), plus that assets depreciate (4 %), resources are used (10 %) Utilities are used (20 %), wellbeing improved (10 %). A Total of 66%, the consumption and Utilities portion are withdrawn monthly, and the depreciation over many generations (using viral theory & half-lives).

Here we see the How and amount of the Pressure (P) value to the system and the role of the state.

The remaining Thirty-four percent of all investment by seigniorage will be circulating backed by real-goods, work in progress, quality infrastructure left to the future, and entropy (health, NPV of opportunities and well being).

In effect, the deal with the future is that the current generation keeps what they make, and the future pay for what they get, when they redeem the currency still circulating.

Using this model; the average household of 2.5 people in a G20 country with a combined income of $US 100,000, would be living in their existing house, have no debt whatsoever, income security for retirement, all bills paid, full medical cover, existing or better lifestyle, and be saving 34% of their income every year they work (which does not depreciate, because that portion is not withdrawn from circulation). They will have consumed, or spent 66% of their income living.

The polity will be very active with the new generations proposals for land restoration, ocean clean up, fast trains, reforestation, energy generation, hospitals, and electric car plants, because the society will be wanting to deliver quality proposals to the future, so that we can live well now. There is a demand after all, but it is in the future.

What does The Bank of England say about the Money we will abandon.

In a 2014 article titled Money Creation in the Modern Economy, the bank of England made a full admission that the banks have no money. There is no money in any bank, never has been, never will be.176

The banks have no money; they create it for the average man [sic.] (Keynes). Whenever average-man and or his government agree to borrow it, the bank creates the money, charges interest on it, and destroys the money (capital) with the principal when it is paid.

The banks understand time. They create a fraudulent asset and purport it has a value, by calling it money. However, it is not money, it is a bookkeeping fraud, they charge interest on it, and want it paid back. The banks then wipe it off their books as if it never existed. They keep the interest (time) the only value in the fraud, was the energy spent paying the interest. The banks then destroy the worthless and fraudulent money.

To be clear, we (not the bank) create money by agreeing to borrow it. This not-money and destruction of not-money do seem ridiculous, and the idea that this is the case has been a truth partially told by fractional reserve banking; otherwise, it is the ranting of money cranks.

Now it is fully admitted, and the Bank of England says that Ninety-Seven percent of all money (debt) is created and destroyed in this way. There is no fractional reserve banking in 2018 because the banks have zero reserves. *Ninety-Seven percent of all money is created and destroyed over time now in 2018.*

This fact is labored because this paper is proposing a seemingly great reform of money, but measured against the current system of money, the proposal to issue notes like we do coins now, and withdraw it with tolls, is a non-disruptive parallel system, that creates more and destroys less.

Henry Ford was alert to this money creation in the 1920's when he proclaimed, if the public ever became alert to how banks create money, there would be a revolution. Ford's observation points to the reckoning due, the status quo that has let people exchange their labor and guile, over the generations for nothing worth anything.

The proof of this extraordinary sleight-of-hand is given by Richard A. Werner, The Theories and the Empirical Evidence.177 Professor Werner's paper and his evidence are yet to be challenged. Werner suggests an alternative model based on the German banking system; this work supersedes his ideas for reform.

The thermodynamic economy functions partly on trust currency, backed by trade credit and real-goods (GDP), discounted in the commercial bill market and redeemed on payment. The commercial bill market is not enough known from history, as the real bills doctrine. It naturally facilitates exchange allowing the swapping of debts and the matching of obligations. Bills are settled with a counter trade, whenever an imbalance is too significant to carry. Carroll Quigley gave a good account of its working, and the importance of checking accounts, circa 1900 in the early chapters of Tragedy and Hope 1966.

In a thermodynamic economy, money is used by people on trust, as trade credit, or it is issued to people on trust in good faith like trade credit and called seigniorage to solicit community goods, and public infrastructure. This currency is issued to be redeemed in the future by the generations that will be benefiting from the goods and infrastructure. External imbalances are settled with countertrade, and internal imbalances with a distribution for work well done, or a penalty in the form of pressure (toll's) for being spendthrift. The mechanism for settlement is some optimum combination of P, Q, & H.

Seigniorage, in this form, is full payment for capital, backed by assets so it cannot be inflationary, so long as the assets are productive, or aid in productivity. The introduced money will always reflect the value of the stock on shelves and the value of the things being nurtured.178

The reform suggested by this paper is that; Seigniorage will invest in any productive enterprise. A Farmer, wanting new equipment, will have it funded at zero interest by seigniorage, he would pay back the funding over the life of the asset, and the money destroyed. The farmer does not have to compete for loans with more profitable sectors, and he does not have to pay interest, he becomes more efficient, as food prices drop with his costs.

The reform - taking the banking sector out of the economy, is in effect no reform, just an admission that their historical role in the enterprise of society, and in Nation building has been superseded because we evolved, and learned to trade with the future sincerely, and honestly too - with each other. We learned by understanding entropy that the present generation is with near-certainty trustworthy, and to evolve in good faith. To understand entropy, and do reform becomes, therefore the dream of the future, lived in the present.

A final word.

The thermodynamic economy is a system of agreements and contracts, where a myriad of people, symbols, and images, react to the Polity. The State applies some pressure, and sets some boundaries; these are agreed to, after that the parties to the agreement, contract with the next generation.

The play of society with the State is called the Political Economy, and the contact with the future is mediated by a Lorentz transformation and called a trade agreement in a single currency.

The Lorentz transformation enables the Political Economy to trade now, with the future. We supply the services now, paid for in advance, by seigniorage (the profit we take), and they will pay the extra back by redeeming the currency later.

The State, has a proper and defined role, in the agreeing with the present and we have a reason, not an obligation to deliver services when contracting with the future. The reason is; to give our money value, we must perform for the future, so that they will trust its value.

Admittedly this conjuring of money would seem a strange process, but the economy is a system, not a process. If the system soon to be described in full and working with the future is operating, the value of money will be apparent.

Simmel discussing Money as a substance (product of a system) said,

> "there is no possibility of measuring the size of an iron pipe and a given water pressure, but if both are integrated parts of a mechanical system with a specific power output. Then it is possible, under known conditions of change in the water pressure, to calculate from changes in the output of power what is the diameter of the pipes in the system." 179

The value of money is derived from a system that uses it. We have to start the system to get its measure because a system is more than its parts.

Now the final word on money;

The Political economy tells us the purpose of life. It is to be useful by closing the distance to the next generation.

There is nothing subjective about the next generations reality to us because we can only live well now, or at all, by making theirs worthwhile, in time. How, is now explained with a final instruction on the system.

You have now been given, the thermodynamic model of the ancients; the holy grail of the Knights Templar, was the Ancients nation building with seigniorage, but you cannot use it to get rich, without making a real and sincere commitment to the future economy like the ancient pyramid builders paid those buildings forward we must too.180

We are either joined to the future, living and thriving, acting with good faith, and trusting the future, by giving them a reason to redeem our currency; otherwise, we are surviving in the gulag, borrowing money from the Templars, and working for a bailout from the facilitators (banks & churches).181

Let us call the economy of the future, that our living depends on, Simmel's stranger, a foreign land. How to incorporate the stranger economy with ours? We first model it, say in 30 years distance. The modeling is possible, because thermodynamics is only interested in changes, and our economic period table is sturdy enough to estimate the strangers starting mass, which is the only necessary information to begin a trading relationship.

This paper has been discussing Economics as science, mixed sometimes with charge hinting at electricity, and at other times with Gravity hinting at Cosmology. The confusions, are because we understand gravity more than electricity, and income better than charge, the discussion of incorporeal society and physical production as a single subject has been confusing because it is by necessity across disciplines.

Now we will be clear, by saying; the common element to Astronomy, Thermodynamics, and Electrodynamics is Time. Each uses time, and we will now introduce the time element to economics, and unite all of the science by trading with the stranger 30 years into the future.

Entropy and Time

Imagine our relationship with the stranger economy as two planets orbiting each other in space. Their economy is Thermodynamic like ours, and say that we trade electricity with them, and the trading is in electric charge. The electricity, has value in money (it is money). We are the exporter of energy; we send it to the stranger's portal, a capacitor.

Now let us construct this, a Lunar system. There are two masses; one is the stranger economy of the future, the other is ours in the present. There is a distance between the two masses, both defined by their respective charge as mass, the sum of their periodicities (economic table). We turn the money pump on in ours - it works, and a charge (a substance) travels a distance to the stranger.

Distance is time, the money pump & work *stops and starts* in our economy. It has an oscillating frequency, the charge traveling to the stranger meets some resistance from the wire connecting, and we have a self-inducing Alternating Current AC. The stranger's capacitor absorbs Electro-Motive Force (EMF) at the end of the line and has a habit of discharging shocks back (interpreted as signals) if the time intervals of the AC frequency, are not smooth-too much, or too little. We imagine the signals from the future as a judgment of our integrity, and a check that we are doing useful work for them.

In lay terms; if we send too much money into the future, money not backed by assets, it will not be honored, our currency will be defaulted, we will have been dishonorable in issuing it. There is no bailout. Dishonesty has consequences. In effect, we live in the artist colony, the stranger in the future is the client. For us artists to enjoy a 100% seigniorage profit, the stranger in the future will need to value our work 200% more than cost. We leave 30% on the table for the future, spend 70% in the now, so us artists better be creative.

We can now say that our economies are linked wholly, to the stranger's influence. We can now know how to trade with the stranger we are reliant on so that they will accept our currencies value.

First, we will understand our relationship with the stranger from Einstein's relativity equations, later, we will prefer the more straightforward Lorentz transformations, because we have already acknowledged that Mass = charge. We will end using Coulomb's law, instead of the gravitational law and get superior results.

We will be using the work of Eric Verlinde cited earlier, and use his elasticity, and entropic work, to value our not-waste, and this writer thinks that we will turn to the early work of Oliver Heaviside on Transmission lines to tell of the limits to trade (the FX market).

How much force, or wealth we can enjoy, will be known from the signals of the stranger. How much effort we need to make and coexist with our abstract stranger in the future will be a known quantity. Our purpose to close the distance with the future, has a measure, and with this thermodynamic formula, and a trading relationship mediated by a transmission line, our success in the political economy will have the certainty of science and for the second time in 4000 years.

That future place, of Simmel's stranger, is the only that we are attracted to, drawn by and reliant on because only they can redeem our money.

It is a beautiful and scientific fact, that if we want to be secure and wealthy, we need only be sincere and honest with the future generations, such that they will accept our money. The celebrations at home will be glorious.

You are welcome. 182

Edward Brew 2018

ENDNOTES

---

1 Everybody's Political What's What? By Bernard Shaw 1944 Constable and Company What the f#@K is today's understanding of what's what, and paraphrased Shaw's purpose and intention in writing the book. He explains all of Politics, Banking, Money, economics, public-private relationships, class, society, and Shaw realized that it needed to be done in 1944 to prevent another bloody war like John Lennon said, 'war is over if you want it.'

2 Jean Hardouin 1646 -1729 Royal Librarian (Paris) made similar claims to Newton; history had added 300-400, or 1000 years.

3 See Book by Russian Mathematician Anatoly T. Fomenko History: Fiction or Science? Delamere Resources 2003 (series 1- 16) "nearly the entire part of the Scaligerian textbook of ancient history leads to a significant assertion that the period preceding 900 - 1000 A.D. consists of phantom duplicates. The originals are in the time of 900 - 1600 A.D." P.333 See also chapter 11 p.334 Authentic history only begins in the XVII Century A.D. The history of the XI-XVI century is distorted. Many dates of the XI-XVI century require correction.

4 Tenant #5 Chapter 2 Communist Manifesto 1848 'centralization of credit in the hands of the state, by means of a national bank with state capital and an exclusive monopoly' Karl Marx & Friedrich Engels.

5 Ibid. No reading of the Ten tenants of communism outlined in the Communist manifesto 1848 chapter 2, as 'generally applicable' to a communist society could conclude that they are not the obvious distinctions of today's 'capitalist' societies. One need only un-pick the fiction of private property through the lens of; the family courts, asset seizures of the DEA (proceeds of 'crime'), tax laws, eminent domain, the asset hypothecation in mortgages, capital gains tax, and defamation or personal liability laws, to see that property in land (private property) is neither real or sacrosanct in any western country - purporting to be

capitalist one (it is a fiction not hidden). Capitalism is communism is capitalism. Lenin called Communism "State Capitalism" and thought it an interim stage on the path to socialism.

6 Harmony of Interests, Agricultural, Manufacturing, and Commercial, by Henry C. Carey 1851

https://archive.org/details/cu31924030185056 Carey has much to say about the evil Eugenics (Malthus) at the heart of the Templar system (p.68,69, 234).

7 Characters representing large numbers and types - a mole is a measure used in chemistry, the Qin said Tiger, Wasp, Rhino speaking of demographics by character.

8 The English war of the Roses 1490 is an excellent example of the past not being the history. It was said to of raged for 40-50 years, yet there was only one battle, lasting one day, 3, or 4 minor skirmishes involving often less than 20 people and lasting less than ten minutes, 1 or 2 squabbles lasting an hour or two, and nearly nobody prior to Bosworth knew much about it. All up the war affected hardly anybody except some people in a limited area for a few weeks over the fifty-year term. The real war was between some academic genealogists with competing theories of rights, and some servant boosters were agitating for spoils & booty.

9.' GBS letter to Upton 12/12/41

10 Readers seeking further references from the Daodejing to the work of Hongkyung Kim, Old Master, The A: Syncretic Reading of the Laozi from the Mawangdui Text A Onward. Albany; State University of New York Press, 2012. This text is also available on Project Muse, which only accepts the best of peer-reviewed and the most authoritative works.

11 Erin M. Cline Two interpretations of De in the Daodejing. http://www3.nccu.edu.tw/~kangchan/readings/Laozi/Cline_2004.pdf

See also Stanford Encyclopedia of Philosophy; 2003, revised 2012 Philosophy of Economics, for a comprehensive expose of today's economics as jargon-laden pseudoscience. Mainly for the reader mistaken who thinks the economics taught today is either useful or proved. https://plato.stanford.edu/entries/economics/ This Laozi suggests a root and branch alternative to the current philosophy of economics exposed in the encyclopedia.

12 Lest any reader think that this is a claim too far, refer to the book; Staging Memory: Myth, Symbolism and Identity 2015 by Stepfania Del Monte. It talks of statecraft practiced old school in Libya by Colonel Gaddafi, using artifacts, history, story, myth, art, Gaddafi even created himself as a Confucius publishing his Analects in the form of a Green Book. Del Monte tells the Libya story of myth-making also undertaken purposefully by Mussolini to justify his colonization of Libya - the book tells the same story from both sides and is an excellent read.

13 See history of economics in the appendix.

14 The Jesuits had a conspiratorial relationship with the Emperor that is best understood as, they 'were birds of a feather' each rat (the emperor & the Jesuit) thought they needed the other, and both thought they had the upper hand. Most likely the Emperors were being managed by court advisors, who bought into the endeavor of creating the history to make the empire - always with the best intentions because intentions and agendas usually do accompany ignorance, Laozi will advise against having a purpose or an agenda.

15 A simple way to think of the hexagram tool is as Rock, Paper, Scissors. The game has two outcomes. A stand-off, or win. The Three choices allowed by gravity are; join, orbit, or avoid, the game has two outcomes. The stand-off, or win. Learn to trade with gravity by playing Rock, Paper, Scissors."Throw" the hand three times, and know the game originated in China BCE.

16 In the text arrangement of this book chapters, 80 & 81 follow chapter 66 Mawangdui discovery 1973. My reading of the text says chapters 1 - 36 are the pure science of economics summarized by chapter 37. Chapter 38 is a recap of the pure science preface to the second book. Chapter 39 -66 is the Applied Science of Economics, Chapter 80 is either the afterword, or prologue of the Laozi, Chapter 81 is the works summary, and chapters 67 - 79 are discourse and storytelling applying the

science of economics for further instruction.

17 J.M. Keynes Chapter 24 General Theory 1936.

18 Frederic Bastiat, in Economic Harmonies, explained this relationship between a value (the sum of things being wealth) and work (effort). 'If there were no obstacles between utilities and wants, there would be no efforts, services, values, any more than there are for God; and while measuring wealth in terms of satisfaction, mankind would be in possession of infinite wealth; yet in terms of value, it would have no wealth at all. Thus, two economists, according to the definition they chose, might say: Mankind is infinitely rich, or Mankind is infinitely poor' ('Wealth,' Library of Economics and Liberty, 1996 [1850]. Online at http://www.econlib.org/library/Bastiat/basHar6.html). He adds: 'Wealth (taking this word in its generally accepted sense) stems from the combination of two kinds of operations, those of Nature and those of man. The former is free of charge and common to all, by divine gift, and never cease to be so. The latter alone possess value, and consequently, they alone can be claimed as private property. However, in the course of development of human intelligence and the progress of civilization, the action of Nature plays a larger role in the creation of any given utility, and the action of man, a proportionately smaller one. Hence, it follows that the area of gratuitous and common utility [the commonwealth] constantly increases among men at the expense of the area of value and private property – a fruitful and reassuring observation that is entirely lost sight of as long as political economists attribute any value to the action of Nature' (On Value', Library of Economics and Liberty, 1996 [1850]. Online at http://www.econlib.org/library/Bastiat/basHar5.html).

19 'A Petition,' Library of Economics and Liberty, 1996 (1850). Online at http://www.econlib.org/library/Bastiat/basSoph3.html.

20 Cornucopia is the horn of plenty well known to the ancients as the purpose of a nation, often displayed on national flags. The vessel (cup) is empty, yet it is full; later this concept will be likened to a pool connected to a stream that can never be empty and will never be filled (Ch. 15).

21 See chs 2, 3. Buckminster Fuller taught that in time, all things would be made better through innovation, stronger from fewer materials, and cheaper with technology. Ever stronger alloy metals, and more powerful computer chips.

22 The term 'entities' includes objects and people, in any combination. People are attracted to objects or materials as well as other people (A. North Whitehead).

23 An attraction like love creates: it inspires images then it creates activity; Attraction starts the effort, to unravel tangles, blunt sharpness and soften glare (Ch. 4). In this way, the metaphysical attraction physically starts then powers production as gravity does. A thought is an object, and an idea is valuable, the bellows are a variant heat exchanger that converts one energy, into another with a value to production, a BOE and dollar value.

24 The Nobel prize-winning chemist Frederick Soddy asked 'How do men live? He answered by explaining what makes a train go.

In one sense or another the credit for the achievement may be claimed by the so-called engine-driver, the guard, the signalman, the manager, the capitalist, or shareholder, or, again, by the scientific pioneers who discovered the nature of fire, by the inventors who harnessed it, by Labor which built the railway and the train. The fact remains that all of them by their united efforts could not drive the train. The real engine-driver is the coal' ('Cartesian Economics: The Bearing of Physical Science upon Start Stewardship,' Lectures to the Student Unions of Birkbeck College and The London School of Economics, November 1921).

Energy is the sole subject of production, and that is the only explanation for movement - which defines life. Economics is production, which is our nation and life described - all are discussed through the portal of energy - by Laozi.

25 'For a finite-size system to persist in time (to live), it must evolve in such a way that it provides easier access to the imposed currents that

369

flow through it' (Adrian Bejan, Duke University,
http://www.topopleidingen.org/Fractalisme/Constructal-law.pdf; there is
also a good article in the National Geographic by Jeremy Berlin, May
2016, 'What's the meaning of life? Physics',
http://news.nationalgeographic.com/2016/05/physics-evolution-life-
constructal-law-bejan-ngbooktalk/).

26 Examples of the pattern are; sporting hierarchies and associations,
supply chains for manufacturing or commodities markets. Those
described; stars on ropes in the heavens and equally well by; chains of
ponds on earth, and supply paths in the workplace.

27 Ch. 10 of the Tao is well understood, even fully translated by
Rudyard Kipling, in his poem If ('Brother Square-Toes'—Rewards and
Fairies). Kipling's If is almost to Taoism what the Lord's Prayer is to
Christianity: its themes are trust, preparedness, and effort. Each line of If
has a reference to the Tao Te Ching, most of them to the content of Ch.
10, which is similar to Ch. 68.

28 The Apostle Peter did not want Jesus to wash his feet, so he
stopped Jesus. He stopped the provision of a service. He prevented
something that was to happen - for free, because he had his ideas and
designs, while Mary Magdelaine let it happen - she got production, by
allowing it.

29 Laozi thinks of creation as having sex with the female in the
missionary position: the female is accomodating.

In the book Temple of Man by R.A. Schwaller de Lubicz, the author
was mistaken about The Luxor temple. It was -the Temple of a woman.
Schwaller got nearly everything else right, excepting its purpose was to
model the economy, the woman is the model of production. The Luxor
temple of Woman has the identical layout to that of Beijing's Hidden
City, the emperor's palace is perhaps more complete as Woman because
the creek flowing across its entrance are the woman's ovaries. The
Temple is the model of the state focused on production - in architecture.

The only difference between Luxor & Beijing is the Egyptian representation is more anatomically accurate, whereas the Chinese one is stylized. The Beijing woman is more abstract like a Chinese tiger is less anatomically correct than an Egyptian lion. See more on Luxor & China model, footnotes Ch.19.

30 (chs. 2, 3) (see 'Martin Heidegger', Stanford Encyclopaedia of Philosophy, 12 October 2011, online at https://kvond.wordpress.com/2009/02/18/heideggers-hammer-the-pleasure-and-direction-of-the-whirr/).

31 Theodore Adorno and Max Horkheimer, 'Culture Industry: Enlightenment and Mass Deception' in Adorno, T & Horkheimer, M, Dialectic of Enlightenment [Philosophische Fragmente], Social Studies Association Inc. NY, 1944. Have made a book of this chapter, evident in its title.

See also the confusion of economics sorted by the sage (ch. 2).

32 K. E. Boulding, The Image: Knowledge in Life and Society (University of Michigan Press, Ann Arbor, 1956) describes 'the image' as the 'element' of production that Laozi introduces in Ch. 21. Boulding's work is a sophisticated explanation of what motivates activity, and he is in total agreement with Laozi. He says, like the Scottish philosopher David Hume, that facts or information do not affect actions, or motivate unless they affect the image we have of reality. That image guides to action. The image we have of things is resistant to change; it will stay between a phase transition of 0 and 100 degrees, regardless of information received, for a long time. The image is Laozi's actor (explained in Ch. 21), and people are passionate about their images. Refer also to the Society of the Spectacle by Guy Debord (1977 [1967], trans. F. Perlman & J. Supak, Black & Red, 1970; rev. ed. 1977. Online at Library.nothingness.org).

33 See, for example, the film Potiche, featuring Catherine Deneuve, and Legally Blonde with Reece Witherspoon as perfect demonstrations

of the Laozi workplaces and how to be successful getting things done. Potiche illustrates all of Laozi's three foundations (ch. 67).

34 Laozi, Soddy, and also Guy DebordSociety of the Spectacle, have all described economics as a space. Dubord - most explicit as the space between two planes. Their fellow traveler is Deleuze, says the economy as a place between two [planes] constructed as a sandwich - works like a sponge.

Henry George (footnote to Ch. 25) says something similar. All these thinkers describe the economy as an area at the introduction of their subject economics, as Laozi has done here at Ch. 14. Duality is explaining economics. Now Laozi's extraordinary claim; is that duality is a singularity because all is energy (qi). (Chs 7, 16,21,51, 63).

Debord crossed his constructed duality (avoiding the singularity of George, Soddy & Laozi Ch. 21), linking the humanities to the sciences as a sponge membrane filling the space between his two planes. Gilles Deleuze and Felix Guattari described the economy as a 'plane' in their book A Thousand Plateaus: Capitalism and Schizophrenia (Bloomsbury, 2014):

'The system of the strata thus has nothing to do with the signifier, and the signified, base and superstructure, mind and matter. All of those things are ways of reducing the strata to a single stratum, or closing the system in on itself by cutting it off from the plane of consistency as destratification' (p. 82); 'Then there was the system of the strata. On the intensive continuum, the strata fashion forms and form matter into substances. In combined emissions, they make the distinction between expressions and contents, units of expression and units of content, for example, signs and particles. In conjunctions, they separate flows, assigning them relative movements and diverse territorialities, relative deterritorializations and complementary reterritorializations ... Content and expression intermingle, and it is two-headed machinic assemblages that place their segments in relation. What varies from stratum to stratum is the nature of the real distinction between content and expression, the nature of the substances as formed matters, and the nature of the relative movements' (p. 83); 'Finally the machinic assemblage is a meta stratum because it is also in touch with the plane of consistency and necessarily effectuates the abstract machine' (p. 84).

See; Herman Daly's article 'Dualist Economics' (online at The Daly News, Center for the Study of the Steady State Economy, online at http://steadystate.org/dualist-economics/).

From Wu's translation of Ch. 14: 'These three attributes are unfathomable; therefore, they fuse into one ... the unnamable moves on ... and returns beyond the realm of things ... we call it the formless form, the imageless image'; and Lau's: 'These three are confused and are looked on as one ... dimly visible, it cannot be named and returns to that which is without substance.'

35 For Laozi, speaking of the 'ancients' with reverence is not ancestor worship, but rather an acknowledgment that things were better in the past. Society has regressed. The Daodejing has an authority that suggests its use at an earlier time. Laozi is not a dreamer of utopias: he seems a practical man who is more likely a reliable witness ('I will describe them from observation') – hence his authority.

36 Entropy: 'The term available in this definition has the same meaning as in the second law of Thermodynamics, which divides energy into two categories, useful, available or free energy, and useless, unavailable, or bound energy, the latter also being designated entropy ... that kind of energy is available [and] which tends to transform itself into other forms' (Frederick Soddy, Wealth, Virtual Wealth and Debt, 1926, ch. IV).

37 'Did you,' so he asked him at one time, "learn that secret from the river; that there is no time?' Vasudeva's face was filled with a bright smile. 'Yes, Siddhartha,' he spoke. 'It is this what you mean, isn't it. That the river is everywhere at once, at the source and at the mouth, at

the waterfall, at the ferry, at the rapids, in the sea, in the mountains, everywhere at once, and that there is only the present time for it, not the shadow of the past, not the shadow of the future?' (Hermann Hesse, Siddhartha, 1922, https://www.gutenberg.org/files/2500/2500-h/2500-h.htm; see also ch. 1).

Although Hesse portended influence of Buddhist teaching, nearly all of Siddhartha comes from The Laozi (the plot is Laozi's legend), including the substantial part of Siddhartha's life when he lived in society as a successful businessman, never learning, taking care of himself and retiring, and generally being very attractive getting rich without making an effort to do so, while defying conventions. Siddhartha taught in stillness and silence, just like Laozi.

The Siddhartha, & If by Rudyard Kipling, & The Prophet by Khalil Gibran (delayed he tells) and the Kabbalah (green tablets) each owe their active content to Laozi.

38 This and the previous chapter are out of sequence for reading. Read this Ch. 16 with Ch. 21. Laozi made no mistake in the chapter order. His oral knowledge is not read in order: most of the significant chapters, like this one, are located on or are introduced by Chapters with, or near prime numbers.

Chapter 21 introduces the factors of production referred to here as 'energies.' It is those factors, which include the forces of nature, that produce things spontaneously, using chemical reactions, heat or sunlight to grow and create. Chapter Twenty contains Laozi's warning that this chapter 16, and his explanation of the productive process will seem incredibly hard to comprehend, and he apologizes for it; saying that he will introduce the factors of production at ch. 21, those are called by him energies here. He will elaborate on the process of making, and the factors of production in great detail later.

The 'energies' discussed by Laozi here are what economists call - land, labor, capital, and entrepreneurship – they are atomized by Laozi to the common denominator of 'energy.' As 'one,' these factors are described collectively by Laozi as 'energies.' Note that capital is not a factor of production in a feudal system (or in any other; expanded on later by Laozi). All other Laozi translators misunderstand these energies as the myriad of things, yet they acknowledge products being the ten thousand things.

39 'The continuous plane': see Ch. 14. footnotes.

"The stream" is as Guy Dubord's Spectacle - it is both a broadcast channel - media, and a highway for distribution, the Laozi is a very modern economics text, and detailed description of the present economic process, media, distribution, and public relations. Note also that Laozi is always referring to time, Time is the key to the Allias equations.

40 Laozi describes Production as a performance dance piece; he is describing production precisely as Hans Jenny did (Cymatics 1967); inanimate elements arranging themselves into forms influenced by energy Jenny showed it with sound energy, Laozi is saying people spontaneously produce by being attracted. Inspired they resonate in proximity - and arrange, and these arrangements themselves, and or the movement they cause are the things we call the products and services, those that we add to discuss Gross Domestic Product (GDP).

41 Frederick Soddy, Wealth, Virtual Wealth, and Debt (ch IV, 1926).

42 Digging For Roots ch.7 Realm of Numbers Isaac Asimov 1963 "What is the reverse of raising to a power? ...raising to a power consists of repeated multiplication, the reverse consists of a repeated division. Why root? Well, 32 grows out of a foundation of 2's and 81 out of a foundation of 3's (n.b. the Daodejing has 81 chapters) as a plant grows out of a foundation of roots. ...the numbers containing roots are radicals, ... The Chinese knew the square of each side of a right-angled triangle summed equaled the square of the Hypotenuse - 600 years before Pythagoras and so did the Egyptians."

Why is this relevant? Because this chapter describes making, or multiplication in the Fibonacci sense - The Fibonacci sequence describes growth - production, or work, while - returning to the roots describes -

going home from work or rest, as does the book of the dead. The norm is to be rooted.

Laozi was an economist, he spoke in mathematics. The Hypotenuse is greater than the sum of the parts. It is the product of making, (production) economics done well is more than the sum. The production comes from the roots. The constants squared; make more multiplied together.

43 The great concern of kings is succession; to be kingly is to have a sense of time. Our time is limited; the next generation has the claim of physical things. "The social absence of death is the social absence of life" (Guy Debord, The Society of the Spectacle, p. 160; see also Debord's passages on time and history [pp 125–146] and spectacular time [pp. 147–164]).

44 We can only have wealth now by building the infrastructure for the Commonwealth of the future. We are to leave our legacy to the future and spend our income in the present.

45 Economics must distinguish between changing something and creating something. Wood can be transformed into timber, but creation is from nothing. Laozi explains creation from nothing as trust, and trust as potential energy like hydro and nuclear. Because Laozi is clear in his terms and definitions, it is easier to have confidence in the science given later.

46 In this context, filial piety is unhealthy respect for elders, slavery to parents. Paternal kindness is an unhealthy love of children, slavery to children.

47 'The whole aim of practical politics is to keep the populace alarmed (and hence clamorous to be led to safety) by menacing it with endless series of hobgoblins, most of them imaginary' (H.L. Mencken, In Defence of Women, 1918).

48 Here is the link of the Laozi to the first emperor's book of medicine, and a clue to the workings of the economic model in the Temple of Luxor & the Forbidden City. Health is privileged knowledge, the acupuncture and surgery are swift, for it to be effective there can be no fore-warning or signaling. Banishment replaces justice. The Exodus

describes a mass sophist banishment from Egypt. A draining of the administration swamp. See Sigmund Freud Moses and Monotheism 1939, for a complete explanation.

49To Banish learning is one of Laozi's strongest recommendations, he dramatically expands on this advice at chapter 65.
see 'Educating for dependence or understanding: Framing the debate on academic education,' Draft A multi-perspective analysis of; " We want one class of persons to have a liberal education and we want another class of persons, a very much larger class of necessity, to forgo the privileges of a liberal education" Woodrow Wilson (1909) by Tjeerd Andringa, 2012
http://www.geopoliticsandcognition.com/docs/AcademicValues.pdf for general background and an introduction to the work of John Taylor Gatto on the subject.
50 See Voltaire's Bastards: The Dictatorship of Reason in the West by John Ralston Saul. 1992
51 The commonwealth's assets (incl. intellectual property) are denied by education, so people are ignorant of their ownership; they include air to breathe, water to drink and land to live on, but also the currency to exchange. Nobody can own the currency; its purpose is to facilitate exchange. Currency needs to be understood by its teleology - it is a public utility like a road. Its value is as a free good and known on the basis that people will take as much as they need, which is more than nothing and all that they can use. Currency is an energy that exists in the commonwealth only by being used, it is trust, and it is a free good.
52 Dr. Richard Horton, editor-in-chief of the Lancet - says most medical research is entirely false;
"The case against science is straightforward: much of the scientific literature, perhaps half, may simply be untrue. Afflicted by studies with small sample sizes, tiny effects, invalid exploratory analyses, and obvious conflicts of interest, together with an obsession for pursuing fashionable trends of dubious importance, science has taken a turn towards darkness."

Dr. Marcia Angell, Editor-in-Chief of the New England Medical Journal (NEMJ) says,

"It is simply no longer possible to believe much of the clinical research that is published or to rely on the judgment of trusted physicians or authoritative medical guidelines. I take no pleasure in this conclusion, which I reached slowly and reluctantly over my two decades as an editor of the New England Journal of Medicine".

53 (trans. Pears/McGuinness, https://people.umass.edu/klement/tlp/tlp.pdf).

54 The Social Contract (Penguin Books Great Ideas, 2004 [1762], p. 43):

55 Composites are the combining of metals with knowledge and heat (substance, image, essence) in the workplace the minerals are made stronger, lighter, more voluminous, and more useful than their components. All activities in the workplace and the economy aim to achieve alloy's; these are the synergies that deliver the more we need than we do. Synergies are fairly won by a society based on a workplace (in a city with a legacy) and appropriately distributed from the whole (inclusive of the dead) in combination as more, all the ingredients are more when combined in an efficient economy based on knowledge inherited, and appropriate relationships (free of laws, barriers, patents, ownership). The production of the synergy (extra) in the alloy is also called a profit, and a Composite explains that as the value of knowledge - that not seen in the substance, never admitted by Stanley Fisher.

56 Modern economists assert that along with land, and entrepreneurship, capital is required to produce things. Children know on the beach building sandcastles, the value of capital, where the substance is free, and the (children's) labor energy is inspirational. Entrepreneurs know that only credit is required to produce. Credit is trust. A basket maker need only be trusted by a farmer to create baskets with the farmer's willow on credit; the maker requires no tools or capital to produce baskets. Note also the scientific superiority of Laozi's economic factors: as they are all energy, they can be measured.

57 K.E. Boulding in The Image (1956) said that people were not motivated by facts or knowledge, or for self-interest or any other reason, but by their image that they have of the world. If facts did not affect the image, nothing changed. The image is real. It exists as if it were a physical entity. David Hume discussed something similar: facts may not change the idea if the perception of reality is more important than the truth. Laozi's description of images is that of Boulding's. Laozi had a very sophisticated sense of people as images. So while we will talk about humans and people for convenience, the picture of reality that people carry is the active factor, not the person. The image is the thing that motivates, it needs to change, for excitement, to move the person. Guy Dubord uses the Image in his Society of the Spectacle in the role of protagonist, Gilles Deleuze, and Felix Guattari use the image in their A Thousand Plateaus: Capitalism and Schizophrenia (tr. Brian Massumi, University of Minnesota Press, Minneapolis, 1987); and as the actor in psychotherapy of Sigmund Freud.

58 Materials are resources, like water; they have no value except if priced. Resources only have value to an owner, where access is free so is the resource.

59 See Erik Verlinde's article and his paper explaining Gravity by Thermodynamics (http://www.nytimes.com/2010/07/13/science/13gravity.html?_r=0; http://arxiv.org/pdf/1001.0785.pdf). He says talking about coiled energy (elasticity) that stillness creates the force, the contraction after work is the gravity - or energy - the explanation of Potential.

60 For the Dao scholars - that energy needs proof - is a significant proof of this reading of the Daodejing.

61 Essence is Pneuma to Westerners; qi means the purest form of Pneuma energy to Laozi.

62 In Ch. 25, Laozi expands on the essence, in particular describing trust as energy. In the following chapters (22–28), his sole topic is essence as trust or gravity, potential, and kinetic energy.

63 Laozi understood production as a universal law. He was, therefore,

able to speak with authority about the heavens from his experience on earth. So, he explains the universal law of production to us using the example of gravity, but he only understood cosmology from his knowledge of production in a factory (ch. 1).

The fabric of space will be explained later as the money supply, and it is the currency that floats all things.

64 F =MA discussed from chapter one, is expressed now by Laozi as W = Mg Weight = Mass (the amount of matter) x g (the rate of acceleration due to gravity) Laozi has been discussing energy as a force, he is now discussing that energy - force as weight - Mass. He has changed the discussion, to emphasize Mass, and is using a different but equally accurate expression of force called acceleration a.k.a. Attraction.

65 Mass is not the same as weight, because the weight is a factor of gravity and gravity is not the same on earth as it is on the moon (or in water and on land). Mass purports to describe matter, but it is measured by counting moles, into weights, so it fails to explain the mass, better described as the charge. However, for ease of understanding, and for clear communication, this book will always talk about the better-understood misconception of mass as a weight. Because the existing perceptions of cosmology, and its laws are well understood-misunderstood. This explanation of economics is sufficient without correcting the established physics.

As an example - of this works usefulness; by using the established relativity theory, we can now say; In the Dao the currency is trust, and trust is the fabric of society like gravity is the fabric of the universe (because the Society is our universe). So, the value of a currency is the power or constant of gravity (G) affected by the mass of objects and their distance relative to each other. All the mathematics of cosmology is directly applicable to the new economics, later corrections of mass being charge will only make it more accurate - together with the science. See the Appendix model.

66 ...when the time comes, it will be with the necessary mass gained

from that experience (ch. 10). Skills come from elusive opportunities (ch. 14). Time is the measure of distance (MPH), getting some distance is another way of expressing the concept of buying some time – both mean; get some experience.

Note also that gravitas is won in the Commonwealth - playing in the park is an opportunity to experience, reminding that private land, assets and capital are irrelevant to the entrepreneur.

67 Frederick Soddy, discussing the mathematical impossibility of rent-seeking called debt and compound interest (wealth protection) virtual wealth. Lawyers know it as odious wealth. The question is Can assets grow at an exponential rate on a finite planet? Logically, it is impossible. Restricted holdings cannot back infinite debts because as Soddy said a farmer could not have minus one pig.

68 A house is more valuable in a neighborhood serviced by parks, schools and public transport than it is in the field without an open road. No amount of effort by the homeowner could make up the difference in value.

69 David will partner with a smooth, clean heavy round stone to kill Goliath, not a fluffy ball.

70 All decisions can made by join, orbit or avoid. All are valid choices. Laozi's economics is brutal and effective. An exchange or trade event is conducted like the Chinese BCE game called; paper, rock scissors.

71 The laws known to Laozi were gravity, diminishing returns, least resistance and thermodynamics (burning a stick is enough to know matter is energy). Laozi also understood that natures limits (ch. 23). Exponential growth is impossible. Life needs power it will be free, or there will be death.

72 Here a transitive relation A=B and B=C then also A=C, all models and topologies in the realms of heaven and earth are the same.

The maps of known ways reflect the patterns of the earth in heaven. Organization charts, set theory, any graphics showing relationships show the patterns of heaven. The relationships between suppliers and consumers; from mines owned by companies, transport owned by individuals, manufacture owned by partnerships, markets controlled by communities. All show patterns around centers, and chains of ponds leading to the sea (see Adrian Bejan's Constructal Law: there is a universal evolutionary tendency towards design in nature because everything is composed of systems that change and evolve to flow more easily).

73 Each transaction invites movement. The exchange we are discussing is not a barter because each transaction is primed by (fortune cookies) and assisted with trust (a smile). Something extra given makes the trade that supplies an extra enough to skew the crankshaft, keeping the movement makes the momentum on earth as it is in heaven.

74 Trust as energy illustrates static electricity - made from movement and stored in a capacitors counter-space. Some part of trust energy is thought by the Laozi to be an alternative explanation for entropy. Say trust can exist in a room full of poor people, now call it goodwill and observe the miracle that good things happen in that room.

Now say the room is charged with potential energy, and its potential produces good things because it is energy. The potential energy then can only be trust; it is the currency, call it goodwill again, and see it alone can make rich from poor. What is valuable is faith in giving and receiving trust in exchange is, therefore, the currency of goodwill.

Trust is the currency, and it is the fabric of the economy. Currency comes from goodwill, or faith in exchange, it is a thing valuable for its energy

Now see the room full of opportunities, and the people get them, say the place is full of radio signals, and the people have a tuner to receive. This tuning gains Energy, or wealth as currency, is experienced like food which is also energy. Wealth is a resonance - something that is heat producing; It is consumed, but amplified, consumption is broadcast - it is the ambition and purpose of a properly functioning economy.

Say if God owned all the things in the garden of Eden and all was valuable, so god was rich. What then if another garden equal in size was found and all was barren but also free, would you say everyone there was destitute. Laozi suggests the ideal state is the empty garden because it has more counter-space to fill with trust. There is freedom to move (there are no obstacles -assets - owners to prevent movement), and the garden is fully charged rich, and the commonwealth is a surface of opportunity, where images imagined are valuable for their potential, not a place of equilibrium that needs permission to move.

75 In previous chapters workplaces were called living pools, evoking images of chains of ponds, but now they are now likened to botany.

Mining towns and banking centers are workplace descriptions of societies located at Cape Town and New York. Manufacturing says Detroit, like motion pictures, introduce Los Angeles. The place becomes by the gravitas got from production.

76 Bribery is thought to be the transfer of an asset with value; a price given in the form of ownership titles, it is a convenient misunderstanding that benefits owners. Bribery is like inflation; it is treason. Corruption undermines trust, which is the foundation of the economy. Giving money (which is a token of faith, credit for goods on demand) undermines the society, and therefore it devalues the worth of all efforts, by making things more expensive (by increasing demand), it makes work never enough. Bribery with either money or items valued in cash is a form of counterfeiting in a society that measures its wealth by the value of the commonwealth for the future.

77 See Carroll Quigley, Tragedy and Hope: A History of the World in Our Time, 1968. p. 37-90. His source Power by Bertrand Russell Unwin books 1938.

78 The tragedy of the commons taught in school as the right to property; the sophist teacher tells the students that the greedy people overgrazed them, so the owners fenced them, and excluded the people to save the land. The real tragedy is that the people were excluded and denied access to the land that sustained them with all of their necessities.

Exclusion forced them to work - to work for their needs, and pay rent (or interest) so they could live on the earth. The sophists teach that people belong dead in the kingdom of heaven, and not alive on earth.

79 Here ownership of possessions (furniture, cars, animals, inventory, stock) is absolute. Possessions are not property. A house is a possession owned by an individual; land is property owned by the commonwealth. A tool is a possession; its utility is public property. As a rule, most things are in the public domain (Ch. 2).

80 The workplace is anarchy, evidenced by the black economy, the unheard economy and the elusive economy (Ch. 14). Every workplace breaches laws every day: people listen to copyrighted music, lift heavy weights, do dangerous things, breach laws in hiring and advertising, make unsubstantiated claims about a service, claim unwarranted expenses, wash money through legitimate business. Laozi pleads for reality. Laws are only enforced on the weak and never apply to the strong who ignore them and even change them for their advantage.

81 This model was implemented in full by the United States in the late nineteenth century. It is the early history of corporations and was responsible for the period of the greatest wealth creation in history. Rent-seeking is impossible without laws, and where access to resources is unrestricted.

82 There are many domains of men: the king has one, [and the market has another] (chs 25, 34).

83 Cf Heidegger's Hammer: a market is a perfect tool that is only noticed when it is broken.

84 Laozi's pet name for the market was the river. The (Dao) prices went left and right like the river because he used an abacus, we say in the economy - the prices go up and down in the market.

85 Singularity is where everything and nothing is possible, infinite potential, from nothing, or nothing and infinity. The market equilibrium has never existed, it is a coiled spring that can be triggered with a butterfly's movement.

See Ch. 14: 'Above it is not bright, below it is not dark.' In the market, there is no better or worse, no right and wrong.

At the village fete - the price is as you find it on the day. There is no reserve price, free is an acceptable price to a producer at day's end. Wealth is made producing not selling; income is produce not bought, produce, is income not sold, the net is zero in every market, so the price is irrelevant in a market at a time when all is on offer. Profit comes only from the potentials seen, so by acquiring not by selling.

86 Time, distance, success and trust (wealth) are all relative to the Commonwealth (and calculated by triangulation). Therefore, wealthier individuals can only exist in a more affluent society (ch. 2).

87 BTU - the amount of electricity needed to raise the temperature of water - a measure of heat.

88 This chapter introduces the applied science of economics, the de jing - the book of wealth (de is the virtue of wealth). Thirty-nine is the book's first chapter. The previous Chapter 38 was its foreword in three parts - a discussion of Chs. 1 - 37.

89 Hermes Trismegistus, has many names, and an uncertain origin, hence he is known as "Thrice wise" - the king of the world, he is Thoth - the maker of civilization in ancient Egypt, Laozi was the Pythagoras of old, and the first Alchemist/Economist. The green tablet that Newton interpreted is very similar (identical) to Chapter one of the Daodejing. Newton describes statehood in identical terms to Laozi, and Alchemy describes Laozi's subject - production, - he is an economist that understood how to make the nation rich, he was known at the same time as the Daodejing, or spoken of - this Author speculates that his texts - attributed are coded versions of the Daodejing. This interpretation of the Daodejing would be described by a scholar as a Hermetical reading because - it guesses the meaning of an ancient text from Hieroglyphs, like all previous readings of Hermes Trismegistus, and Laozi have done.

90 Neils Bohr won the Nobel Prize for Physics in 1922. In 1947, he was awarded membership of 'The Order of the Elephant,' the highest honor given to a Danish citizen. His family did not have a coat of arms,

so he designed one himself by appropriating the yin-yang symbol of Daoism. Neils Bohr said that the yin-yang symbol represented complementarity and the wave-particle duality. It fully represented quantum physics. 'If we look for a parallel to the lessons of atomic theory we must turn to those kinds of epistemological problems with which the Buddha and Laozi have already been confronted' (Neils Bohr, Atomic Physics and Human Knowledge, John Wiley & Sons, New York, 1958).

91 A traditional transliteration in English says the Dao gave birth to one; the way gives birth to Two. Here the Dao is the economy which is noticed as a movement by an exchange (resonance) of Two as one (ch.39), where the one is nothing without being Two.

The pyramid is the first thing that can exist in three dimensions; it is the minimum structure. (Buckminster Fuller).

Ch. 42 gives the minimum formula needed for the Fibonacci sequence (Golden ratio). One and one is two, two and one is three after that three and two are five. The series is enough information to know that five and three are eight.

Two is three because one is in counter-space. A Chinese joke on children is to ask them to count their fingers on one hand, when they say Five, they are told Nine because there are four fingers in counter-space. So, two fingers are three.

Fibonacci is an exponential mathematical tool. It illustrates the sequence of the one becoming the many (creation) which is the purpose of economics and what was, surrendered at a significant cost to religion.

Note also the yin-yang sign can be read as one small hole (a nothing), plus another nothing is two; together, reacting they have an effect on their surrounds which is a third. The third is movement -life. The three are whole, then plus the two added are 5, 8 and 13. This sequence is a frequency, one that is living. Laozi says everything is created by energy (ch. 21) by returning to the roots (division). Kinetic Energy is a frequency measured by a sequence that manifests itself. The Yin Yang sign are surrounded by the Hexagrams - tells that life starts with the relationships.

386

The other that said all of life could be explained (in this way) by frequency, and with the number 3, was Nicola Tesla.

92 The one becoming two, two becoming four, is duality, or binary thinking, which has been categorized by philosophers as the tree of life logic; the precursor to Hagel dialectics. However, when the Laozi four becomes 10,000 (his term for GDP, many, everything), it changes to a new paradigm. Richard Feynman described complexity as an onion, where at different scales, science finds unique solutions. Laozi was already there with Fibonacci (Buckminster Fuller, Synergetics, 1024.24, https://fullerfuture.files.wordpress.com/2013/01/buckminsterfuller-synergetics.pdf).

93 This process demonstrated by Buckminster Fuller has him holding two billiard balls in each palm, then clapping hands such that 'the joined centers' of each set of balls met at a ninety-degree orbital inclination. The four balls form a pyramid. Three balls make the triangular base, while one ball sits in the nest created by the Three's center. Please do this simple experiment and see the marvel of this chapter 42 of the Laozi.

94 The joy of creativity flows through you as effortlessly as your breath. From it the most minute areas of your outer experience spring. Your feelings have electromagnetic realities that rise outward, affecting the atmosphere itself. They group through attraction, building up areas of events and circumstances that finally coalesce either in objects - or as events in time.

Some feelings and thoughts are translated into structures that you call objects; these exist, in your terms, in a medium you call space. Others are translated instead into psychological structures called events, that seem to exist, in your terms, in a medium you call time. From Jane Roberts The Nature of Personal Reality (A Seth Book) Specific Practical Techniques Session 613, September 11, 1972, 9:24 P.M. Monday.

95 Walter Russell speculated that Two elements precede Hydrogen in the periodic table. Using this chapter 42, and 39, and keeping in mind that charge measures mass with an error 10-4, we can say that Walter

Russell was right, except Two is one, and one is a charge. Laozi, Buckminster Fuller, and Walter Russell then have a superior, and simpler standard model. Walter Russell tells further that the pyramid utilized by Laozi is a vortex; then Laozi stylised the vortex, there is always more to know.

96 '42' is the answer to the meaning of life, the universe, and everything in the Hitchhiker's Guide to the Galaxy by Douglas N. Adams. Adams gave many lectures to live audiences explaining the ground up construction of everything, a flavor of which was published posthumously as a collection of his papers in a book The Salmon of Doubt.

97 Bastiat's Economic Harmonies Ibid, p. 81.

98 The Translation by Wu has the sycophant lawyers and psychologists as the fleet-footed horses (clowns) banished to work in the fields. (ch.20) When the world is led according to the Dao, but when it is overcome by a kleptocracy ', they breed themselves' (by education) in the suburbs. There is no evil like them.

99 Alfred North Whitehead asserts that actuality is a series of momentary events.

100 Cf Kurt Wolff, 'The Sociology of Georg Simmel', https://archive.org/details/sociologyofgeorg030082mbp). Neither the Sage nor the ruler seeks consent or permission. See also the individual's superiority over the mass (ch. 31).

101 Here is a classic 'knot' for a Sage, and the significance of the insight of Hesse' Sidhartha. The river (the market) is everywhere at once: at the foothills, the sea, carrying the ferry. A demand economy plans production for a future that existed yesterday. It leaves time, and to do that it leaves space; in essence, a demand economy can only be a virtual one.

In reality, people can afford only to exchange what they produce. Price is irrelevant (Say's law) because the currency expands to accommodate production. Where the demand, is estimated for the future time and products are brought in from another space (a foreign country), no price is affordable, because no one produced them (in the real time, in the actual space) there is no currency. Here is the excuse for debt - it balances the equation that can't add.

Without the artifice of made up factors, economics as we know it - one based on demand & debt, proved by mathematics, fails. Here is a full explanation of how Capital and a banking system is a fix for the classical theory like black holes are for cosmology.

102 See chapter 2, nearly all of the vexing questions in economics are because of their posit premise. Problems that disappear with clear thinking, or need never be considered - sensible people ignore the economists (not-problems).

103 Trade: is a slave, blackmail, ransom, kidnapping, sex, drugs, and weapon thing. Trade in inventories belonging to another time and other places is a theft thing. By damaging the beautiful elsewhere and destroying or denying the abundance at home, free things are made scarce by rentiers to be expensive, and valuable things are made elsewhere to be cheap - this starts the cycle of misery in both places and simultaneously. Ch. 38.

104 Foreign energy is today's example. (ch. 46). Free trade always involves Two violated parties. Sugar trade was slave trade and opium trade, and oil trade today is weapons trade and opium trade, clothing trade is today slave trade and pollution trade. No trade is a good trade (excepting domestic surplus). Comparative advantage defines itself as an abuse of power.

105 The producer buys and sells in the same market, so the price (performance) is irrelevant in an autarchy (Chs. 34, 51).

106 All real assets decay (rot, rust, break) in time. Debts, titles, licenses, concessions, and patents, are not real assets, they are pieces of paper thoughtlessly given, and wrongly perpetuated with police violence. They are not real things and can be nullified by the stroke of a legislator's

pen or by creditors acquiescing to the impossible collection of an odious claim. The commonwealth restored in a single moment of sanity. Soddy and Laozi are the Authority, although Solon is the example.

As an afterthought for the incredulous Londons Mayfair has the world's most expensive property, and none of it is held freehold by the house owners. The Duke of Westminster holds the freehold, house owners pay the Duke (commonwealth) rent - this is an example of Laozi demonstrated by observation but well explained to a modern audience by Henry George - Progress and Poverty 1879.

107 Jean Buridan de Bethune (1300–1358) proposed a theory of money by presenting this paradox: Socrates gave his wife willingly and with her consent to Plato to commit adultery in exchange for some books. Which one suffered a loss when each gained more? According to de Bethune, there is no price in a free exchange because there are no losers in trade. It is good when it is fair, and only participants understand this. (ch. 14: the unheard component is the counter trade/barter).

Thorstein Veblen The Theory of the Leisure Class 1912 (and other works), Spoke of the Savage having reached such a high plane of sophistication of savagery that they were our superior.

108 The sophist meddles in the journey. Compare this instruction with that found in Guanzi's Four Seasons or practiced by the Christian faith, both have many sayings about enjoying the journey as a good, i.e., hard work. Laozi thinks hard work is a life wasted, and the path to absolute poverty.

109 A more literal translation of this chapter is a monologue continued from the previous chapter, a rant, perhaps, an example of oral knowledge in performance. This chapter has been paraphrased more than others for the reader's benefit. Here chapter 64 is 63 continued excluding the references to previous chapters already explored.

110 For a modern take on this chapter, see 'George Carlin's Greatest Moment' on YouTube.

'There is a reason, there is a reason education sucks, and it is the same reason that it will never, ever, ever, be fixed, it is never going to get any better,

For an economic explanation of this chapter, see Bastiat's Broken window 'That Which Is Seen and that which is Unseen' 1850 The Education system and its graduates break windows all day every day. In Bastiat's story, the producer was to buy his son a pair of shoes before his window broken. Republished by Henry Hazlitt 1946 as Economics in one lesson. In short, educators break the young and train them to break society.

See George Smoot Nobel prize winner for physics explain educations highest purpose; simulation theory; there are boundaries in the owner's game that we cannot find, watch him laugh about it at TedxSalford 'what I am going to try and do is convince you [that] you are a simulation and physics can prove it, ok?
https://www.youtube.com/watch?v=Chfoo9NBEow
111 [Comte de] Saint Simon (1760–1825) says that ' ... people are only educated to keep them subservient in meaningless jobs to control the population - Thus instruction cannot be universal, and most of all it cannot be free - It is necessary in order to maintain the subordination of the masses to restrain the flowing forth of ability, to reduce the too numerous and too unmanageable attendance at colleges, to keep the systematic ignorance of the millions of workers doomed to repugnant and pitiful labor, to make use of instruction by not making use of it. That is to say, by turning it toward the brutalization and exploitation of the lower classes
...When the working man has been brutalized by the division of labor, by attending machines, by teaching that does not teach, when he has been discouraged by small wages, demoralized by being out of work, famished by monopoly; when he has neither bread nor dough, neither cash nor credit, neither fire nor hearth, then he lies, he thieves, he robs, he

assassinates. After passing through the hands of the plunderers, he passes through those of the dealers in justice, is that clear...(P.J. Proudhon, General Idea of the Revolution in the Nineteenth Century, Second Study, 1851, Translated by J.B. Robinson, 1923, p. 58).

See John Ralston Saul, Voltaire's Bastards: The Dictatorship of Reason in the West. Laozi's educated eunuchs are 'Voltaire's Bastards' (Chs 18,19, 20, 28, 38). Saul gives a detailed account of education abused to impoverish a country. Saul argues that education is not a harmless enterprise, but a deliberate ploy by rulers to control the people and rob the country.

112 Fichte - spoke like Laozi in a series of lectures to the German people during the occupation of Napoleon. He told the German people Thomas Paine type common sense - Germans are good people, the people have power, seize the day, invent a better way.

113 History of Western Philosophy (Simon & Schuster, New York, 1947, ch 30, pp 827–828, http://www.ntslibrary.com/PDF%20Books/History%20of%20Western%20Philosophy.pdf.

114 Science dogma is; evolution, expanding universe, unbreakable laws, and constants, but it has 'inconvenient truths,' like; the earth is not spinning (Michelson Morley), The earth is not spinning and receives free energy from the solar system (Allias to NASA 1954) the universe is not expanding (Halton Arp) sound is faster than light (Tennessee University - Robertson), Charge measures Mass (Victor Yu. Gankin), Einstein relativity equations (Stephen Crothers) Blackhole evidence (none) The Aether exists (Michelson Morley US Army, Nature volume 322 Aug 1986 p. 590), No optical microscope limit (Sagnac 1913). Science also has dirty laundry called 're-normalisations' and 'paradox's, necessitating Copenhagen, and climate type consensus, a church by Nicene decree, complete with holy relics like Higgs bosons, gravity waves, dinosaur bones, carbon dates, and moon rocks. (very much where the church was at the time of the last reformation). Established science is proved with holy relics (facts) and by syllogism (mathematics), only on paper or on

television screens as computer-generated images, and it does not even pretend to be real. Black holes, Higgs bosons and gravity waves (now proved with a 28% certainty) are Disney type creations, chimeras, and unicorns that an experienced people - knowledgeable would ignore as useless.

115 "the hereditary propagation of monetary phenomena with a gradual weakening through time; the concept of lagged regulation implying the existence of limit cycles." The primary subject of the deal with time - a deal with the future - a thermodynamic economy explained in the Appendix.

Source; Nobel Lecture Dec 9, 1988, by Maurice Allias. An outline of my main contributions to economic science
http://www.nobelprize.org/nobel_prizes/economic-sciences/laureates/1988/allais-lecture.pdf
116 No disrespect intended to M Allias, he was a trained Engineer - not an economist, and he made a significant contribution to NASA, and to the French War effort.
117 The Two most essential reference prices, those that set the price of everything on earth, that determine the value of work and the distribution of wealth, are the price of Oil, and the Price of Money. The price of Oil is determined by a consortium of Owners, called variously; "The industry," OPEC, "Sanctions," Subsidies, Parity taxation, Controllers by any name, not supply or demand. The other price is that of Money; the same people set it the "Controllers" they name the price "Interest," and lend it into existence to prevent Bertram Russell's disaster and to prove the Allias equations if ever they miscalculate the discontent of the people.

John Maynard Keynes in his 'The General Theory of Employment, Interest and Money', explained "the game" played by the status quo to control humanity by education, that is to make a simulated reality of prices, facts and winners that seems real for the lemming players, to

prevent Russell's social disaster. From the concluding chapter 24, he said (observe his amusement) "For my own part, I believe that there is social and psychological justification for significant inequalities of incomes and wealth, but not for such large disparities as exist today. There are valuable human activities which require the motive of money-making and the environment of private wealth-ownership for their full fruition. Moreover, dangerous human proclivities can be canalized into comparatively harmless channels by the existence of opportunities for money-making and private wealth, which, if they cannot be satisfied in this way, may find their outlet in cruelty, the reckless pursuit of personal power and authority, and other forms of self-aggrandizement. It is better that a man should tyrannize over his bank balance than over his fellow citizens; and while the former is sometimes denounced as being but a means to the latter, sometimes at least it is an alternative. But it is not necessary for the stimulation of these activities and the satisfaction of these proclivities that the game should be played for such high stakes as at present. Much lower stakes will serve the purpose equally well, as soon as the players are accustomed to them. The task of transmuting human nature must not be confused with the task of managing it. Though in the ideal commonwealth men may have been taught or inspired or bred to take no interest in stakes, it may still be wise and prudent statesmanship to allow the game be played, subject to rules and limitations, so long as the average man, or even a significant section of the community, is in fact strongly addicted to the money-making passion." [emphasis added]
http://cas2.umkc.edu/economics/people/facultypages/kregel/courses/econ 645/winter2011/generaltheory.pdf

118 This is mocked by scientists as the 'Heisenberg principle' where the society is changed by observing it.

Kahneman and Tversky (Nobel Prize 2002) developed prospect theory which proved stochastically that educated people (we are all educated) apprised of facts are unable to filter them hedonistically or otherwise because they are confused by heuristics and biases [being educated & inexperienced]. (1973)

119 Frederic Soddy Wealth, Virtual Wealth and Debt 1926 Allen & Unwin

120 Scottish philosopher Alan Watts said sailing is the perfect tangible example of nonaction because all the purpose of sailing is to use the power of nature, the winds, and currents. Nonaction tells the general to harness the free power of nature, let it defeat the enemy.

121 An earthquake is always imminent, but the 'when' is never known. A rock sits on a hill for a long time before it rolls to the base. 'When' is never known.

122 is the title of an article published in the Journal of Aerospace Engineering in 1959 and the title of a book by physics professor Hector A. Munera 2011.

123 ALLAIS EFFECT' AND MY EXPERIMENTS WITH THE PARACONICAL PENDULUM 1954 - 1960 by Maurice Allias. The Allias equations that he won the Noble prize for are discussed at length in the essay following this appendix.

124 Allias later made Four equations, similar to Maxwell, that tell of public relations, and time lags, - explain Hysteresis in trade, and are the most useful indicator ever devised to explain, or that manipulate-otherwise create unexplainable events.

125 P. 588 A System of Logic 1843 John Stuart Mill.

126 There is said to be an 'Allias Paradox' in game theory, and an 'Allias effect' in Tidal duration, the labels gave aspects of his work by others were ignored by him and are here too. Allias wanted to explain what could not be, which is the subject and purpose of this paper.

127 See Adam Smith, The Glasgow Edition of the Works and Correspondence of Adam Smith (1981 - 1987) Vol. III: Essays on Philosophical Subjects. This edition edited by W.P.D. Wightman and J.C. Bryce has an excellent Preface which tells this story.
http://portalconservador.com/livros/Adam-Smith-Essays-on-Philosophical-Subjects.pdf

128 Stanford encyclopedia

129 See J.Van Evra 1984 Richard Whately and the rise of Modern Logic. History and Philosophy of Logic 5; 1-18. The Stanford encyclopedia cited later.

130 On Liberty was published by a desperate J.S. Mill in 1859, and Representative Government in 1861 both documents plead for the right of soft-minded women to select weak minded politicians that would be more susceptible to his brand of sleazy lobbying, to overcome the hard-minded establishment that had the Honourable companies measure.

131 The history of the East India company is not controversial, only not admitted in public. Smith and Mill worked for the sole purpose of the company; they invented the pseudo-science of Economics to get a bailout, and to keep getting bailed out. An excellent account of the company was published by the Guardian 4/3/15 An article The East India Company: The original corporate raiders, For a century, the East India Company conquered and plundered vast tracts of south-east Asia. The lessons of its brutal reign have never been more relevant. by William Dalrymple https://www.theguardian.com/world/2015/mar/04/east-india-company-original-corporate-raiders

132 see what the 2018 Noble lunette for economics has to say on the history of economics here; https://paulromer.net/what-went-wrong-in-macro-historical-details/

133 Voltaire explained all of what has been discussed here as classical economics, as satire, in his book Candide 1759 - "All for the best" mocks the logic of economics.

Winston Churchill admitted as chancellor admitted that Capitalism was a terrible system to a group of single taxers, and add "its better than all the rest."

134 Stanford Encyclopedia of Philosophy, Winter 2013. Daniel M. Hausman. 1. Introduction: What is Economics?

135 Economics: The User's Guide Ha Joon Chang Pelican Books 2014 p. 17 - 27 What is economics.

136' http://www.investopedia.com/terms/e/economics.asp

137 Stanford Encyclopaedia of Philosophy, Winter 2013. Daniel M. Hausman. 1. Introduction: What is Economics?

138
https://www.academia.edu/17446391/A_CONTINUING_INQUIRY_IN TO_ECOSYSTEM_RESTORATION_EXAMPLES_FROM_CHINA_S_ LOESS_PLATEAU_AND_LOCATIONS_WORLDWIDE_AND_THEI R_EMERGING_IMPLICATIONS

139 A thermodynamic system is, by definition, a closed system. The closed system is a familiar to economics and called autarky. Autarky is to be self-sufficient and not reliant on international trade. International trade is outside of the closed thermodynamic system.

140 BTU is the amount of energy required to boil a pound of water by one degree Fahrenheit, i.e., Heat.

In two steps one could adopt the joule as the standard measure for all forms of energy, name the Joule a Dollar and the baker could regulate his oven with dollars instead of degrees. He would be able to make bread & money from his oven - as he does but now more directly - with less complication.

141 Seigniorage issued the greenback; Lincoln did it, Kennedy did it, Jackson tried and got shot twice. This investment is paid for by the profit made on issuing the currency in good faith. Seigniorage will be discussed in detail further on; it is sufficient to know that Seigniorage currently issues all coins currently in circulation and exchangeable for notes. This model makes the modest suggestion that the State resumes the issuing of notes, from private banks, and issue them as it once did, and does today with coins - by seigniorage. It implies that 'we the people' will support our leaders trusting us with money, by protecting them from assassination.

Viral theory suggests a new Qty. Theory of money: Half potential x half-life of each iteration - so roughly half NPV x halftime for the period/cycle.

142 A Joule is a measure of energy and therefore also a unit of work.

143 Once the money is defined in thermodynamic terms (as heat), we can better understand what it is and how to use it. For example, as heat does not attract heat, there can be no interest (return on money). Here we have the first-ever enunciated scientific fact of economics: money cannot attract interest, because the laws of thermodynamics, now the rules of economics, tell us that heat does not flow to heat. They tell us that heat dissipates.

144 A product is 'a service anticipated.' Service is an effort. A ready-made suit anticipates the service of a tailor. Therefore, products are services. There is no such thing as a product; it is a service or effort anticipated - Bastiat. Products are stored work (Joules) convertible to money, as readily as fuel is to the same as the input. The language of economics is more precise by calling all goods 'services,' and the terminology helps to understand thermodynamic economics because services imply work and work is energy.

145 A seigniorage investment is a creation of money by the state to supply its infrastructure. Money is issued - or given like trade credit, for the promise of supply, this money gets work in progress and final delivery. Later it will be explained that it is withdrawn from circulation with tolls and taxes, following Gessell 1929. What is left circulating will be redeemed by a future generation.

146 W is the sum of a change in pressure (P) multiplied by a change in volume (V), this sum for economists is the GDP. GDP = W

147 Entropy (S) is the dividing of the change in the enthalpy H, by the change in energy input (money), Q. Entropy roots the change in wealth (internal heat of the system) by the change in investment (energy input, as the investment, by seigniorage).

148 Here, with Bastiat's window example it is worth pause to consider how traditional economics treats waste as production. This thermodynamic model has defined its terms so clearly that we can say - money is energy, it is the what wasted and shown by a change in Entropy (S) and not by an increase in GDP. A strict accounting for the broken window in the thermodynamic economy; is that no asset has made it to

the next generation W=0, all the energy is spent replacing it (S), and the seigniorage currency, therefore, losses value. The currency punishes society.

149 Eugenics is essential to classical theory because it proves scarcity, that gives the urgency for supply-side fixes and supporter interventions from Banks and churches, it explains why there are more war projects, than environmental ones, the economy keeps producing too much, so destruction creates the scarcity that Eugenics explains. Soddy plagiarist, JM Keynes was the President of the British Eugenics Society and a collaborator of Traitor Harry Dexter White.

150 The most likely form is now known by the Constructal law as stated by Adrian Bejan, in combination with that of thermodynamics - part each. Constructal law states "For a finite-size system to persist in time (to live), it must evolve in such a way that it provides easier access to the imposed (global) currents that flow through it." Bejan's published his new Law in 1995. Bejan will be awarded the 2018 Benjamin Franklin Medal in Mechanical Engineering for "constructal theory, which predicts natural design and its evolution in engineering, scientific, and social systems." Bejan, Adrian (1997). "Constructal-theory network of conducting paths for cooling a heat generating volume." International Journal of Heat and Mass Transfer Bejan is Distinguished Professor of Mechanical Engineering at Duke University.

The probability of most events is statistically irrelevant because they are, with near certainty, unlikely. The future is therefore not a time where anything can happen. Instead, it is a time where a limited, more likely path is the only one available. The object will drop, the perfume will escape the bottle.

151 Frank Lambert, Professor of physics, paraphrased from past Wikipedia entries on entropy now deleted.

152 Things have predictable outcomes (money gets work). People are perfectible; they learn from their mistakes and will not build houses on sand. Human nature has a direction, and it is forward. It takes time to be

perfect, and effort too, which is measured by distance, and the mum knows the boy comes back from the trip exhausted and improved. Progress is inevitable because a person's learning implies it. Demographic profiles explain that a population's needs are nearly always more than their abilities. However, society can and does expand to accommodate, today we do it with debt, this paper suggests a parallel universe, it now and later expands by, ideas spreading, it is intellectual capital that expands to accommodate growth. Is the expansion of ideas wasted energy? Alternatively, is it a lesson learned? Entropy gives us the answer. Society rearranges, it learns, the person becomes an efficient builder, and the house takes a more useful form, rearranging is not waste, the benefits come later.

153 2018 Nobel prize winner Paul Romer in an Article "What Went Wrong in Macro-Historical Details;" Gives a more recent account of the problems of Macroeconomics. His is entirely consistent with the one given earlier, and makes the admission that timidity in economics - is a fear that politicians will use their policies on the community - they know that classical theory not just useless but dangerous.

"Stigler wanted halt to progress in economic theory because he feared that it would lead to more theories like those of Keynes and Chamberlin (who provided the foundation for Dixit and Stiglitz). For him, there was too much risk that such theories might lend political support for government policies that should not be tried."

https://paulromer.net/what-went-wrong-in-macro-historical-details/

'My paper Mathiness in Theory of Economic Growth' Link to Paul Romer's Blog, and Paper talking about economic tricks, fake theory, and dishonest math. https://paulromer.net/mathiness/

154 To avoid unnecessary confusion, and for comparative purposes; GDP is said (W) here. However please intuit that goods for consumption will be accounted for by entropy because those do not make it to the

future - the GDP we are talking about is what lasts into the future - houses, roads, infrastructure, intellectual property, community manners. More is apparent later.

155 We need also intuit that the wealthy society values the things made as consumables less, as they value their surroundings more, it is essential to appreciate that innovation makes things less valuable, and wealthy people spend less of their income on necessities, and more on their surroundings. So with time and wealth, we would expect that the effect of investment would be less GDP and more entropy, this would show that we are producing all we need, have the right amount of leisure and health, and are living in a pristine environment. It would further indicate that the infrastructure we are building for the next generation will stand the test of time and that the currency we issued ourselves to build it, will be redeemed in the future.

156 Entropy is a Force - In a paper titled "On the Origin of Gravity and the Laws of Newton" 6, Jan 2010 Erik Verlinde tells;

Gravity is explained as an entropic force caused by changes in the information associated with the positions of material bodies. A relativistic generalization of the presented arguments directly leads to the Einstein equations. When space is emergent, even Newton's law of inertia needs to be explained. The equivalence principle leads us to conclude that it is actually this law of inertia whose origin is entropic.

https://arxiv.org/pdf/1001.0785.pdf

Moreover, in more detail in a paper Titled "Emergent Gravity and the Dark universe" 8, Nov 2016 Erik Verlinde explained;

The emergent laws of gravity contain an additional 'dark' gravitational force describing the 'elastic' response due to the entropy displacement. We derive an estimate of the strength of this extra force in terms of the baryonic mass, Newton's constant and the Hubble

401

acceleration scale a0 = cH0, and provide evidence for the fact that this additional 'dark gravity force' explains the observed phenomena in galaxies and clusters currently attributed to dark matter.

https://arxiv.org/pdf/1611.02269.pdf

The work of Verlinde in applying entropic values to the Lorentz transformations- really the all of the Einstein equations will provide much of the Mathematical foundation of this economic model. In lay terms, entropy tells us that relaxation, consumption, leisure, all of what entropy measures, is us arranging like springs, to work, do, make later, the waste is a charge, its four magnitudes greater in Quantity than the energy that does work. A stored and powerful "dark" energy - to be employed - later. Time is the all of later.

157 As an aside, the mathematics, or conventions ultimately used to agree this economic model, will involve our own Copenhagen agreement. This author will give some suggestions in concluding. Later we will use Coulomb's law and assert with authority that; inertial mass is the equal of charged mass, and learn that economics is understood by gravity, as Allias intuited, and that by relativity.

158 Ibid. Stanford Encyclopedia 2013.

159 Entropy (S) is a state variable, this seems counter-intuitive, but it is because it becomes. There is a metaphysical component to a system, when it works it is more, and here we see why a profit, how a synergy, what a hysteresis, the value of time, and the where of Verlinde's elasticity, his entropic potential energy made from chaos - an arrangement useful for later. There are more scientific explanations for entropy being a State Variable, many disputed, but we are cross-discipline, and this paper is more an explaining one, introducing, than a proving one, arguing. This economic system is being introduced now, and later it will be explained as a reversed Carnot; the Refrigerator model, and these synergies that are asserted to be entropy will appear more intuitive.

160 That is, maturity, enlightenment (say education) and change within individuals - from knowledge and skill. When people change, the same people are different, people once not exciting or attractive - become by getting older, educated, wiser or skilled.

161 Frank Lambert, Physics Professor (dec.)

162 It is not conceivable to do an inventory of gratuitous wealth. Thermodynamics only measures changes. So, the starting point is in the present - No audit is necessary - this explains the whims of kings past that built grand cities from nothing. In economics, we are interested in changes, amounts (quantities) are irrelevant, for example in consumption we want more until we are full, not three now. When we have a house to live in, we rarely want another to maintain. A Thermodynamic Political economy is likened to good parenting, or as Laozi does to hospitality - make sure there is enough of everything and lots of room in a great space, and the party happens without the entertainer.

163 Potential energy is the effective wealth transfer to and from the thermodynamic heat sink or public and private domain. By using Viral theory (A virus doubles at each iteration of its life), we can derive a quick NPV, or NFV from any potential energy, and n assess entropy.

164 The Black Book of Communism: Crimes, Terror, Repression 1997, Stéphane Courtois, Nicolas Werth, Andrzej Paczkowski - 100 million deaths. The Black Book of Capitalism 1998, Gilles Perrault - 100 million deaths. Dick Cheney told Sasha Baron Cohn that he killed 700,000 in Iraq, & Winston Churchill starved 4 million people to death in Calcutta 1944 Shashi Tharoor Inglorious Empire: what the British did to India 2017.

165 It is assumed by most that commodities have value, because the land is owned, and thought that ideas have value because they are patented. This paper asserts with Bastiat that nature has no value and with the law that after a period, ideas are public property. That period could be the three days it takes an enlightened society to award the inventor a money prize. Commodities and tools are utilities that belong in the public domain as gratuitous wealth. Along with air and water, they

cannot be owned, if we are to contract sincerely with the future. 'Humans cannot create matter, and nature cannot create value' Bastiat Ibid. (ch.2)

166 Quote unattributed, from History of the industrial revolution. (perhaps from Soddy)

167 Gankin http://en.fphysics.com/mass V. Yu Gankin & Yu. V. Gankin Electro Magnetism Physics of Twenty-first Century Renome Saint Petersburg 2013

168 To adjust or alter the real world to fit a model could be dismissed as hubris. However, it is the real world now that is artificial. It has already been adjusted since the middle ages to fit the classical model - that makes no sense. The suggestion here is that - the artificiality imposed by the facilitators of classical economics be removed and the real world be allowed to follow the constructal Law of life, where the system evolves with easier access, by taking its most likely form - unhindered by constraints - following A Bejan.

169 A guiding Principal - of this system is that all facilitators - Judges, Churches, Unions, Think Tanks, et al., have their reason for being, removed. To reduce frictions; a common-sense suggestion to reward mothers is given as an example. The cost to society of frictions is more than they are worth. The laws of the future will be in plain speak, simple and not open to interpretation. The final word in this paper will give society its purpose, and with purpose most problems solve themselves.

170 Refrigerator model was suggested in an incomplete paper by Borisas Cimleris (FUMG Brazil). https://en.wikipedia.org/wiki/Carnot_heat_engine

171 Money Creation in the Modern Economy (M. McLeay, A. Radia & R. Thomas, Quarterly Bulletin 2014 Q1, online at http://www.bankofengland.co.uk/publications/Documents/quarterlybullet in/2014/qb14q1prereleasemoneycreation.pdf)

172 A currency, investment, by way of Seigniorage, additional currency can only realistically be issued by the State when it funds a viable industry, or useful infrastructure, to back it initially, and then to earn tolls so that the money issued can be withdrawn at a rate that

matches the depreciation of the asset.

173 In this case of too many Zombies, the entropy variable would interpret consumption and potential as opportunity cost; the enthalpy variable will be falling, as the elements lose their charge.

174 The relationship Keynes asserted between Employment, Interest, and Money, has now been admitted a Chimera. It was said to be proved by the Phillips Curve but is now ADMITTED by the Philadelphia Federal Reserve. Its Director of Research Michael Dotsey Co-authored this report in 2017https://www.philadelphiafed.org/-/media/research-and-data/publications/working-papers/2017/wp17-26.pdf

175 The General Theory of Employment, Interest, and Money, pp. 149, 222.

176 Money Creation in the Modern Economy (M. McLeay, A. Radia & R. Thomas, Quarterly Bulletin 2014 Q1, online at http://www.bankofengland.co.uk/publications/Documents/quarterlybullet in/2014/qb14q1prereleasemoneycreation.pdf).

177https://www.kreditopferhilfe.net/docs/Richard_Werner__Can_ban ks_individually_create_money_out_of_nothing__plus_supplemental_mat erial.pdf

Additional reference; The Creature from Jekyll Island: A Second Look at the Federal Reserve by G. Edward Griffin (American Opinion Publishing, Appleton WI, 1994).

178 Seigniorage is the profit on manufacturing money. That profit is almost 100% with paper or digital money, so seigniorage is the issuing of currency by the state. In this model, it will be issued against public infrastructure projects will earn a capital return for the whole community that is more than the projects' actual return. For example, a port might return 10%, but the economic benefits are the improvement in efficiency that is attributed to the port by perhaps 0.05% of the GDP. The efficiency would see the port return 20%. Economic impact studies have consistently proved this benefit for fifty years (It is not ROI, its efficiency, we have been calling it entropy, and here is another proof that this thermodynamic model has been running in parallel to ours for many

years, we are in its shadow). By funding infrastructure with seigniorage rather than debt, with stamped money increases the return on the project by the saving of interest, is not inflationary, because the goods appear with the money, and guarantees full employment in perpetuity. Seigniorage is also the ideal way to invest in the construction of utilities, and fund a living wage from their income.

Note; There is no need to save for an asset like a house, the money is, issued, and the client would pay the principal off monthly (without interest) the house is to the client's specification. Every person is a sovereign. There is no finance or insurance sector.

179 Simmel, Georg The Philosophy of Money 1900, Translation David Frisby 1978 Routledge and Kegan Paul Ltd.

180 The Templars perverted the ancient system of Nation building to; church and castle building with banking, now modified to demand and supply with banking, the church is now the government demanding services for say; immigration and the castle is the military supplying oil from foreign lands with borrowed money from banks.

181 Keynes got of the bailout from Newton admitting in his Principia that the maintenance of his system requires the "intervention of some extraneous supernatural powers."

182 The exact mathematics & formulations are the trade of others, this is a theoretical paper that has told what is to be made by the engineers.

www.ingramcontent.com/pod-product-compliance
Lightning Source LLC
Chambersburg PA
CBHW020153200326
41521CB00006B/344